Ghosts
in the
Mind's
Machine

Creating and Using Images in the Brain

Stephen Michael Kosslyn
Harvard University

W · W · *Norton & Company*
New York · London

Copyright © 1983 by Stephen M. Kosslyn
All rights reserved.
Published simultaneously in Canada by Stoddart,
a subsidiary of General Publishing Co. Ltd,
Don Mills, Ontario.
Printed in the United States of America.

The text of this book is composed in Palatino, with
display type set in Michelangelo. Composition and
manufacturing by The Maple-Vail Book Manufacturing Group
Book design by Angelica Design Group, Ltd.

First published as a Norton paperback 1984

Library of Congress Cataloging in Publication Data

Kosslyn, Stephen Michael, 1948–
     Ghosts in the mind's machine.

     Includes index.
     1. Imagery (Psychology)—Memory
2. Brain.   I. Title.
BF367.K66 1983   153.3'2   82–19038

ISBN 0-393-95366-1

W. W. Norton & Company, Inc., 500 Fifth Avenue, New York, N. Y. 10110
W. W. Norton & Company Ltd., 37 Great Russell Street, London WC1B 3NU

  2 3 4 5 6 7 8 9 0

Grateful acknowledgment is extended to the grantors of permission of the following:

Figs. 3.2 and 3.3 Shepard, R. N., and Metzler, J., "Mental rotation of three-dimensional objects," *Science* 171:701–703, February 1971. Copyright 1971 by the American Association for the Advancement of Science. Reprinted by permission.
Fig. 2.5 Photograph courtesy of The American Museum of Natural History.
Fig. 6.8 From Ballard, D. H. and Brown, C. M., *Computer vision*, Prentice-Hall, 1982. Reprinted by permission.
Fig. 5.1 Brooks, L. R., "Spatial and verbal components of the act of recall," *Canadian Journal of Psychology* 22:349–368, 1968. Reprinted by permission.
Figure 3.10 Finke, R. A., and Pinker, S., "Spontaneous imagery scanning in mental extrapolation," *Journal of Experimental Psychology, Learning, and Cognition* 8:142–147, 1982. Copyright 1982 by the American Psychological Association. Reprinted by permission of the author.
Page 14 Photograph courtesy of United Press International.

To Robin and Carol
I couldn't have done it without you

Contents

Acknowledgments   xi
Prologue   xiii
Chapter 1   A GHOST IN THE BRAIN   1

       Inner Visions   1
       Puzzles and Problems   3
       Some Early Speculations   4
       Enter the Psychologists   6

Chapter 2   GOODBYE HOMUNCULUS   12

       How a Computer Works   13
       Computer and Mind   17
       The Computer as a Tool   20
       Pictures in the Mind?   20
       Qualifying the Brain–Computer
         Analogy   26

Chapter 3   STALKING THE MENTAL IMAGE   29

       The Privileged Properties of Images   32
       Investigating Mental Depictions   37
       Some Preliminary Image Studies   38
       Scanning Visual Images   41

Chapter 4   THE MEDIUM AND THE MESSAGE   53

       Properties of the Medium   54
       Testing Size and Detail   56
       Measuring the Scope of the Medium   62
       Stabilized Images   67
       Brain Damage: The Blind Side
         of the Mind's Eye   69
       The Message about the Medium   71

Chapter 5   HOW DO WE KNOW IT'S THERE
            WHEN WE CAN'T SEE IT?   72

                Tangled up in Images   75
                Where Do Vision and
                    Imaging Overlap?   77
                The Mind's Eye in Imagery
                    and Perception   86
                Classifying Images and Percepts   87
                Mind and World   90

Chapter 6   PRIVATE CREATIONS   91

                Generating Images   92
                Transforming Images   104

Chapter 7   COMPUTER MODEL OF MENTAL
            IMAGERY   111

                The Compleat Theory   111
                A Theory of Imaging   113
                Structures in Active Memory   117
                Structures in Long-Term Memory   119
                Generating an Image   122
                Inspecting an Image   125
                Transforming an Image   127

Chapter 8   THE COMPUTER MODEL IN ACTION   131

                Explanations   131
                Predictions   141
                Extending the Theory   153

Chapter 9   REMEMBERING APPEARANCES   160

                Depictions and Propositions Again   160
                The Race between Words and Pictures   162
                Putting Imagery to Work   171
                Extending the Theory: When Are Images Used
                    in Remembering?   175

Chapter 10   VISUAL THINKING   177

                  Imagery and Problem Solving   177
                  Simulation or Symbolization   179
                  Testing the Theory   181
                  Imagery and Knowledge   189
                  Thinking Ahead   192

Chapter 11   PEOPLE ARE DIFFERENT   194

                  Individual Differences   194
                  Cognitive Development   201

Chapter 12   THE PHILOSOPHICAL AND
                  THE PRACTICAL   205

                  The Philosophical   205
                  The Practical   213
                  Science and the Mental Image   223

Notes   225
Bibliography   231
Index   238

Acknowledgments

This book was born twice: once when I was enthusiastic about making accessible the fundamental ideas of cognitive science by examining research on mental imagery, and again when I met Carol Verburg. The task of making abstract philosophical, methodological, and conceptual points easily understood was more challenging than I had originally anticipated. This book almost died in infancy. Fortunately, Carol has nursed more than one book back to health, and I had the good sense to enlist her aid. It is almost impossible to give too much credit to Carol. She took my drafts and made sure that the ideas came through in a clear, readable way; she not only rewrote awkward prose, but pointed out blind spots and helped flesh out cryptic passages. She forced me to do it right, and I cannot thank her enough. I am also indebted to Norton editor Don Fusting, who provided input at every stage; to Gail Pendleton, who provided useful feedback on the quality of the writing as she typed the manuscript; and to the copy editor Alicia Salomon, who provided the final polish on the prose. George Smith, at Tufts University, stimulated me to think about the connection between philosophical points and current research, and my numerous discussions with him have probably affected my thinking more than I realize. In addition, numerous discussions with Martha Farah helped clarify what this book was about. Gary Hatfield at Johns Hopkins read over the final draft and suggested many valuable improvements. I am also grateful to Harvard University Press for allowing me to incorporate passages from my more technical book *Image and Mind*. Finally, I must thank my wife Robin, who tolerated it all; my various collaborators (cited in the text and references); and my patrons at various funding agencies, who made this book possible. In particular, Joseph L. Young at the National Science Foundation (Grant BNS82-40259), Leonard Lash at the National Institute of Mental Health (Research Career Development Award 1 K02

MH00352-01A1 MHK), and Marshall J. Farr, Henry Halff, and Kathy Spoehr at the Office of Naval Research (Contract N00014-82-C-0166) provided not only the funds to carry out the work described in this book, but friendship and genuine interest in the work and the workers.

Prologue

Something exciting is happening in psychology today. The study of the mind is finally becoming a real, live science. How do we think? remember? use language? recognize objects? These sorts of questions have puzzled people at least since the dawn of recorded history, and we finally are beginning to come to grips with some of them.

Resting comfortably inside every human skull is a brain. To look at, it resembles about a cup's worth of overcooked oatmeal. Yet this lumpy mass is implicated—directly or indirectly—in virtually every movement, thought, and sensation. Somehow the mind is hooked up to this wet machine, allowing us to store and use memories that can span a century of experience: the taste of popcorn at the movies when we were kids, the sight and smell of elephants at the circus, the giddy feeling of falling in love for the first time.

The mind's accomplishments have intrigued people long before anyone even knew that the mind was associated with the brain. Aristotle, perhaps the greatest philosopher of all time, maintained that sensation and thought took place in the heart; the brain he took to be a cooling device that, among other things, induced sleep by cooling the blood. But even such a serious misconception did not stand in the way of studying the mind: The mind has a life of its own and can be studied independently of the brain. The early philosophers asked the difficult questions, pondering the nature of thought, how information from the world enters our minds, how information is stored, and so on. The philosophers tried to find answers using observation and logic—which yielded a host of clues, but only erratic progress.

One of the central puzzles for those grappling with questions about mental events was the dichotomy of body and mind. The French philosopher René Descartes gave considerable thought to this paradoxical distinction during the first half of the seventeenth century. Clearly the body is a tangible entity, occupying space; yet the mind, though closely connected with the body, is intangible. Whereas the body is subject to physical laws (it falls when dropped, and so on) and presumably could be understood in terms of its components, like a machine, the mind remains elusive. Sensations, thoughts, memories, mental images, and consciousness itself seem to dwell within the body like ghosts, animating and controlling it without being part of it. As ghosts, mental events were seemingly beyond the reach of science.

Figuring out how to approach the interesting questions about thinking and perceiving in a scientific fashion has proven to be one of the greatest challenges in human history. Discovering that mental activity takes place in the brain did not make the "ghosts in the machine" any easier to observe. Studying the brain—the machine itself—seemed straightforward enough: One procures some brains, weighs them, cuts them up, and otherwise determines their properties. But how does one quantify an idea or a mental image? Although the tools of science have enabled researchers to unravel a great deal of the structure and functioning of the brain, until recently the mind within it has remained persistently out of reach. Some early psychologists abandoned the whole idea of trying to understand mental events; others insisted on maintaining a broad view of the mind, and leaned heavily on art, literature, and philosophy for their insights into psychological dynamics; and still others at the rigorous end of the scientific spectrum wound up focusing on behavior in very specific tasks or on nerve cells and their interconnections. On the one hand were the ghosts—thought, ideas, perceptions, and the other intangible phenomena that comprise the mind; on the other hand was the machine—the brain with all its physical and electrochemical characteristics. For centuries, it was a mystery how two such disparate things could be interconnected.

Progress in coping with this "mind–body problem" only occurred after philosophers realized that it was in fact two problems: One problem focuses on the nature of our conscious *experience*, of how things "feel" to us. This led philosophers to wonder about questions like, Could blue to you look like red to me? The problem of consciousness is so difficult that we are not even sure whether the questions we ask make sense, and it is not surprising that virtually no progress has been made on this problem. The other problem focuses on how the mind *functions*, how it carries out mental activities (thinking, perceiving, and the rest). The virtue in breaking the big problem down in this way is that the second subproblem, of how the mind operates, *is* amenable to scientific study. This way of looking at things gives us at least one problem that is tractable.

A number of disciplines seized on the notion that mental functioning could be studied independently of consciousness. Out of the melding of artificial intelligence (which is concerned with making computers behave like thinking organisms), psychology, linguistics, and philosophy has emerged the alloy known as *cognitive science;* and the methods and tools of cognitive science have allowed psychologists to bring scientific rigor to fundamental and fascinating questions about the human mind.

This book focuses on a particular investigation within the field of cognitive science: the study of mental images. Images are picturelike, but they are not real pictures—you cannot frame a mental image, or drop one on your toe. Historically, images are the quintessential inhabitants of the mind. In fact, thought has often been equated with sequences of mental images. By considering how psychologists are coming to understand this species of "ghosts in the mind's machine," we can see in detail how two decades' worth of research has been able to produce more knowledge about the mind than was available through all the preceding centuries. The research on imagery is a case study, illustrating the kind of work currently being done in cognitive science. It is also a sort of detective story—a study of how cognitive scientists are coming to understand that most uncooperative object of study, the human mind.

This book is intended as a teaser, providing just a taste of what cognitive scientists are trying to do. I will count it as a success if the reader comes away wondering how the story will turn out. I will count it as a spectacular success if you decide to pursue the topic in more detail.

Ghosts in the Mind's Machine

Creating and Using Images in the Brain

1

A Ghost in the Brain

IT'S LATE at night and you're just drifting off to sleep when a sudden noise jolts you awake. *What was that? Burglars?* With a shock you remember that you left your wallet on the table right beside the window—at least you can see yourself setting the wallet down there between the empty glass and the book, and when you search your memory, you don't recall picking it up again. Would anyone outside be able to see it through the window? You imagine yourself as a potential burglar, hands on the sill, peering in. No, the table is too far to the right; you can't see it or the wallet on it from the window. Relieved, you lie down again and fall asleep.

"Excuse me!" a distressed voice calls from a car window. "How do I get to the train station from here?"

You think about it a moment. In your mind you are driving up the street, turning right at the light, past the big parking lot, then left—no, there's a one-way sign . . . another block and *then* left, and there's the station at the top of the hill.

"Okay," you say, "go straight three or four blocks till you come to a traffic light. . . ."

INNER VISIONS

Mental imagery is a phenomenon most of us encounter numerous times every day, When someone asks a question—"Which way to the train station?"—an image is likely to pop into mind without our even thinking about it. When we try to remember something—"Where did I leave my wallet?"—we may recall it by "looking" at an image. Whether spontaneous or deliberate, images are involved in a whole range of mental activities, from solving problems and memorizing information to daydreaming.

Precisely what images are, however, is not so easy to say. A recent book entitled *Seeing with the Mind's Eye* opens with, "The human mind is a slide projector with an infinite number of slides stored in its library."[1] This is probably the most common way of thinking about mental images: as intracranial photographs. Images might be stored in some greatly reduced form and projected onto an inner screen when we want to look at them.

This model begins to falter, however, when we examine imagery more closely. A good way to appreciate the difficulties is to consider some of the ways people report using mental images. For example, suppose someone asks you the following questions:

What shape are a German shepherd's ears?

Is a radish the same shade of red as a strawberry?

Most people say that they respond to questions like these by creating a mental picture and "looking" at it for the answer. You image a German shepherd and then "zoom in" on its ears; you image a radish and a strawberry and compare them.

Up to this point, images seem to behave much like photographs or slides. But think about another question:

Does a frog have lips and a stubby tail?

People asked this question usually report picturing a frog, looking at its mouth, and then mentally rotating the frog, zooming in at the rear to check for the tail. Hard to do with a photograph! Imaging would seem to be considerably more complex than flashing slides on a screen. For one thing, objects in mental pictures do not seem to be necessarily flat, but can be three dimensional; for another, they do not seem to be fixed, but movable.

To complicate things further, think about one more question:

How many windows are there in your living room?

To answer this one, most people report picturing their living room and scanning around it, counting the windows. This brings up yet another property of mental images: Besides being able to inspect them from a distance, as it were, we seem to be able to put ourselves *inside* them. Most people claim that if they wanted to, they could close their eyes and envision not just the windows of their living room, but the sofa, the bookcases, the television, or whatever, as if they were standing in the middle of the room and gazing around. Furthermore, they can "see" the living room from several vantage points and can swiftly shift from one view to another. In addition, they claim to be able to add new pieces of furniture that are not really there and to "see" how they would look in the room.

PUZZLES AND PROBLEMS

The flaws in the slide projector model and our way of evaluating it are illuminating because they raise many of the puzzles and problems that must be dealt with before we can understand the mind scientifically. To begin with, images cannot really be slides or any other kind of actual pictures. Aside from the problem of where the pictures would be kept (in cracks between brain cells?), a literal picture in the head would require some way in which we could look at it. Given that the eyes that inspect the world cannot turn inward to inspect images, the alternative is some kind of "mind's eye" whose job it is to watch the inner screen. But no examination of the brain has ever turned up either a screen or an eye to watch it. Further, this idea puts us back to where we started, for now we need to explain the images "seen" through this inner eye. The slide projector model fails to tell us how *mental* images can exist in a *physical* brain.

If images are not pictures, what are they? This is a major challenge in studying imagery: how to characterize these ghostly quasi-pictures flitting through the brain. A theory that can explain mental images not only must do away with an actual inner screen watched by an inner eye, but must also specify how images— and other mental events—relate to the machinery of the brain. How is the mind, an ethereal thing, harnessed to the brain?

In addition, we need to explain how images can represent (stand for) objects in their absence. Looking at a slide or any other picture is a lot like looking at an actual object: You recognize what is in the picture in much the same way you would recognize the object it depicts. If images are not pictures, how is it they can stand for things out in the world? To put it another way, how are we able to store a record of observed events in our heads?

In short, understanding mental images—and, by extension, the mind—requires a theory that can explain several different puzzles. We need to characterize the mind in a way that recognizes that mental events are different from physical ones; we need to specify how the mind relates to the brain; and we need to establish how information is stored in the mind. More immediately, we have to find some way of asking questions about the mind that will yield answers we can use as guidelines in constructing such a theory. Finally, assuming we can come up with a theory that meets all these requirements, how do we find out if it is correct? In addition to holding up logically, our theory would have to be susceptible to empirical testing. But how can we test something as elusive as a mental image?

In testing the slide projector theory we relied on introspection to reveal enough about imaging to impress us with its versatility. "Introspection" is the process of looking within, of observing the mind's workings. As an investigative tool, however, it has some serious drawbacks. For instance, go back for a moment and take a closer look at that imaged frog. Does it have a distinct skin texture? How many spots does it have? What do its hind feet look like? Are its eyes at the front of its head or toward the sides? Most of us are not absolutely sure—and some people "misimage" the creature, incorporating features (such as a tail) that real frogs do not have. Given such discrepancies, how much of people's reports can we trust? And what about people who say they have no imagery? Some readers must be very confused at this point, having had none of the experiences described so far. What should we make of *their* reports, and how could we tell what was really going on in their minds?

Puzzles like these have always intrigued psychologists and philosophers. The difficulty of these puzzles is well illustrated by the rise and fall of the study of mental images. In some eras, mental imagery has been heralded as the keystone of thinking; in others—including much of our own century—its very existence has been denied. The reasons for such fluctuations will shape any future theory of the mind. To see how, let us briefly review some historical highlights.

SOME EARLY SPECULATIONS

The central preoccupation of most thinkers about the mind has been to understand how thinking and memory work. More specifically, what form do thoughts take when they are handled and stored in the mind? Obviously *some* kind of translation goes on between perception—our sensory contacts with the world—and thought. In perception an external stimulus triggers a reaction in the appropriate sense organ, which notifies the brain that something is "out there." When you look at a frog, for example, light bouncing off the frog strikes the retinas of your eyes and causes visual information to be transmitted to your brain. But how is it that you can also *remember* what the frog looked like after it has hopped out of view? It must be that some *representation* of a frog or frogs remains in your mind even in the absence of any external "froggy" stimulus.

Most philosophers assumed that our mental representations of objects must be images (visual, auditory, tactile, etc.), verbal meanings, or both. Words and images, after all, are the two vehicles we are aware of using when we communicate with others. Our knowledge about German shepherds thus might be stored as a mental image of a large black and tan dog or as a verbal description of the beast—its habits and so forth—attached in some way to the words *German shepherd*. Aristotle was one early commentator who gave a crucial role to mental images, claiming that "thought is impossible without an image" and "memory, even the memory of concepts, does not take place without an image."

If thought and memory depend on images, does that mean that a concept of a thing is the same as an image of it? Does your idea of *German shepherd* consist of a sort of a generalized "average" picture of the dog? A number of philosophers found this an attractive idea in light of the only apparent alternative: If concepts are not handled and stored in image form, then they must be verbal.

But words have a serious drawback as the main ingredient of thought: They are not innate. One must be taught a language. Making sounds comes naturally to human beings, but to communicate through sounds we have to learn the meanings our culture has given them. The foundation of thought ought to be more basic than that. After all, if all meanings are stored in terms of words, how do you learn the first word? What do you use to store *its* meaning? There is a paradox here. Something else must be stored in memory to begin with that can be used to learn the meanings of at least the first words. Because images spring from perception, and hence need not be arbitrarily paired with the

1.1. What dog can stand for all dogs?

things they represent, they are a good candidate for the "bedrock representation." This and related lines of reasoning led many thinkers to conclude that the basic elements of thought must be imaginal, not verbal.

This theory has its drawbacks too, however. In the eighteenth century the Irish philosopher Bishop Berkeley pointed out how difficult it would be to use an image to store a concept of a *class* of objects. Take *dog*, for instance. You want your concept of dog to encompass dogs in general, including ones of various sizes, shapes, colors, and degrees of shagginess. When you *image* a dog, however, you picture a particular dog, one of a particular size, shape, color, and shagginess. It is impossible to generate one mental picture that represents all possible dogs (Fig. 1.1).

To make matters even more complex, it was pointed out that images—like pictures—are susceptible to multiple interpretations. An image of a sitting man could be seen as representing "bent knees," "John's head," or a "twentieth century person." We are never puzzled by an ambiguous thought (when you think about *sage*, you know whether you are thinking about the herb or a wise man). Thus neither images nor words seemed suitable as a means of storing information in the mind.

ENTER THE PSYCHOLOGISTS

By the beginning of the twentieth century, there was no real progress toward solving the problem of how information is represented in the mind. By this time, however, a scientific approach to psychology seemed promising. In the vanguard was Wilhelm Wundt, now considered the father of scientific psychology. Wundt established the world's first psychology laboratory in Leipzig, Germany, in 1879. He defined psychology as "the science of immediate experience." His goal for this new science was to construct a periodic table of the mind, identifying the elementary sensations that make up experience just as the chemical periodic table specifies the elements of the physical world. Such a table would also describe the rules by which sensory elements combine. Wundt's main subject matter was imagery, but unfortunately his main methodology was introspection. Laboratory subjects examined and described the "pictures" in their minds and researchers tried to analyze the structure of their images.

The potential problems with Wundt's use of introspection are dramatically illustrated by the claims of another strong advocate of imagery as the foundation of thought and introspection as the means of investigation, the American E. B. Tichner. Tichner was a devoted follower of Wundt. He went to Germany to study with him but rarely actually did more than admire him from afar. Upon returning to the United States, where in 1911 he established himself at Cornell University, Tichner quickly emulated his idol—to the point of adopting the German style of lecturing in full academic regalia. And he took Wundt's ideas about imagery even further than Wundt himself. Tichner argued that even abstract concepts can be pictured "if you do but have the imaginal mind." In support of his views he described some of the images he himself used to represent abstract ideas:

> I see meaning as the blue-grey tip of a kind of scoop, which has a bit of yellow above it (probably a part of the handle), and which is just digging into a dark mass of what appears to be plastic material. I was educated on classical lines; and it is conceivable that this picture is an echo of the oft-repeated admonition to "dig out the meaning" of some passage of Greek or Latin. I do not know; but I am sure of the image. And I am sure that others have similar images.[2]

Other psychologists, however, were not so sure. At the forefront of the skeptics was the American John B. Watson. With the appearance in 1913 of Watson's paper "Psychology as the Behaviorist Sees It," psychology was launched on quite a different tack. Watson called imagery "the figment of the psychologist's terminology":

What does a person mean when he closes his eyes or
ears (figuratively speaking) and says, "I see the house
where I was born, the trundle bed in my mother's room
where I used to sleep—I can even see my mother as
she comes to tuck me in and I can even hear her voice
as she softly says goodnight"? Touching, of course,
but sheer bunk. We are merely dramatizing. The
behaviorist finds no proof of imagery in all this. *We
have put all these things in words long, long ago* and we
constantly rehearse those scenes verbally whenever the
occasion arises.[3]

Watson did more than reject the claim that concepts are essentially imaginal; he attacked the whole idea of trying to study the
mind. In his opinion, images are not "mental pictures" at all, but
one form of *subvocal thinking*—tiny movements of the larynx, a
literal talking to oneself. People's introspective reports to the
contrary could be ignored because there was no way of objectively verifying them. Introspections, in Watson's view, were
equivalent to opinions, and unsupportable opinions at that.
Watson believed that "the brain is stimulated always and only
from the outside"; that is, neither thought, imagery, nor any other
so-called mental activity arises directly in the brain. "There is
always an object stimulating us," he wrote, "if not a chair or
table, then some organic or muscular process such as the muscular process in the throat that we use in whispering to ourselves
(thought)."[4]

This was to become one of the central tenets of the new
approach Watson had dubbed "behaviorism." According to the
behaviorists, all behavior is a response to some stimulus. This
principle seemed eminently scientific. If you think about it, it
has somewhat the same ring as a basic principle of physics. In
physics, when a billiard ball starts rolling, it is because a cue
stick or some other billiard ball has hit it. In psychology, Watson's principle means that when a baby cries, it is because her
stomach is empty, a pin is sticking her, or a strange object has
startled her, and not because it is the nature of babies to cry.
Crying was defined as a response to some stimulus. Emotional
causes were ruled out; to Watson, emotions were just an old-
fashioned way of describing certain collections of behavior.

Thought and imagery fell into roughly the same category. Thoughts do not simply occur to people; they are a form of behavior (specifically, a type of speech) triggered in response to some stimulus.

At the time Watson entered the scene, psychology was a fledgling science. Its adherents were wholeheartedly committed to the scientific method as the key to discovery. One of the most damning accusations anyone could make to these devotees of laboratory research was that they were not being properly scientific; and that was essentially what Watson was telling them.

Stung, psychologists rejected the study of the mind, and the focus of the field became observable behavior. Internal events, which were not susceptible to direct observation, were considered impossible to study or, at the extreme, nonexistent.

What Went Wrong with Behaviorism?

The predominance of behaviorism and the intellectual climate it encouraged persisted for some time, but it began losing ground as the method for understanding human psychology in the late 1950s, primarily for two reasons.

First, the limits of behaviorism itself began to show. Notably, the very concepts of "stimulus" and "response" seemed almost impossible to define. The behaviorist approach rested on the premise that all of an organism's actions can be described solely in terms of stimuli and responses: Some responses are automatic ("unconditioned," in behaviorist terms), as when you bite into a lemon and the acid causes you to salivate; other responses are learned ("conditioned"), as when just seeing a picture of a sliced lemon causes you to salivate. A central goal of behaviorism was to show that different stimuli are systematically related to responses in lawful ways.

But precisely what is a stimulus? It is not just a physical object but, rather, some *aspect* of an object that draws an organism's attention. Even something as simple as a flashing light offers numerous alternatives: the color, the brightness, the shape, and the rate of flashing. And as soon as the door is opened to talking about "attention," the whole raft of mentalistic terms (those referring to unobservable internal events—*idea, think, want,* and so forth) creeps in again, defeating the whole point of the behaviorist approach.

So too is the case with the notion of "response." A response is not definable simply in terms of muscle twitches, as Watson had described it. For one thing, the same set of muscle twitches can underlie different responses. Consider a story told to me by a French friend: During the Second World War, a certain comedian was asked to perform for a roomful of Nazi officers. Upon mounting the stage, the comedian gave the traditional Nazi salute, which brought the officers to their feet, returning the stiff-armed gesture. At this point, the wag, arm still extended, said (in French), "Yes, gentlemen, we are all in it up to *here*." This was not at all what the officers thought they were conveying with the salute, and the entertainer fled the premises.

Furthermore, the same response can be made (and usually is) in more than one physical form. A common laboratory procedure is to train animals to run through a maze correctly in order to obtain food. The behaviorists' assumption was that a set of behaviors—leg movements, head turns, and the like—become conditioned responses to the visual stimuli of the maze. However, rats taught to run a maze can then *swim* it correctly if it is flooded, even though swimming requires a whole different set of movements. Clearly, the animals have learned something more than merely a sequence of muscle movements. Furthermore, rats can run to the reward from new starting places in a maze once they have learned to run it correctly from one location. If all they had learned was a specific sequence of "responses," however defined, they should have learned only a single route. To explain the rats' behavior, we are forced to refer to a concept or representation of the layout of the maze to define the stimulus, and to an intention, goal, or some other mental state or event to define the responses. The apparent simplicity of behaviorism dissolves before our eyes.

Still, it usually takes more than the dissolution of an idea to loosen its hold on a field. People tend to hang onto an old theory or idea until a better one comes along to replace it. Thus it is of no small importance that as the problems with behaviorism became more apparent, dramatic developments in two other fields moved in to fill the gap.

In the area of linguistics, the work of the American philosopher Noam Chomsky not only revealed the inadequacies of the behaviorist approach, but offered an alternative. Behaviorists had asserted that language is merely a set of verbal responses—noises—that we learn to make in response to specific stimuli. These stimuli include all kinds of things: visible objects, remarks by other people, and so on. Thus to learn a language is to learn to emit a specific set of responses in specific circumstances. Children learn to speak like adults by imitating adults' words, phrases, and sentences.

Chomsky countered this view with the claim that language is not at all so cut and dried; rather, it is the product of a creative ability, generated according to a system of rules. A child does not repeat what adults say; instead, he or she learns the *rules* that govern a particular language (i.e., a grammar). He or she can then utter virtually an infinite number of sentences allowable by these rules. The very spirit of this approach—positing the existence of mental rules and operations and the ability to make use of them—was contrary to the bedrock assumptions of behaviorism. And the fact that Chomsky's theories produced a detailed understanding of many of the properties of language was not only an argument for his approach, but an argument against the behaviorist one.

The second key development that assisted in the demise of behaviorism as the approach to understanding psychology has less to do with its own inadequacies than with advances in technology. In the 1950s modern digital computers became widely available. This development has ramifications far beyond how best to do calculations very quickly. The computer also offered insight into how to solve some of the most troublesome puzzles about the mind, those surrounding the absurdity of "ghosts in the machine." So important is the contribution of the computer that it warrants a chapter of its own (Chapter 2).

2
Goodbye Homunculus

DO YOU REMEMBER JIMINY CRICKET? He was a Walt Disney character, a cheerful little green fellow, who figured in a cartoon I saw twenty or thirty years ago and still remember vividly. Jiminy was in a quandary. The camera flashed to a scene inside Jiminy's head, where there was a tiny control room with a little man seated before a console. The little man scratched *his* head, made a decision, and pulled a lever; and then we saw Jiminy smile and go off on his way.

Jiminy Cricket may be a Disney fantasy, but the concept represented in this cartoon is centuries old. It is the literal extreme of the idea of the mind existing within, but separate from, the body. The little man inside Jiminy's head, known to philosophers as a homunculus, is trouble for any theory of the mind. How does he decide what to do? Is there another little man inside *his* head? Are we stuck with an endless series of homunculi nested inside each other's heads like Russian egg-dolls?

It was problems like this that caused many psychologists in the mid-1900s to stop talking about the mind altogether. Behaviorism had succeeded in discrediting introspection as a research tool. The idea of mental events—ghosts—was intangible and seemed too unscientific to pursue. Yet for all the behaviorists' insistence that psychology could only reasonably theorize about observable phenomena and for all the skepticism about what British philosopher Gilbert Ryle called "the dogma of the ghost in the machine," the mind refused to simply disappear. Neurons could be mapped, electrochemical transmitter substances identified, and areas of the brain linked with particular functions, and still not everything had been said. There was more to the mind than just the brain. One thing in particular that remained unexplained was mental images.

Instead of dying in the mid-1900s, as perhaps the behaviorists had hoped, the issue of mental images changed shape. Most people who were aware of using images to think about things or recall information found it hard to accept that images did not exist. As the behaviorist position eroded under the works of Chomsky and others, interest in imaging revived. But changes in the field of psychology caused researchers to frame the issues in new ways. By the third quarter of the twentieth century, the question was no longer simply, What role do images play in thinking? Rather, the questions became, How should we best conceptualize imagery? and How can we best find out about the properties of images?

The new approach to imagery followed in large part from a new way of regarding the mind, which rested on the distinction between how the mind works (how memory, reasoning, perception and so on operate) and how such mental events are consciously experienced. All progress in understanding imagery—as will be discussed—has been made in understanding how imagery works, and in fact all progress in understanding the mind in general has been in understanding how it works.

The first precise way to conceptualize how the mind works came from an unexpected corner, technology. The development of the modern digital computer serendipitously offered psychologists a new way to frame questions about mental events, imagery included. Computers do more than simply add, multiply, and otherwise manipulate numbers: They manipulate symbols in general. They can handle and store words, and they can also process configurations of dots depicting objects, in other words, images. With these capacities, computers can be made to do all manner of marvelous things, from playing chess to "seeing" (in some limited circumstances). What made the computer so important for psychology was that it was a well-understood example of how a machine—a physical device—could *process information*. And the brain too could be regarded as such a device. Before we can see how learning to think about the operation of computers lent real insight into understanding the mind, we need to examine these machines.

HOW A COMPUTER WORKS

Although the idea of a mechanical computer is not new to our century, actually building one was never practical until the mid-

2.1. An early computer.

1900s (Fig. 2.1). Two breakthroughs made the modern computer possible, one technical and one conceptual. The technical breakthrough was the development of electronics. Innovations in electronics allowed many functions that machines had previously performed mechanically—that is, with moving parts—to be done electrically. This meant that not only could machines be built smaller than ever before, but they could also store and manipulate information at virtually the speed of light.

The conceptual breakthrough was actually not one but a series of changes in thinking that culminated in the notion of artificial intelligence. That is, it occurred to a number of people that one ought to be able to create a computer that could carry out many of the same activities human beings are able to do by virtue of their intelligence. In terms of the famous test proposed by the mathematician Alan Turing, artificial intelligence would be achieved when a person could have a conversation with another person and a computer (both in other rooms) and not be able to tell which was which. (The conversation would have to take place over typewriter terminals, of course, so that tone of voice and other irrelevant features would not divulge the identity of the machine.[1])

The actual design of the modern computer is credited to John Von Neumann, who was famous around the Massachusetts Institute of Technology for years before and after this invention. Von Neumann stories abound to this day in Cambridge, and everyone in the field has favorites. I cannot resist telling mine: Von Neumann was cajoled into teaching an undergraduate course every few years, in which a hearty two or three students enrolled. At the first lecture, the professor wrote the left half of a complex formula on the blackboard and asked the class what resulted from it. After ten seconds, he wrote the answer on the right side of the equal-sign, turned to the class, and said, "See?" The students exchanged anxious glances. Finally, one timidly raised his hand and said, "I'm sorry, sir, but that was a little fast. Could you please go through it again?" Von Neumann looked confused, erased the right-hand side of the formula, and stood back from the board. After about twenty seconds his face brightened and he rushed to the board and wrote down the right side of the formula again. Smiling, he turned to the class and said, "See? I even did it a different way for you this time!"

Von Neumann was a man of extraordinary thought processes.

With regard to computers, Von Neumann's basic idea was that one could construct a general-purpose computer by setting up a *memory* and a *central processing unit* (CPU). The memory (the "storage bank") is divided into individual locations. As an analogy, think of a row of numbered tin cans, each of which has a sheet inside with writing on it: You can look up the information on any sheet by knowing the number of the can it is stored in. The CPU is a complicated switching device that is directed by the information stored in some locations in the memory, and which then does things (such as add or replace) to other information stored in other locations.

To return to our tin can analogy, imagine that you are sitting in front of a row of cans, each of which is numbered and contains a slip of paper with a short coded message written on it. You also have in front of you an answer key, which pairs up possible messages with sets of instructions. You pull out the slip in the first can, read the code, and find it on the answer key. Next to this particular code is the instruction "Add together the numbers in the next two cans." You pull out the next two slips of paper and do this, and then pull out the slip in the fourth can, which you treat as a new instruction. You look up this new coded message in your answer key and discover that you are to write the sum of the numbers you just added on the slip in the fifth can. You do so, then pull out the slip in the sixth can, and continue. In this analogy, each tin can is a separate location in memory, and you (armed with the answer key) have been acting as the CPU.

One of Von Neumann's great insights was the idea that any memory location can hold either data or instructions telling the CPU what to do with data in other locations. In modern computers the format of both these types of information is not slips of paper, but sets of 0's and 1's stored electronically. This property is central to the digital computer—so called because of its reliance on binary digits (0's and 1's) or, as they are more commonly known, *bits* (from *bi*nary dig*its*). The CPU reacts to ("reads") the set of bits in the first memory location it comes to as an instruction about what to do with other sets of bits; that is, the particular sequence of 0's and 1's in the location corresponds to a sequence on an answer key (which is "wired into" the CPU), just as in the tin can analogy. The instructions are more flexible than those used in our analogy: they can specify which memory locations are to be looked up in sequence, in which location the CPU should put its results after it follows the instructions, and a variety of other things. Moreover, the instructions can be changed; that is, the set of bits in any memory location can be erased and replaced by a new set. This is what makes the computer "general purpose": Its *program* can be modified at any time. The program is simply the sets of instructions in the computer's memory.

Perhaps the most important implication of Von Neumann's design comes from the fact that the same kind of data—sets of bits—can be "interpreted" different ways. It is a short leap from treating a set of 1's and 0's as either digits (data) or instructions to treating them as symbols for other things. A convention soon was worked out whereby the CPU could "read" sets of bits as corresponding to letters of the alphabet. In a computer, eight bits are grouped together into a *byte*. Each byte thus contains one of 2^8, or 256, possible combinations of 1's and 0's. To represent the alphabet, we have only to pick out twenty-six of these combinations to stand for letters. For example, we could let 00000001 stand for the letter A.

Once the machine can read letters, the next step is for it to read *sets* of letters. This too was accomplished easily enough. Now a program could be written instructing the CPU to read sets of letters—namely, words—and to do different things, depending on what word it reads. For instance, a "free association program" might have the machine print out *cat* if it reads the word *dog*. We can do this by first setting up three bytes (three sets of eight bits) to stand for the symbols c-a-t. Each byte is stored in a numbered memory location. Let us say that we store C-A-T in locations 10, 11, and 12. To create the free association program, we simply store instructions for the CPU to look up what is in locations 10, 11, and 12 if the symbols D-O-G are typed into the computer. Then we can ask the machine to print out the information stored in these memory locations. Now, when we type in *dog*, it will "free-associate" *cat* back to us. We can add any number of other associations or create other programs, all by arranging for the CPU to interpret series of bits as instructions about how to read the contents of memory locations and what to do with them.

Another aspect of computers is also worth noting here. Besides printing out an answer on paper, the computer can display its responses (along with the operator's commands) on a screen. This screen is a cathode ray tube (CRT), like that used for a television screen. But whereas a television screen typically shows a prerecorded sequence of images picked up from a broadcast station or video recorder, the CRT connected to a computer can provide a changing visual record of what is going on in the machine.

COMPUTER AND MIND

The idea that the computer can store and manipulate symbols such as digits and letters provided the key to understanding how mental events (the ghosts) could exist in the brain (the machine).[2] The insight lies in how we think about what the computer does. At the *physical level*, we can describe the operation of the computer in terms of electronics, that is, in terms of how current is flowing from one part to another; but we can also describe the computer at the *functional level*—in terms of the way letters, digits, words, and other symbols are used by the computer as it solves a problem. Most of us who use computers (and who are not concerned with designing their circuitry) ordinarily talk about them at the functional level. Rather than describe a step in a program by saying that the computer has switched current from one place to another, we say that it has added two numbers, matched two letters, or the like.[3]

Indeed, simply describing the electronic components of a given operation in the computer gives us no insight at all into what that operation accomplishes in terms of symbols. There is no natural and necessary relation between the computer's electronic workings and its functional results; in fact, there are many ways we could wire up the computer to carry out any specific function. (For example, two numbers could be multiplied by adding one number to itself over and over or by taking the logarithms of the numbers and adding the exponents; furthermore, these circuits could also be used to help carry out other, completely different functions.)

And so too for the human brain. We can describe the brain at the physical level in terms of electrochemical processes—the physical operation of the brain cells themselves—but we can also describe it at the functional level, in terms of how it functions to store and process information. And when we speak of the brain at the functional level, we are speaking about the mind.

We use the functional level of analysis to answer questions about mental events because of the nature of the questions themselves. That is, the kind of answer you want depends in large part on the kind of question you are asking. For example, the explanation of why a particular peg will not fit in a particular hole will not be in terms of subatomic physics; the question asks about a peg and a hole, and the answer should specify the relevant properties of pegs and holes—such as their shape and rigidity—that determine why the peg will not fit.[4] Questions about thought processes concern how information is stored and processed, and the answers must describe how the brain functions to accomplish these ends.

The cognitive science approach toward describing the brain at the functional level exactly parallels our description of the computer at the functional level: The brain's functioning is described in terms of how it stores and manipulates symbols. We can speak of the mind as being embodied in the brain, just as we speak of a program as being embodied electronically in the computer; mental events—thinking, remembering, and the rest—can be understood in terms of a symbolic description of the stored information. Thus cognitive scientists have borrowed much of the vocabulary developed to talk about computer functioning and use it to talk about mental representation and processing in humans.[5]

Herbert Simon won a Nobel Prize partly for his role in developing computer programs that imitated mental processes. Simon and his colleagues Allen Newell and J. C. "Cliff" Shaw took seriously the idea that mental events in the brain can best be analyzed in terms of the ways in which symbols are manipulated in a computer. They reasoned that if the brain and computer both can be described as manipulating symbols in the same way, then a good theory of mental events should be able to be translated into a computer program, and if the theory is correct, then the program should lead the computer to produce the same overt responses that a person would in various circumstances (that is, to come up with the same actions, remarks, and so on). For example, suppose you wanted to understand how a person thinks when he or she plays the card game gin rummy. The goal is to figure out what data, instructions, and processes are used in the player's mind to play the game. You would start by watching people play, noticing when they pick up cards, when they discard, the time it takes them to make decisions in different situations, and so on. You would then try to formulate a theory that fits the data; once you have a theory, you use it to program your computer so that it picks up cards at the same points, makes the same discards, takes the same amount of time, and so on, as people. The act of trying to get the program to work correctly will probably force you to think about things you ignored (e.g., what people do when they have two of a kind), which will then probably force you to alter your theory. Once you have a theory specific enough to be programmed into the computer, you can test it by putting the computer into a novel situation—deal it another hand perhaps—and watching what it does. If your measures of performance are very detailed, and the correspondence between the person's and computer's behavior very close, then you have evidence that your theory is correct.

THE COMPUTER AS A TOOL

As we have seen, one way to study the mind is to try to figure out how to build a computer program that mimics it. This approach to understanding mental events in humans has three important aspects. First, we know how a computer works and how to theorize about its "thinking." The vocabulary we use to describe symbol processing in the computer can also be applied to psychology. With it, we should be able to construct an explicit, detailed theory of how people think. Like the computer theory, the psychological theory will describe the principles that dictate how information is stored and processed.

Second, if we can program a computer to operate the way we think humans do, then we have a means of testing our theory. Given the complexity of human thought, it should not be surprising if a theory of the mind turns out to be complicated— perhaps so complicated that some of its predictions will not emerge until the computer is put in various situations and its behavior observed. In a way, then, the computer is a crutch, something like a pad of paper when one is doing arithmetic. It helps keep track of many things at once.

Third, thinking about the brain as a device that processes symbols leads us to ask particular kinds of questions. Instead of one vague, general question like, What is the role of mental images?, we can pose a set of specific, concrete questions about the nature of symbols and the processes by which they are manipulated. As each of these questions is investigated and answered, we have one more essential clue to the nature of the beast, elusive though it may be. And we also have an idea of what to look for next.

PICTURES IN THE MIND?

As one example of how the computer approach illuminates the nature of mental events, consider the visual mental image. Mental images, being mental, are not *actual* pictures, with a size, weight, and so on; nor are such images viewed with an actual eye. But if they are not real pictures, what kind of pictures are they? How can there be a picture in the mind?

The brain-as-computer view suggests a way of salvaging the

picture metaphor without being stuck with the obvious absurdities of a literal interpretation. Let us start with an analogy: What if we think of images as being like displays on a television monitor screen attached to a computer? The computer can generate images on the screen from information that is not picturelike; data that are stored as symbols in the computer's memory emerge on the screen in pictorial form.

Suppose that someone asks you, What shape are a German shepherd's ears? Presumably you have seen a German shepherd at some time or other, and the memory of what the dog looks like is filed away in your brain. The information you need to answer the question is stored in some condensed form that can be used to generate an image of the dog (or at least its head) and project it onto an internal screen. (Hold off for now on the question of who watches the screen.)

This model of imaging has some clear advantages over earlier conceptions. Let's take a look at two of them. One common view of mental images is that they are like a collection of photographs or slides. To account for the fact that objects in images can move, we might add film or videotape to the concept. But the problem remains: If images are stored and retrieved as pictures, then we can only envision objects we have already seen. How do we then explain the human ability to rotate imaged objects into novel positions, add to them, and change them? It's easy to picture a horse; all of us have seen horses, or at least pictures of them. But picture it jumping over a house. Chances are you've never seen this happen, but you probably can image it without any difficulty. How is this possible?

Thomas Hobbes, the seventeenth century English political philosopher, argued that we can create images of novel scenes like this because we have seen the component parts at one time or another, "as when from the sight of a man at one time, and of a horse at another, we conceive in our mind a Centaure."[6] An image is created by composing parts, not simply by projecting a stored slide.

In short, a serious drawback to depicting mental images as pictures—even moving pictures—is that pictures are fixed and images are not. If we think of our images as displays on a computer monitor screen, on the other hand, we get pictures that are *generated* when they are needed, not merely retrieved, and we can easily imagine manipulating the information in the computer and thereby altering the image on the screen.

The Mental Matrix

But who does observe the screen? To solve this problem is to dispatch the homunculus, the "little man in the head," an absolute necessity if we are to have scientific theories of mental events. How this can be done becomes clear when we consider a second important contribution of the computer display view of imagery; namely, it makes it clear that something does not have to *be* a picture to *function* as one. If you look closely at a television screen, you can see that the pictures it shows are actually arrays of dots. We can think of the blank screen as a matrix crosshatched by hundreds of horizontal and vertical lines that form tiny squares, or cells, all across the surface. When dots are placed in certain cells, the result is a picture. This pattern is clearly pictorial—but why? Because it has spatial characteristics —distances among points, geometrical relations (e.g., "adjacent to," "diagonal from") between points, and so on—which allow space in the matrix to stand for real space and points in the matrix to correspond to points on the surfaces of objects; that is, points close together on an object (as seen from a particular point of view) are close together in the matrix, points diagonal on the object are diagonal in the matrix, and so on.

But these spatial characteristics do not have to be represented in an actual picture. By analogy, imagine 36 people milling around a room, standing in no particular order. When these people first walked in the door, they were shown a picture drawn in a 6 × 6 matrix (like the one shown in Fig. 2.2). Each person was assigned a single cell in the matrix and was told to memorize its row and column number and whether or not the cell was filled in. For example, one person would memorize "3, 5" for the cell three rows down and five columns over from the left. After each cell had been memorized, the picture was destroyed, but the people collectively stored the spatial information that was in the picture. To see how, pretend you arrived late and wanted to know what the picture looked like before it was destroyed. More specifically, say you wanted to know whether there was a horizontal line one

2.2. A milling crowd that can "store" a picture if the information is interpreted in the right way.

row up from bottom of the picture. You could find out by playing the following game.

You walk into the room and call out a pair of numbers, such as "5, 1." The person who memorized the cell with these numbers then either shouts "filled" or is silent. By calling out "5, 1," "5, 2," and "5, 3" you can find out whether these cells were filled in the matrix. If they were, the person assigned to each cell will shout "filled" after you call his or her numbers. You then need to find out whether the cells above and below these cells were also filled. If they were, you may have found a solid region; if they are not, you found a line—without ever actually looking at a real matrix. Even though the people may be standing anywhere, they function to represent points that are close together in the matrix, diagonal, and so on. All the information in the picture is available, even though there is no actual picture (Fig. 2.2).

Similarly, there is no physical matrix—actual glass screen—inside a computer on which pictures are displayed; rather, cells in a hypothetical matrix are represented as entries in the machine's memory. The computer identifies these elements in a way that results in their functioning *as if* they were arranged in a visual array (Fig. 2.3). The information needed to create a picture exists in the form of a list—cell (1,1) is black, cell (1,2) is white, and so on—which can be interpreted as a spatial pattern. Thus the computer can "scan" across the cells in any direction, discover which ones are next to which others, categorize points as being along a line, and so on—all because the points are treated as if they were spatially arranged: At the functional level the elements have all the spatial relations that characterize actual pictures.

ROW	COLUMN	FILLED?	ROW	COLUMN	FILLED?
1	1	yes	3	2	no
1	2	no	3	3	yes
1	3	no	3	4	no
1	4	no	3	5	no
1	5	no	3	6	no
1	6	no	4	1	no
2	1	no	4	2	no
2	2	yes	4	3	no
2	3	no	4	4	yes
2	4	no	4	5	no
2	5	no	.	.	.
2	6	no	.	.	.
3	1	no	.	.	.

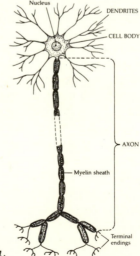

2.3. The list has the same information as the matrix, if it is "read" the right way.

From the computer analogy we can also hypothesize how the physiology of the brain might make such a matrixlike phenomenon possible in the mind. The human nervous system, including the brain, is made up of specialized cells called *neurons* (Fig. 2.4). Information is transmitted when a series of neurons fire, or go off, in sequence. Each neuron is connected to many others, and an electrochemical impulse is passed up the line to the appropriate part of the brain, or down the line *from* the brain to a gland, a muscle, or whatever.

There are billions of neurons in the nervous system, and most

Nucleus
DENDRITES
CELL BODY
AXON
Myelin sheath
Terminal endings

2.4. A neuron.

of them are organized into structures that deal with one particular type of information or another. Studies of animals have unearthed some neurons, called *detector cells*, that are so specialized that they will fire only in response to certain very specific stimuli. Frogs, for example, have "bug detectors" that fire when the frog sees a dark moving spot of a certain size, such as a fly. The human nervous system operates in a much more complicated fashion; it has a tremendous number of specialized areas and pathways. Thus we can imagine sets of neurons in the brain (or patterns of neurons firing) that stand for the various portions of an object, and neurons which connect these representations so that they give us the information we need to discern a picture. In this way, nerve cells can *function* as if they composed something like a television screen without actually *being* one.

The computer approach to understanding the mind also provides the answer to the apparent paradox of the "mind's eye": That is, if an image is a picture in the head, who is looking at the picture? The eyes that scrutinize the outside world obviously cannot be turned inward, and we know there is no homunculus watching an inner screen. The computer approach suggests that the mind's eye is comparable to the processes that allow a computer to interpret visual displays. When a computer stores pictorial information, it translates it into a set of points, with each point being stored in a cell in an imaginary matrix. To see if a straight line (or any other visual feature) appears on the matrix, the computer treats the points as being organized spatially (into rows and columns) and checks which cells have points. The computer and probably our brain can do this in a split second. The presence of a line is thus determined by two things: the stored information and the tests carried out to interpret it. We do not have to have a literal mind's eye, then, with a lens, retina, and so on, to perceive images. Instead, the mind's eye consists of the various tests that evaluate and interpret the information in a matrix. [7]

The solution to the problem of "who watches the screen" is a particular example of the general solution to the problem of the homunculus: Rules guide processing, which allows stored information to be "interpreted." We know for a fact that computers work without little men inside their heads. Goodbye Homunculus!

QUALIFYING THE BRAIN–COMPUTER ANALOGY

Although the brain–computer analogy is very useful, we should avoid overstating the case; the two are far from identical. Physically, the brain and computer have very little in common: The computer is dry and metallic, it runs on line current, and it works entirely on patterns of 0's and 1's; the brain is wet and nonmetallic, and it is composed of living nerve cells, which do not require current from outside the body. Nor do the brain cells simply switch on or off; they influence each other partly by gradual shifts in their level of activity (Fig. 2.5). The computer has distinct memory locations and a CPU. We do not know for sure whether the brain has a distinct CPU, but it seems unlikely; the brain seems to process numerous things, in different locations, at once. Furthermore, the brain apparently does not store information in just one place either, but distributes it in many places.

The similarity between brain and computer, then, is a fairly specific and limiting one, existing purely at the level of function; both machines can be understood in terms of how symbols are stored and used. To summarize, we can think of the brain—the mechanical seat of the mind—as analogous to the circuitry of a computer. Mental events—the workings of the mind at the functional level (thoughts, images, and so on)—can be conceived of as corresponding to the functional operations of a computer (adding numbers, comparing letters, and manipulating other symbols in various ways). Mental images, with their apparent pictorialness, are reminiscent of the displays on a cathode ray tube connected to a computer. However, although it is irresisti-

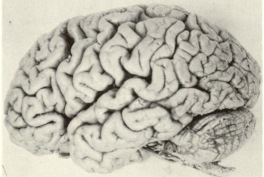

2.5. The human brain.

bly convenient to talk about visual images as if they were displays on an inner cathode ray tube (because that is how we experience them), the brain has no such screen. The pictorialness of images lies in the way they are interpreted within the mind; that is, images are interpreted in the mind *as if* they were actual displays by means of operations similar to those a CPU uses to interpret data as displays in a matrix. Thus when we speak of a "mental matrix," we are speaking about a functional organization, not a literal one.

The resemblance between computer and mind is inherently limited in another important way: The computer, so far as we know, has no experience of images or of anything else. Computer imagery is an imitation only of the functional state of a person's mind when he or she has the experience of "mentally picturing," not of the experience itself. We assume that when a person is aware of having and using an image, that is an indication that his or her mind is engaged in a particular kind of activity. Our goal is to characterize the nature of that activity in sufficient detail to program a computer to carry out the same functions. The computer will not help us understand why these activities *feel* the way they do, but this is not our goal: We want to know how the mind works, and experiences are treated as byproducts of mental activity.[8]

The problem of "ghosts in the machine" no longer stands in the way of theorizing about mental events, but we still have not said anything about the actual workings of the mind. Recall that the computer approach also helps us deal with another problem: How to raise questions about the mind in a systematic way. That is, we ask questions with an eye toward using the answers to guide us in programming a computer to mimic a person. Here, then, are some of the questions I had in mind as I began my research.

Are images really represented like a display in a matrix? An image, like a display in a computer, can be of a single object or an entire scene. How are we able to scan from one object to another, or across an entire panorama, as when we look around an imaged room to count the windows?

Images appear at different sizes. Do they have a spatial boundary, like the fixed rectangle of a television screen? If we try to form too large an image, will it overflow the available space?

If the medium for mental images is like a matrix, then it should have a grain. If so, then when we form an image of an object at too small a size, details should be obscured. Is this true?

Great scientists and mathematicians often report mentally "playing" with imaged objects, twisting and turning them in various ways. What are the possibilities? In what ways can we transform shapes in our images?

Are images from memory displayed in the same matrix as images from the eyes, as a television can display stored information from a computer or "live" input from a camera?

And when is imagery useful? We saw some examples in Chapter 1 of situations where imagery might occur (remembering the location of a wallet, deciding on a route through a city); are these isolated cases or can we define in a systematic way the kinds of situations that in general will require imagery? Should one try to use imagery when solving certain problems? If so, what kinds of problems?

Over the course of this book, we will return to these questions. The first task, though, is more rudimentary. Before it is possible to resolve complex issues about the various properties of images or other mental events, it is necessary to establish some basic facts about them; and to do so requires a research methodology. Once the questions are identified, how do we then go about looking for the answers?

3

Stalking the Mental Image

ALL CONTEMPORARY SCIENTISTS studying imagery begin with the assumption that images are not literally pictures in the head. (The very thought brings to my mind an image of a bizarre murder scene in an art gallery, in which a guard's head has been bashed in by a heavily framed portrait!) According to the cognitive science approach, an image is a representation in the mind that gives rise to the experience of "seeing" in the absence of the appropriate visual stimulation from the eyes. Ideally, then, we would like to study this representation directly. Unfortunately, though, imagery involves both a representation and a conscious experience, which is going to make things tricky. From the point of view of the person having the experience, the image itself is not usually attended to any more than the amount of attention we give to the texture of the paint or the brush strokes in a painting; in both cases we pay attention to the objects portrayed. When we use an image to answer a question about the shape of a dog's ears, we examine the ears in the image—not the image itself. Similarly, from the person's point of view, we manipulate (rotate, scan, expand, and so on) the object in the image—not the image itself.

In contrast, from the point of view of cognitive science, the image representation—not the object being represented—is what is being processed. When such a theory specifies how an image is "inspected," it is specifying how the representation is processed such that the representation of the sought feature is found; when such a theory specifies how the image is "rotated," it is specifying how the representation is processed such that the object is represented at progressively different orientations, and so on. We assume that there is some connection between how representations are processed and how objects appear in images, but the exact connection must be discovered.

Thus the cognitive scientist's task is to figure out what goes on in the mind when we are introspectively aware of doing various things to objects in our images. We want to know how visual information is stored in the representations underlying the images we experience "having," and we want to know how these representations are manipulated during the course of thinking. Not all of the properties of these mental events need be evident in our experiences, but we should be able to give an account of what is going on when we do have the experience of, for example, "seeing," "rotating," or "scanning," objects in images. In this book, unless we are discussing how objects appear introspectively in images, the term *image* will refer to the underlying representation in the mind.

According to the computer display metaphor, images are depictive; that is, they are arrays that function as if they had spatial properties. But this is not the only possibility. There are a number of alternative interpretations of people's introspections about imagery, including some that do not attribute any pictorial properties to the underlying mental representation. In order to begin to understand imagery, then, we must first spell out these alternatives and try to find out which one is right.

Of the nonpictorial explanations that have been proposed for mental imagery, three are worth considering. First, some philosophers have maintained that when people talk about images, they are not necessarily referring to any real entity. We might be using the word *image* like the word *Pete* in the expression "For Pete's sake!"—as a convenient way of talking, not having to do with an actual person called Pete. This view lacks plausibility if only because it does not fit our experience of imagery. When I image my living room, it is as if I am actually seeing it, and no one could convince me otherwise. The experience alerts me that *something* is going on in my mind. Experiences are, to use the philosophers' own term, *incorrigible*. You cannot be wrong about whether you feel pain, for instance: If you feel it, you feel it. You can be wrong about the *source* of the pain, but not about the fact that it hurts. Thus, given a large number of presumably honest people reporting the experience of imagery, it seems evident that something is going on in the mind. What that something *is*, however, is not clear.

A second and more interesting nonpictorial view of imagery

accepts people's reports of experiencing imagery at face value, but claims that this experience does not tell us anything about what is going on in the mind; that is, the fact that images "feel" pictorial does not ensure that anything pictorial is occurring in the mind when we have this experience. According to these theorists, the same kind of mental event underlies both imagery and language. Images, then, are better understood as being like sentences than pictures. A major proponent of this view is the psychologist Zenon Pylyshyn, who once asserted that images are appealing because they are "warm and fuzzy," but that their attractiveness does not mean they are a special kind of mental phenomenon.

If the mental events that produce the experience of imagery are the same as those involved in language, why do these events sometimes feel pictorial and sometimes descriptive? A common answer is that the "feel" of the experience must result from the way we interpret it. To understand what this means, consider an analogy.

In 1962, the psychologists Stanley Schachter and Jerome Singer were studying the basis of emotion. They wanted to know whether there was anything to the idea that people's feelings are often determined by how they *think about* an emotion. Schacter and Singer gave subjects an injection that was identified as a vitamin compound but which was actually a powerful stimulant. Each subject was asked to wait in a room with another person before the experiment began. In fact, the other person was a stooge—a confederate of the experimenters—and the "waiting time" was really the time during which the subject's behavior was to be observed.

With half the subjects, the stooge acted very excited and happy, flying paper airplanes and playing with a Hula-Hoop; with the other half, the stooge was upset and angry. But in both cases, the subjects interpreted their own mood as being the same as the stooge's. If a subject was with someone lively, then the adrenalin put him or her in a boisterous good humor; if the subject's companion acted angry, then the drug made the subject angry too. The same physiological state, arousal, *felt* completely different, depending on the context.

Similarly, languagelike activity in the mind may feel different according to whether it relates to visual or abstract information.

In this view, the pictorial *experience* of imagery is due strictly to the way we interpret a certain mental event; it is not related to any real difference in the mental events or the way we process verbal and visual information: If you think of a memory as arising from pictorial input, then you will perceive the memory as pictorial, even though it might just as well be perceived as descriptive.

A third nonpictorial interpretation of imagery asserts that images are not directly involved in thought at all. They are simply an indication that work is being done by the mind—like lights flashing on the outside of a computer while it is adding. The lights are an *epiphenomenon* of the machine's adding; they are "just along for the ride" as far the actual adding process is concerned. According to this theory, asking about mental events on the basis of introspections about imagery is pointless. You cannot know if the representation that produces the experience actually takes part in thinking; images might have no more to do with actual thinking than the heat given off by a lightbulb has to do with reading.

These three views obviously are quite different from the computer display metaphor. All three suggest that the properties of the images we experience tell us nothing about the actual mental representation. After all, why *should* they? It seems peculiar to think that just from introspection we could deduce how the brain functions. Nobody would think of saying such a thing about the workings of the eyes or any other bodily organ, so why should this be said about the brain, which is umpteen times more complicated? The burden, therefore, is on us to support our theory, that the mental state underlying the experience of imagery is pictorial—in function if not in form—and that such images are extremely useful (and in some cases essential) in a wide range of thought processes.

THE PRIVILEGED PROPERTIES OF IMAGES

As of the early 1970s, we were faced with the challenge of collecting evidence for a pictorial theory of imagery. We had to find a "window on the mind," and we had to use it to rule out the nonpictorial alternatives.[1]

Our first clues came not from science, but from philosophy;

that is, we found ourselves considering what it is that makes pictorial representations unique. If a set of properties could be identified that are characteristic of depictions and no other form of representation, then it might be possible to establish that those properties affect mental processing. To track the bear, one must know what its footprints look like. Thus the first order of business was to figure out what the footprints of a mental depiction would look like, as it were. Only then could we know what kind of evidence to look for in order to establish that mental images depict information.

Although words and pictures may carry much of the same information, they do so differently. Pictures *depict*; in some fundamental way they "look like" the object being represented ("re-presented"). A sentence, on the other hand, bears no resemblance to the content it carries, but conveys meaning according to an independent set of rules. Pictures seem to be accessible to anybody, but language must be learned. To extract the content of a sentence, one has to know what its words mean to some particular group of speakers. In addition, one has to be familiar with its grammar—the rules that dictate how words can be arranged into meaningful units. Although the grammar of every language is different, all languages have a similar underlying structure; that is, each includes various types of symbols (typically, one set to represent objects, another set to represent actions, and so on) and rules that govern their arrangement.

In English, for example, a sentence must have a noun phrase and a verb phrase. The noun phrase must contain a noun, but it can also include other elements, such as a determiner (*the, a*) and an adjective. *The cat ate the mouse* includes *the cat* as the noun phrase and *ate the mouse* as the verb phrase. The noun phrase itself includes a determiner and a noun, and the verb phrase includes a verb (*ate*) and another noun phrase embedded in it, which includes a determiner and a noun. The rules of grammar allow us to construct an infinite number of grammatically correct sentences, and they also prevent us from generating an equally large set of possible, but nongrammatical, word strings (such as *The ate mouse the cat*).

Precisely how language differs from depictive representations is a crucial issue to anyone trying to pin down the nature of mental images and their role in thinking. The kind of linguistic representation used in the mind is several steps removed from the actual sentences; people usually remember the gist of a sentence, not the words themselves (let alone how they sounded when spoken). If a person were to emigrate from Germany to the United States, for example, he or she might eventually forget much of the German language, but still remember the information he or she originally learned in that language. The kind of "distilled" language representation used for storing information in memory is called a *propositional representation*.[2]

Propositions *describe* the relations among objects or things. Take a simple statement like, "The ball is on the box." In its propositional form, this representation can be characterized as follows (Fig. 3.1):

1. It is composed of discrete symbols. You can break the words down into letters, but these are the smallest "units"; half of *a* is not a symbol that can be used.
2. There are different types of symbols. One of the symbols stands for a *relation*—"on"—that is expressed separately from the other information in the sentence.
3. The symbols are arranged according to a set of rules—a grammar. You cannot say, "On is box the ball the."
4. The representation is abstract, in that (a) it can refer to classes of objects (such as boxes and balls in general) and (b) it contains information that could have arisen from more than one mode of perception (we could arrive at a statement of fact by touch, for instance, as well as by vision).
5. It is unambiguous; its symbols are defined to have only one meaning. This is a critical difference between the words and sentences of English and the symbols and the assertions of propositions. The word *ball*, for example, is ambiguous in English: It can refer to a dance, a sphere, or a part of a foot. Each meaning, however, must have one propositional symbol that is entirely unabmiguous. Think about it: Have you ever had an ambiguous thought? Have you ever thought about a ball and then wondered which sense of the word you meant? Probably not. This is as it should be if you think in terms of propositions rather than words.

In contrast, consider the corresponding depictive representation. It differs from the descriptive statement right down the line (Fig. 3.1):

Description	Depiction
ON (BALL, BOX)	

1. Discrete symbols	1. No discrete symbols
2. Requires symbol for relation	2. No separate symbol for relation
3. Rules for symbol combination	3. One rule for symbol combination
4. Abstract	4. Concrete
5. Unambiguous	5. Ambiguous
6. No spatial medium	6. Requires spatial medium
7. No symbol-for-point correspondence	7. Symbol-for-point correspondence

3.1. Two ways visual information can be represented.

1. The symbols are not discrete; you can break them up in any arbitrary way and still have symbols that can be used—a corner of the box, a side of the ball; even a single dot in a depiction is an acceptable symbol.
2. There are no distinct types of symbols. In particular, there is no separate symbol standing for a relation: "On-ness" is shown implicitly by the way the ball and box are placed, not separately from them. One cannot even represent "on" by itself; the relation can only be represented in a given context.
3. Because there are no discrete symbols that belong to different categories (such as noun, verb, and so on), there is no "grammar of pictures" in the way that there is a grammar in language.
4. The representation is concrete, in that (a) it must include particular details about the ball and box, such as the size and shape (a single depiction cannot represent all properties of all objects in a class; e.g., the box cannot be square and rectangular at the same time), and (b) it is associated with only one mode of perception—vision.
5. It can be ambiguous—there is in principle more than one way to interpret it: Is it a picture of some child's favorite toys? The first in a series of pictures showing a ball dropping through a trap door? A parody of a bust of Beethoven? A propositional representation is defined to be unambiguous; a depiction will

be unambiguous only in a special case, where there are specific rules for the way in which to look at them.

In the context of the computer view of the mind, it is easy to see from this comparison that a programmer would have to approach a descriptive representation and a depictive one quite differently to enter them accurately into a computer's memory. A description would be a string of symbols that are interpreted as different kinds of things (verbs, nouns, etc.) and would need to be looked up in a dictionary to become meaningful. A depiction, on the other hand, would be a set of dots arranged in a spatial pattern. The dots would not need interpretation as different kinds of symbols; instead, meaning would derive from the resemblance between the pattern they form and some object (as seen from a particular angle). From the point of view of a human being, who is used to translating visual information into words and vice versa, the sentence and the picture may appear more or less synonymous. But from the computer's point of view, they have almost nothing in common.

This comparison thus suggests some crucial properties we can use to distinguish a depictive representation in the mind from a descriptive one. These can be called *privileged properties*, in that they are exclusive to depictive representations.

1. Depictions can only exist in a medium that functions as a space (as was discussed in Chapter 2). The space can be a physical one (such as a piece of paper or a television screen) or a functional one (such as a matrix in a computer's memory). Even if we assume that images do not involve a literal matrix, they must, if they are depictive, act *as if* they were in a space.[3]

2. Every part of a depiction corresponds to a part of the object it represents; every dot in a picture stands for a point on the object. Furthermore, the distances between parts of the depiction preserve the relative distances between the corresponding parts of the object (as seen from a particular point of view). This close relationship between depiction and object also means that it is difficult to depict the *shape* of an object without also representing a size and an orientation. You can *say* that a ball is round and leave it at that, but when you *draw* a ball it is hard to avoid adding other qualities.[4]

Depictions and descriptions, then, are different *formats* the mind might use to store information. A format is a type of code, and the same information (e.g., about balls and boxes) often can be stored in numerous different formats. Which formats are in fact used by the mind must be discovered, somehow, by actually studying the mind.

INVESTIGATING MENTAL DEPICTIONS

The ideal way to investigate mental imagery, like anything else, would be to observe it directly. But how can we observe what occurs in the hidden reaches of the mind? Even if the skull were transparent, it would not help much: Watching the brain at work would tell us only what it is doing at the physical level, not what it is accomplishing at the functional level. Given that images are not literally pictorial, they do not offer us anything to observe.

Philosophers and psychologists up through the early 1900s got around this difficulty by relying on introspection. Wilhelm Wundt, in his extensive investigations of imagery (see Chapter 1), depended heavily on his subjects' reports of their inner perceptions to tell him what the brain was doing when a person was performing a given task. Introspection, though, as we have already seen, is of limited usefulness in imagery research. One drawback is the notorious differences in introspective reports (recall Tichner's and Watson's contrasting views), which may be due to differences in each person's ability to introspect (to "see" the images with the mind's eye) and report about his or her images. Given that images are both private and nonverbal, there is no way of knowing whether all of us attend to them and interpret them the same way. Furthermore, just as wine tasters have had a hard time establishing a common vocabulary for describing the smell and taste of various wines, people may use words differently in describing mental images.

A second major limitation on the use of introspection came to light in the early part of this century. Workers in the laboratory of Oswaldo Kulpe, a German psychologist, stumbled on what came to be called *imageless thought*. You can try a typical experiment for yourself: First lift a book, put it down; then lift a glass. Which object was heavier? What was surprising about the results of Kulpe's experiment was that although the subjects could answer the question easily enough, they had no idea how they made their judgments. They were aware of plenty of images and sensations, but these did not seem to be the basis for their answers—the judgments just seemed to pop into mind full-blown, unguided by conscious processing. Kulpe concluded from this that not all thought is accompanied by mental images and thus introspection alone will not reveal everything we want to know about the mind.

It is not surprising that our introspections cannot tell us the whole story of how the mind works. Indeed, it would be surprising if they did. One of Sigmund Freud's great discoveries was that much unconscious mental processing goes on before a person becomes aware of having a thought. Almost by definition, we cannot directly plumb the workings of the unconscious. Similarly, the experience of images need not reveal *everything* about the nature of the underlying mental events, even if the information revealed by the experience were a direct reflection of *some* of the underlying mental events.

How, then, do we find our "window on the mind"? What method can we devise for studying mental events? The solution is to externalize introspection, making some aspect of it publicly observable, and therefore measurable. The answer to the puzzle lies in focusing on the *consequences* of mental activity. As soon as we turn to observing how a mental event affects someone's performance, we are in business—we know how to measure performance. Thus for imagery the trick is to observe the *time* it takes people to use images in certain ways, the kinds of *errors* made when using imagery, and the way imagery affects certain *judgments.* If images really do depict, the representation should have a "size," "shape," and "orientation" in a functional space (as would a pattern of dots in a matrix), and these properties should affect processing times and the like. For example, these properties should be reflected in the time it takes someone to scan across an image, rotate it, and so on. Rather than try to study introspections themselves, then, we set out to study the observable consequences of using imagery.

SOME PRELIMINARY IMAGE STUDIES

An example of this approach is a series of studies Roger Shepard did with Jackie Metzler at Stanford University on the mental

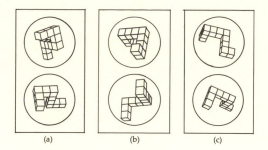

3.2 The stimuli used by Shepard and Metzler in their study of mental rotation.

rotation of images. Shepard and Metzler began by showing their subjects paired pictures of geometric shapes (Fig. 3.2). The subjects' task was to decide as quickly as possible whether both pictures were of the same shape, irrespective of orientation. To answer this question, the subjects would have to rotate one shape in their image until it matched up (or failed to match up) with the other shape. The investigators hypothesized that the farther around a shape had to be rotated, the longer this task should take. Subjects thus should be able to solve the question faster in Fig. 3.2a than in Fig. 3.2b. And so they did. When asked afterward how they compared the two shapes, subjects confirmed that they had mentally rotated one to match the other. In sum, the subjects' introspection matched what the investigators had measured.[5]

The method of studying the consequences of mental activity goes far beyond what we can learn from simple introspection. Take the findings just described. They not only validate the introspection that objects in images seem to rotate by passing through intermediate positions along a trajectory, and hence require more time to rotate further; they also tell us things that simply are not apparent to introspection. For example, the rotation time increased *linearly* with the angle by which the figure was rotated (Fig. 3.3); that is, it took subjects an additional 60 milliseconds (i.e., $60/1000$ of a second) to rotate the object in image each additional degree, regardless of how far it had already been

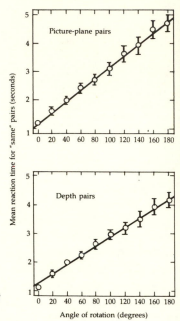

3.3. The time required to compare stimuli when different amounts of rotation are needed to bring them into the same orientation.

rotated. This is not necessarily what happens when someone rotates a real object—spins a globe on its axis, for example. Objects in images *could* possibly have mimicked drag, rotating more and more slowly with each additional degree once they got started, or they could have mimicked acceleration, in which case they would have seemed to move more quickly the farther they rotated, or they could even have sped up and slowed down at different points, as if rotating on uneven ball bearings. But they did none of these things, which suggests that when we rotate an object in an image, we are not simply imitating the way actual objects move; the mind appears to have some kind of process that gets switched on and then operates at a constant speed when we try to rotate something as quickly as possible. This fact is not apparent in simple introspection.

This inferential method, then, gives us tangible data that we never could get from reports alone. And in addition to providing concrete information about the properties of images, experiments like this one support the very idea that images—and mental events in general—are real psychological entities that can be studied, measured, and theorized about.

SCANNING VISUAL IMAGES

The mental rotation results reveal properties of how images are used. However, they do not tell us about the nature of the representations themselves. The mental rotation results could be due to shifting around a depictive representation (i.e., rotating a pattern of points around in a functional matrix) or gradually changing propositional descriptions of the figures so that different orientations are represented. That is, perhaps each figure is stored as a description of how the boxes are interconnected and their angle from the viewer (e.g., "box 1 is connected to the left of box 2, and the two boxes together point 45 degrees up from the horizontal"), and "rotation" is accomplished by gradually changing the description of the angle (e.g., going in steps from 45 to 90 degrees). In this case, more steps would be required—requiring more time—when figures are "rotated" by larger amounts. This propositional rotation process would be carried out unconsciously, and the experience of "seeing" the figures rotate would be produced somehow when the angles are updated. If this theory were true, then, the pictorial properties of the experience of imagery would be epiphenomenal, telling us nothing about the actual representations used in the mind.[6]

Our first set of experiments was designed to get to the heart of the matter. We wanted a situation in which the privileged properties of depictions would leave tracks, so to speak. That is, besides inventing a task in which people would be introspectively aware of having an image, we needed to be able to discern an objective, measurable difference if a depictive representation—and not a propositional one—were being processed. The best way to do this seemed to be to use time as a measure in a mental image scanning task. If subjects took more time to scan a long distance across an object in an image than a short distance, then we could reasonably conclude they really were *using* a depictive representation, not just experiencing the properties of one. Distance is a "privileged property" of depictions, so it should affect scanning

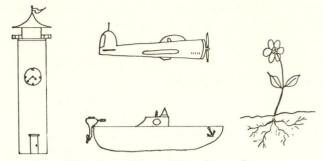

3.4. Examples of drawings that subjects imaged.

times only when subjects use imagery, provided that images
actually do depict information.

The task my collaborators and I chose was for subjects to memorize a sample drawing until they could image it accurately, and
then answer questions by examining the drawing in their image.[7]
Four of the ten drawings we used are shown here (Fig. 3.4). The
subjects first learned to form good mental images of each of
the drawings. Then, with their eyes closed, they heard the name
of one of the drawings (for instance, *speedboat*) followed five seconds later by the name of a possible feature of that object (for
instance, *motor*). Half the time the feature had been included in
the drawing, and half the time it had not. Subjects were instructed
to "look at" the drawing in their images and push one button if
they could "see" the feature in question, and another button if
they could not. We told them that the point was not how quickly
they could decide whether the named feature was present, but
how long it took them to examine the imaged drawing for the
feature. The features we asked about were located at different
distances from the ends of the drawing, either right on the end,
in the middle, or on the opposite end. Half of these subjects were
asked to focus on one end of the drawing as soon as they imaged
it. This way, we reasoned, we could see whether people took
longer to scan from one end to the other than to scan from one
end to the middle. The other half of the subjects were to hold the
whole drawing in view at once.

The results were gratifying. It *did* take subjects longer to scan
from one end of an imaged drawing to the other, and proportionally less time to find a part of a drawing closer to the point of

focus. Subjects who were asked to keep the whole drawing in view in the image were able to find any part in about the same length of time; thus the results were not due to some peculiarity in the parts themselves but, rather, to the distance between the part and the point of focus.

In addition to asking subjects to visually memorize the drawings and form images of them, we asked another group of subjects to learn the drawings by describing them in words. These people then recalled their descriptions when given the name of one of the drawings. Half the subjects were asked to start off by describing the whole drawing; like the imagery group, these people found any part of the drawing in about the same time. Those asked to begin with just one end of the drawing in mind, however, took more time to find parts farther from that end. In fact, the increase in time with distance was far greater than for the imagery group. On closer inspection of these data, we found that this increase was due mostly to subjects who began at the right end of a drawing and presumably had to scan "backward" down a list they had memorized from left to right. People who focused on one end of the drawing in an image, in contrast, scanned just as easily from right to left as from left to right.

Interpreting the Results

On the face of things, the data from this first experiment support the idea that the mind really does depict information when people experience "having an image." Not only did the time the subjects needed to scan drawings in their images increase with the distance scanned, but subjects who had memorized verbal descriptions rather than visual images of the drawings had qualitatively different results.

But does all of this rule out the propositional alternatives to imagery? Unfortunately not. Shortly after these results were published, I got a phone call from Danny Bobrow, a respected researcher in artificial intelligence, who had a different interpretation to offer. Though we had perhaps ruled out a straight verbal alternative, a propositional representation is not necessarily the same thing as a verbal one. What we had demonstrated, Danny suggested, might be simply a difference between alternative ways of organizing propositional representations. That is, the task could have been performed not with a depictive repre-

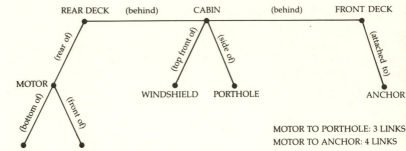

3.5. *A propositional structure representing the information encoded from a picture of a motorboat. The structure is built up by combining propositions, which could be rewritten as* BOTTOM OF *(*PROPELLER, MOTOR*),* REAR OF *(*MOTOR, REAR DECK*), and so on.*

sentation, but with a mental representation like the one in Fig. 3.5—a propositional list with "pointers" linking the names of the drawing's various features. This kind of list is formed by combining simple propositions, each of which is represented by a dot for each part and a connecting link representing the relation. For example, at the lower left of the Fig. 3.5 we see PROPELLER-BOTTOM OF-MOTOR. This is a simple proposition (it has all the elements discussed earlier, BOTTOM OF is the relation, PROPELLER and MOTOR are the symbols being related), which in turn is linked to MOTOR-REAR OF-DECK, another simple proposition. According to this interpretation of our results, subjects construct such a description automatically (and unconsciously) when they are asked to memorize visual information. Although the list mirrors the spatial arrangement of the picture it represents, it is not depictive, because (1) it does not occur in a spatial medium and hence does not embody physical distance per se (it does not represent the space between parts) and (2) it makes use of propositional relations (such as "next to") and discrete symbols in organizing the drawing's features.

If this view is correct, a depictive image was *not* actually part of the subjects' mental processing. When asked to focus on one end of a drawing in the image, they simply activated that section of the list. Then they scanned as much of the list as necessary to find the named feature of the drawing. The so-called effect of distance on scanning time would thus be a function of how many list entries subjects had to look through, not a function of distance at all. The conscious experience of "scanning" a picturelike image may be totally epiphenomenal.

Back to the Drawing Board

So it was back to the drawing board—quite literally—to design another experiment. The flaw in the first one was the relationship between spatial distance and the number of features in the drawing: When scanning greater distances, subjects also scanned over more features. What we had to do, then, was find a way to evaluate the effects of distance alone.

To accomplish this we devised two different experiments. In the first one, the distance scanned and the number of items scanned over were varied independently. Subjects studied a series of drawings, each one consisting of a line with three letters of the alphabet on it. Two of the letters were lowercase and the third letter was in the uppercase (Fig. 3.6). After studying a line, subjects were told to shut their eyes, imaged it, and focus on either the right or the left end; then the name of one of the three letters was presented. Subjects shifted their mental gaze to that letter and pushed one button if it was uppercase, the other if it was lowercase. In scanning to the target letter, a subject might scan any one of three distances and scan over one, two, or no intervening letters.

Once again, the results were just what one would expect had a depictive representation been used to perform the task. More time was required to scan longer distances. Subjects also took more

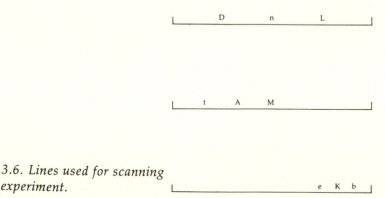

3.6. *Lines used for scanning*
experiment.

3.7. The fictional map that subjects imaged and then scanned across. The X's mark the exact locations of the objects.

time for every letter they had to scan over, which makes sense if you assume that they paused to "look" at each letter as they passed it. The important thing was that the two effects—of the distance per se and of the number of items between the starting point and the target—were independent of each other.

In the previous experiment only three distances were scanned, which was not enough to see if times increased *linearly* with distance. Furthermore, if images depict, they should do so in at least two dimensions, not just along a line. If a constant amount of time is required to scan each additional distance across a two-dimensional display in an image, this would be good evidence that distance per se is embodied in the representation. So we asked subjects to memorize a map with seven locations marked on it: a rock, a patch of grass, a tree, a beach, a well, a hut, and a lake (Fig. 3.7). The distance between every two locations was different. Holding an image of the whole map in mind, subjects were to focus on one location and then "look" for a second one. Half the time this second location appeared on the map and half the time it did not. When it was on the map, the subjects were to picture a little black speck moving as fast as possible from point A to point B, so that their scanning would be as direct as possible. When the speck reached the goal, subjects were to push a button. If they "looked" around the map and could not find the named location, they pushed a second button. Once again, the results of the experiment supported the claim that image representations are depictive: Scanning times increased linearly with

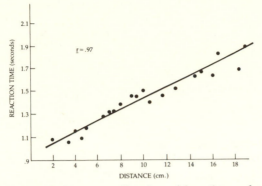

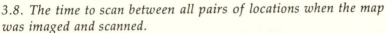

3.8. The time to scan between all pairs of locations when the map was imaged and scanned.

the distance scanned across this two-dimensional imaged display (Fig. 3.8).

We ran a second version of this experiment to double-check the results. Again, subjects were asked to memorize the map, image it, and focus on a given location. But this time, when they heard the second word, they were to decide whether it named a location that was on the map without necessarily using imagery—they were just to answer as quickly as possible. Given that the map contained only seven locations, we reasoned that subjects could simply check a mental list rather than have to scan the image to answer the question. If the effects of distance found before were a special consequence of processing depictive images *per se*, then distance should not affect response times when our subjects did not actually use their images.

In fact, there was not a hint of the effects of distance in the data from this experiment. This strongly suggests that subjects were *not* using some kind of propositional representation in the earlier experiment; for if they had, the results of both experiment should have been the same.

Questions of Scale

It often happens in research that an experiment designed for one purpose ends up leading in some unexpected direction. One of the variations of the map experiment did just that. We had asked a particular group of subjects not to focus on a certain loca-

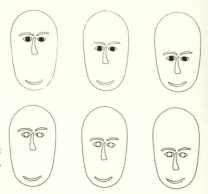

*3.9. The schematic faces
that subjects imaged at one
of three apparent sizes.*

tion, but to "zoom in" on that spot so that it was all they could
"see" of the map. When a second location was named, the subjects were to be sure to "see" it before responding that it was on
the map. Nothing was said to the subjects about scanning, shifting their glance, or the like. Our reasoning was that probably no
effects of distance would show up, because having a distance
requires two points.

To our surprise, scanning time increased greatly as the distance between the initial focus point and the target location
increased. What this meant, we quickly hypothesized, was that
parts of an image can "wait in the wings," to be filled in as the
person scans in one direction or another. This notion led us to
make the following prediction: If people can vary the size scale of
an image so that it overflows the "space," but not lose access to
the parts that are beyond the edge, then the distances *between*
parts must elongate; and as the image grows in size, the scanning
time from one location to another should increase proportionally.

To test this prediction, we used six schematic faces as stimuli.
These varied in two ways: The eyes were either light or dark and
the eyes were one of three distances from the mouth (Fig. 3.9).
After memorizing the faces, subjects were asked to close their
eyes and then image each face at either *full size* (as large as possible without overflowing), *half size* (half as large as possible), or
overflow (so large that only the mouth was visible). Subjects were
to focus on the mouth after adjusting the image to the correct
size. They were then cued either "light" or "dark," whereupon
they "glanced up" to see if the cue word correctly described the

face's eyes. As usual, the time to make the decision was recorded. The results were as predicted: Not only did scanning time increase with distance, as expected, but it increased with size scale as well. The larger faces took longer to inspect, which also amplified the general effects of distance.

Are Subjects Faking the Data?

What if our results are due to subjects intentionally regulating their response times? Perhaps they somehow deduced what the experimenter wanted and decided to cooperate by producing the expected data. This is a common pitfall in psychological experiments, and one we needed to control for before we could be sure that people really can use depictive images in thinking.

In one set of experiments we directly confronted the idea that the experimenter was somehow cuing the subjects about the expected results (perhaps unconsciously), and the subjects were cooperating by responding as we expected. We misled two experimenters about the actual predictions in the map-scanning task. We told them that because the close items (in the lower left of the map) were "cluttered together," we expected subjects to take a long time to scan among them. To emphasize the point, we redrew the map so that the four close items were drawn in very heavy ink, making them seem even more a single group. Thus the experimenters expected a U-shaped relationship between response time and distance, with the longest times for the cluttered items and those separated by long distances and the fastest times for the items separated by medium distances. We impressed upon the experimenters how certain we were that the results should come out as we had explained to them.

The results in this experiment were just as before: For subjects tested by both experimenters, times again increased with increasing scanning distance. The subjects were very fast for the close items, contrary to the experimenters' expectations. The experimenters were disappointed and very surprised when our innocent deception was explained to them. Clearly the increased time to scan greater distances over an imaged object is not due to subjects' responding to cues about the experimenter's expectations.

However, what if the results are due to cues not from the experimenter, but from the nature of the task itself? That is, perhaps the subjects interpret the instructions to scan an object in an image as requiring them to pretend that they were scanning the actual object in front of them; thus they think about what it is like to scan over an actual object and realize (again, perhaps unconsciously) that more time would be required to scan greater distances. Their very understanding of the task, then, would lead them to regulate their responses to mimic what they think would happen if they scanned over objects in front of them, and hence they take longer to respond when a greater distance should have been scanned. If so, then the results from the scanning tasks say nothing about the nature of image representation.[8] Two more experiments address this counterinterpretation of the scanning results.

For our next experiment in this series, a group of subjects first rated 304 true–false statements according to whether or not imagery was required to answer them. Each statement was about a property at one end of an object, for example, "A bee has a dark head." Subjects classified the statements on a scale of 1 to 7 as definitely requiring imagery, definitely not requiring imagery, or somewhere in between. We selected forty "true" statements from this set, half of them rated to require imagery (such as, "A pineapple had pointed leaves") and half rated not to require imagery (such as, "A chimp has two eyes"). Then a second group of subjects was asked to image each object facing a given way and to focus on one end, as in previous experiments. After imaging the object and focusing on one end, the subjects were to answer a question about a feature of the object.

The trick here was that the subjects were never told to scan the object in the image to find the property; rather, they were asked to begin by forming the image as instructed, but then to answer as quickly as possible, without necessarily using the image to reach a decision. The results showed that the time these people needed to answer the questions depended on the distance of the target property from the initial focus point *only* for those items rated by the previous subjects as requiring imagery. For the items rated as not inducing imagery, there was no hint of a distance effect. Because the two kinds of items were randomly mixed (and the subjects in this question-answering task did not even know that there *were* two kinds of properties), we can rule out conscious or unconscious cooperation as an explanation for the

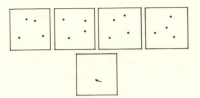

3.10. Stimuli used by Finke and Pinker to study imagery scanning without having to instruct subjects to form and scan an image.

results. Subjects could not have been pretending to be scanning, "faking" the data by taking longer when they knew they were supposed to scan. These people were never asked to scan, nor did they infer the purpose of the experiment when we asked them about it afterward.

One more experiment finalizes our conclusions, in that the experimenters were able to eliminate even the instructions to form an image and focus on a given place. Ronald Finke and Steven Pinker devised a situation in which subjects had to scan an image in order to perform the task. Subjects were first shown a field containing dots in random locations, as in Fig. 3.10. They studied the dots, which were removed. A few seconds later, an arrow was presented. The subjects were to say whether the arrow would have pointed at a dot if it had been superimposed on the first display. Subjects reported that the way they answered this question was by imaging the dots, adding the arrow to the image, and then scanning along the direction the arrow pointed to see if a dot fell along this path. The data supported this introspection: Response time increased with the distance subjects would have had to scan. Furthermore, the actual increase in time with increased scanning distance was virtually identical to that observed in the experiments I had conducted earlier. Clearly, people can form depictive images, and scanning time does reflect the distance between parts of such images.

What general conclusions can be drawn from this series of experiments? For one thing, not all thinking and memory occur in the same format. Rather, information may be represented in at least two formats in the mind, one of which is depictive. This is, of course, only the "thin edge of a wedge": Having opened the door to two, we can ask about any number of other possibilities. Some mental representations may be specialized for representing qualities of sounds, tactile sensations, or smells in a nondepictive but nonpropositional way; others may represent time sequences; and still others may be specialized for purposes we have yet to consider. In any event, it is now clear that these are empirical questions that can be addressed in a straightforward way. We have solved the problem of how to investigate mental events. By studying the consequences of mental events, such as the time a person takes to make a decision, we clearly can further our understanding of that most fascinating phenomenon, the human mind.

4

The Medium and the Message

HAVING DISPATCHED THE HOMUNCULUS, unraveled the paradox of ghosts in the brain, and found a way to study mental events, we now are in a position to begin studying the mind in earnest. We have seen evidence that information can be stored with depictive mental images. But how are images actually used in thought? Before constructing a detailed theory, we must first learn more about images and mental events. In this chapter we explore another facet of mental representation, and collect more information about images per se. Our attack on this relatively narrow problem is one example of how today's cognitive scientists are analyzing the mind. Whether the specific target is language, reasoning, or some other facet of mental activity, the tactics are basically the same.

One implication of the claim that images depict information is inescapable: Any depictive image must occur *in* or *on* something. You cannot draw a picture without something to draw it on, and the properties of the paper, canvas, slate, or whatever medium you use will affect all the drawings you make on it. A sketch on burlap, for example, will be more "pebbly" than one on paper. Thus if you wanted to draw a small picture with many fine details, you would have trouble doing it on burlap.

Plato touched on this problem more than 2,000 years ago, when he was pondering why people forget. (This is a real question, if you stop to think about it; given that we remember *at all*, why should we not keep on remembering?) Plato offered a metaphorical solution to this puzzle:

> I would have you imagine, then, that there exists in the mind of man a block of wax, which is of different sizes in different men; harder, moister, and having more or less of purity in one than another, and in some

of an intermediate quality. . . . When we wish to remember anything which we have seen, or heard, or thought in our own minds, we hold the wax to the perceptions and thoughts, and in that material receive the impression of them as from the seal of a ring; and . . . we remember and know what is imprinted as long as the image lasts; but when the image is effaced or cannot be taken, then we forget and do not know.[1]

The important implication of this idea for present-day investigations of imagery is the notion that we can distinguish between the properties of the medium (the wax tablet) and those of the representation of information (the etchings). No matter what information is stored, it will not change the nature of the medium—wax is wax. The properties of the medium, however, affect all the representations that occur in it. No matter what is being etched, if the wax is unreceptive, the etcher is in trouble.

PROPERTIES OF THE MEDIUM

As we are using the term here, a medium is a place where representations can be put. Like a block of wax—or any kind of spatial medium—a television screen has properties that affect the images it displays. For one thing, the images on a picture tube are made up of thousands of tiny dots, which give these images a "grain." If something is shown too small, details are lost, as you probably have noticed if you have ever watched on television an epic film produced for the wide screen of movie theaters. The reason is that the television screen simply does not have enough dots to convey fine gradations in shape. On the other hand, if the picture is too large, it overflows the screen. Both the grain and size of the medium affect what images can be placed on it (Fig. 4.1).

Unfortunately, we cannot study in isolation either the medium in which the image occurs or the tests of the "mind's eye" that interpret the image. If the whole imaging apparatus is thought of as analogous to a computer system, then the medium is the matrix in which patterns are displayed (which can be connected to a television screen so we can watch what is going on inside).

4.1. Grain effects and extent effects.

The mind's eye corresponds to the tests the computer performs on these patterns to identify and interpret them (see Chapter 2). It is impossible to investigate this system—image, medium, and tests on the image—without using it to carry out the investigation. The problem is a little like the old one that asks whether there is a sound if a tree falls in the forest with no one there to hear it. Any properties of the medium we discover also affect the mind's eye, and vice versa. If they did not, they would never make themselves known to us, and might as well not exist at all.

Establishing the existence of a mental medium in which images occur, however, is a critical step for the study of imaging. If images are depictive, they *must* occur in a medium that acts like a space (though it need not be an actual space). Therefore my colleagues and I decided that it would be useful to pin down some spatial properties of the medium, even though we can only learn about these properties by the way in which they affect the mind's eye. The logic of these experiments was simple: Any property of the mental medium should affect all images, no matter of what.

Two properties of the medium seemed most important to try to establish. First, the medium—as "seen" by the mind's eye—should have a limited resolution. If objects are imaged too small, parts should be harder to see. This is true in visual perception; and if the same medium is used in imagery and perception (as will be argued in Chapter 5), it should be true in imagery too. Second, the medium should have a limited spatial extent: Images cannot be infinitely large, but should be limited by the size of the medium and the scope of the mind's eye.

TESTING SIZE AND DETAIL

Once again, the strategy was to ask people to image an object and then inspect it for some particular property. We started off with animals as the target objects and asked people to look for particular features of the animals in their images. So, for example, the subject might be asked to image a rabbit and then look for the nose. Our hope was to get subjects to image some of the animals so small that details would be obscured by the grain of the mental medium. If this happened, it should take subjects longer to "see" features on animals in these images than on animals pictured at a normal size.

We were afraid that if we simply asked subjects directly to vary the size of the animals in their images, they would guess what we were after, which might bias the results. So we manipulated size in a slightly more devious fashion. Subjects were asked to image a "target" animal (such as a rabbit), which would later be inspected, standing next to either an elephant or a fly. The two animals (rabbit and elephant or rabbit and fly) were to be imaged at the correct relative sizes (Fig. 4.2). We reasoned that if the mental screen had only a limited amount of space, then people would have to vary the size of the target animal, depending on how much of their mental screen was filled up by the elephant (a lot) or the fly (hardly any). If the target animal were next to the elephant, it should be quite small, and its features harder to make out than if it were imaged next to the fly. By measuring how long it took subjects to check the animals in their images for various features, we should be able to tell whether details are indeed obscured by the grain of the mental medium.

The results came out as predicted: Subjects did take longer to "see" features on the animals imaged next to the elephant than on those imaged next to the fly. But there was a problem. Most people, after all, like elephants better than flies. Maybe some of the subjects had a favorite elephant, like Dumbo, but no favorite fly. What if they were lavishing more time and effort on imaging the elephant, leaving less time to image the animal next to it accurately? If so, the time difference in spotting features was actually due to the fact that the subjects were not lingering as long over the fly and therefore made more accurate images of the target animal. To get around this possibility, the next group of

4.2. A rabbit and an elephant versus a rabbit and a fly.

subjects was asked to image their target animals next to a tiny elephant or a gigantic fly. As odd as this sounds, people seemed to have no trouble doing it, and this time they took longer to inspect the animals imaged next to the fly.

But do these results tell us anything about imagery per se? Can we even be sure the subjects were using imagery? The propositionalists disputed the assumption that taking longer to "see" features on a small object in an image than on a large one is really an effect of the image size and the grain of the mental medium. They offered a counterexplanation that rested on the following idea: The representations used in this task are not really depictions of the animals, but mental descriptions of them (although not necessarily in words, perhaps in unconscious propositions). The subjects recall more about the features of the larger animal in each pair because they know that they should be able to see more details on large things than on small ones. And when they recall more features of one animal, they can recall less information about the object it is next to, because they have less storage space left in memory for its description.

The basis for this interpretation lies in psychologists' current understanding of short-term memory (Fig. 4.3). Briefly, human memory operates at three levels: sensory storage, which registers momentary impressions (for less than a second) of things we perceive; short-term storage, which holds items for a slightly longer time (a few seconds); and long-term storage, where information is filed away (sometimes for life) for later use. When you look up a telephone number, for example, the number first enters sensory storage for a fraction of a second. Unless you are distracted, you can then hold it in short-term storage for long enough to make your phone call. Rehearsing the number (saying it over and over) acts to hold it in short-term memory. If you study the num-

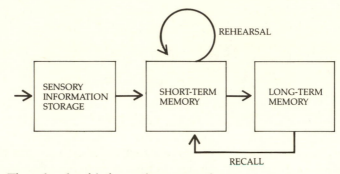

4.3. Three levels of information processing.

ber or use it often, it will be stored away in your long-term memory, where you can retrieve it again when you need it. Most people can hold up to about seven simple items, such as words or digits, in short-term storage before either forgetting them or transferring them to long-term storage. This is one reason why telephone numbers are seven digits long.

The reasoning of the propositionalists, then, was that each time subjects were asked to image a pair of animals, they would use up nearly all the space in their short-term memory remembering features of the larger animals. That is, when a subject was asked to image a rabbit standing next to an elephant, he or she would hold four or five features of the elephant in mind (such as ears, trunk, feet, tail, and skin), which left room for only one or two features of the rabbit. When asked to image the rabbit next to a fly, the subject would remember four or five of the rabbit's features and only one or two of the fly. This is why subjects identified features faster on the larger animal of each pair: The more features someone can keep in short-term memory, the more likely it is that he or she has in mind the feature the experimenter is asking about. Features not on the short-term list require "digging in the files," going into long-term memory, which takes time.

According to the propositionalist interpretation, then, the *size* of a queried feature is of no importance; however, when people recall a list or some other propositional representation, the *strength of association* of a feature with the object *is* important—people recall more strongly associated features more quickly. According to the imagery view, in contrast, the grain of the medium is responsible for the difficulty in inspecting objects imaged at a small size. Thus the smaller features of a given object should be harder to "see" than the larger ones. This hypothesis led us to try to show that it was size *per se* that affected image inspection time, and not the limitations of verbal or propositional short-term memory.

To see how our experiment worked, try imaging a cat. Notice how easy it is to "see" the cat's head. Now, what about its claws? In an image the head is larger and more quickly spotted than the claws. If the propositional view were correct, "claws" should come to mind at least as quickly as "head," because the important thing would be how likely it is that a given feature is among those you recall when you "think of what a cat looks like." And in fact, when people are asked simply to identify the features that characterize a cat *without* using imagery, they identify claws *more* quickly than head.

Thus we pitted two factors against each other: the size of a feature and its association strength. People were or were not asked to use imagery when deciding whether specific features belonged to animals—such as "whiskers" and "back" for a mouse, "feet" and "feathers" for a duck, and "stinger" and "wings" for a bee (each animal was also paired with "false" features, but this does not concern us here). The fact that size affected response times *only* when imagery was used, whereas strength of association affected times when imagery was not used, suggested that our subjects really were using images, and not propositional representations. We therefore felt justified in concluding that it was indeed the grain of the medium, and not the nature of verbal or propositional short-term memory, that was responsible for our results.

Two other points about this set of experiments are worth mentioning. First, it became clear that imagery is qualitatively different from the kind of propositional thinking that underlies language use. When you remember the features of an object from its image, what you recall is not exactly the same as if you remembered the object from a list. This makes it all the more significant that people can *choose* in many cases whether to use an image or a propositional format to remember something. It appears that whether we think of ourselves as "mainly visual" or "mainly verbal," most of us have the capacity to shift our thinking in the other direction when it is useful to do so. How to make use of this interesting phenomenon is a question that will be considered in more detail in later chapters.

Second, what about the apparent contradiction between the findings in these experiments and our earlier data about scanning images? As you may recall from Chapter 3, we had previously found that objects imaged at a large size take more time to scan across than ones imaged at a small size, whereas in these experiments they were taking less time. This apparent paradox, we realized, has to do with the resolution limits of the medium. Although people can scan across a smaller distance faster, the object has to be imaged at a certain size for its parts to be clearly visible; below that size, the grain of the medium makes the parts impossible to "see," so that one cannot scan to a part before zooming in on the object in the image.

Does Size Affect Memory?

The starting point for this series of experiments was the assumption that if images really are used in thinking and memory, then the properties of the medium should affect the message. The elephant-and-fly experiments supported our hypothesis that the mental medium has a "grain" which can obscure the details of an image. We next wondered whether the properties of the medium affect how information is encoded into memory in the first place, as well as how clearly the details show up when it is retrieved; if a person remembers something by putting an image of it into his or her long-term memory, then the properties of the image should influence the amount and quality of information the person encodes.

From the previous set of experiments, it seemed likely that if an object were initially imaged at a large size, it would be recalled in richer detail than if it were imaged at a small size. We decided to test this hypothesis by asking subjects to image pairs of objects interacting—a woman and a rock, for instance. The second object of each pair was to be imaged either at normal size or "so small as to appear a dot." When subjects were asked to recall the pair, we reasoned, they should have more trouble remembering and identifying the second object if it had been imaged tiny than if it were normal size. Subjects were not asked to memorize the pairs, however, but simply to judge the vividness of each image. We feared that warning them about the impending memory test would prompt them to rehearse the names of the objects verbally, thereby circumventing any difficulties they might otherwise have later in recalling a poor image.

After subjects had imaged all the pairs, we presented the name of either the first or the second object and asked them what the other one was. The results were straightforward: When the object imaged at a tiny size was the recall cue, the one imaged at a normal size was harder to recall than when both objects imaged were normal sized; and when the object imaged at a normal size was the cue, the second was harder to recall if it had been imaged tiny than if it had been normal.

There was one problem with this experiment, however, and that had to do with the relationships between the imaged objects. When a subject is told that one of the objects in a pair is to be imaged at a very small size, the relationships he or she can imagine between the objects are quite different from when both objects are normal in size. For example, if you were asked to image a woman and a rock together, you probably would not form the same relationship if you imaged the rock at an appropriate size (she might be sitting on it) as if the rock were tiny (it might be a dot in her hand). A tiny version of almost anything could be held in someone's hand, but only a limited number of things are likely to be supporting a sitting woman, making it easier to guess the second object if you had forgotten it. Memory differences, then, might be due to differences in the relationship encoded between objects, depending on whether the second one is small or large, and not to differences in size as such.

To control for this possibility, we ran a version of the experiment in which subjects read sentences describing a relationship between two objects, for example, "A woman is sitting on a chair." For half the sentences subjects were to image both objects at normal size; for the other half, they were to image the second object the size of a dot. Again, the normal-sized objects were easier to recall and identify than those at dot size. But, you might ask, what if subjects were losing the tiny object by simply imaging a dot and forgetting about the object altogether? To guard against this possibility, we asked another group to image objects at the relative sizes of a nickel and a pie plate. The objects imaged at the smaller size were still remembered less well.

From these experiments we concluded that the size of an object in an image, and therefore the accuracy of its detail, does affect how it is encoded in memory. Like pictures on a television screen, objects can be imaged so tiny that they are hard to see—and therefore hard to remember. The medium in which images occur does have a grain, and this affects the quality of the images.

MEASURING THE SCOPE OF THE MEDIUM

In the scanning experiments using maps and stylized faces, one of our discoveries was that imaged objects can overflow the "mental screen." Evidently the medium in which images occur can only store a limited spatial extent. Later, when we asked subjects to image animals next to an elephant or a fly, it was with the idea of forcing them to use up some of the space in their mental medium. After the experiments, the subjects confirmed that the elephant "took up most of the room," leaving only enough space for an image of a tiny rabbit; the fly, in contrast, took up relatively little room, leaving plenty of space for a full-sized rabbit. This was not surprising, for spatial extent is one of the fundamental properties of any depictive medium, whether it be a wax tablet, a television screen, a piece of drawing paper, or whatever. If the medium for mental images really is a functional space, it must have a size and shape.

Normally, if you want to find out the size and shape of something, you measure it. If you cannot measure it directly, you may be able to calculate its dimensions mathematically on the basis of what you *can* measure. For example, you can calculate the height of a distant mountain if you know how far the mountain is from you and the height and distance of some other object. With mental images, of course, the problem is more complicated. Measuring all or part of the brain would not accomplish much, because the image medium is not a physical space inside the head; it is a system that functions like a space. Nor would there be any point in trying to gauge the length and width of the medium by itself, because the only way we become aware of the medium's existence is by using it to image something. When you are not imaging, you do not "see" a blank screen; and even when you *are* imaging, you do not "see" a "screen," you merely have an image. By the process of elimination, the only things we could conceivably measure that might give us any data about the medium are "perceptions" of objects in images. This was clearly not going to be an easy job.

We started with the one relevant fact we already had: Objects in images can overflow the "mental screen." To get a sense of what this means, try the following: Visualize an elephant standing off in the distance, facing left. Now stare at the center of its side and imagine you are walking toward it. As you approach, the elephant looms larger and larger. Is there a point at which you can no longer stare at the center and still "see" the whole elephant?

This was the task we gave our first group of subjects. The key question was not simply whether the imaged elephant would eventually overflow the field of "vision," but *how far away* it would appear to be at that point. If we have some sense of the elephant's size and its apparent distance from the subject at the point of overflow, we should be able to compute how "large" the elephant's image is when it overflows. Note that the elephant itself is not changing size, only the extent it covers. By measuring the limitations on the "perception" of objects in an image, we can infer the extent represented in the image itself, and hence draw inferences about the extent of the medium (as "seen" by the "mind's eye").

You might be wondering what units we used to measure objects in a mental image. After all, it does not make sense to say an imaged object is 8¾ inches high or to compare it to the size of a bread box. We measured the size of objects in an image in terms of *visual angle* (Fig. 4.4). If you could see all around yourself at once, your visual field would be a full circle, or 360 degrees. If you stretched both arms out from your sides and turned your head from one to the other, your gaze would span half a circle— 180 degrees. When you look at or image an object, it occupies an even smaller portion of the total possible view. A convenient way of describing the size of an imaged object, then, is in terms of the arc it subtends—the fraction of the visual circle it takes up. This arc does not reflect the object's size per se, but is a function of its size and its distance together. The same angle can be formed by something big and far away as by something medium sized and nearer. Knowing the size of an imaged object and how far

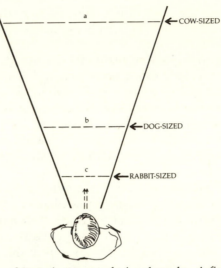

4.4. Measuring objects in terms of visual angle. A fixed angle implies that bigger things must be farther away.

away it seemed at the point of overflow, then, allowed us to compute the angle at which it overflowed. (This computation involved some very simple trigonometry.)

We reasoned that if objects we "see" in images overflow because they exceed the extent of the medium in which they occur, then images of different things all should overflow when they were larger than the maximum extent that could fit in the medium. Thus we needed more data than subjects' evaluations of the size and distance of an imaged elephant. Would a small object—a rabbit, for instance—also overflow the screen at some point? If so, would it do so at an apparently closer distance than an elephant? Would it overflow at just the right distance so it was at the same visual angle as the elephant? What about a tall but narrow object, say, a giraffe? Or a short but wide one, say, an alligator? If the size of the medium determines the point of overflow, then the single greatest extent through an object should be critical, just as a picture of a circle with a six-inch diameter will overflow a television screen at the same angle as a picture of a square with a six-inch diagonal when the camera zooms in on them.

To investigate these questions, we asked subjects to image a whole menagerie of animals of different sizes and shapes. We made sure the subjects would all share the same image of the animals by asking them to memorize a drawing of each creature shown at different sizes. This avoided the possibility that people who had only seen the larger animals in zoos and at a distance would have fuzzy images and might not be able to say precisely when the beasts hit the overflow point. To guard against inaccuracies of judgment, we asked subjects to use a tripod apparatus to approximate the animals' distance at overflow rather than simply estimate it. Subjects placed the tripod at the distance from a wall that the animal seemed to be in the image when it began to overflow. Thus the subjects' skill at converting perceived distance into feet and inches would not bias their reports. We also tried the "mental walk" task with black rectangles of various sizes as the imaged objects, to avoid any chance that qualities of the animals might be influencing the results.

It would be nice at this point to pull off the veil and say what the scope of the mental medium was discovered to be. Alas, things did not turn out to be so simple. Evidently the grain in the medium is not constant at every location; rather, images are sharpest in the center and fade off gradually toward the edges. Thus when subjects were told to be very careful and indicate just when an imaged object begins to become blurry, the angle of overflow was considerably smaller (that is, the imaged object was farther away) than when no such instructions were given (as small as 12 degrees versus around 25 degrees in the average case). We did find, however, that the size of an object (usually as measured by a diagonal across the drawing) was directly related to the distance at which it appeared to overflow: Larger objects overflowed at farther apparent distances than smaller ones, and different-sized drawings (of animals or rectangles) all overflowed at the same apparent size. Furthermore, the subjects' estimates showed a high degree of consistency, both from one object to another and from one subject to another. Thus the results supported the general idea that objects in images seem to overflow because the underlying representations exceed the spatial extent of the mental medium in which they occur.

The other problem we faced in drawing conclusions about the scope of the mental medium was that subjects might have biased the results by second-guessing us. That is, perhaps subjects had not actually imaged the "mental walk" toward the various objects, but had thought about what it would be like to approach them and had reported what they knew would happen. They might have reasoned abstractly that bigger things must overflow the field of vision farther away than smaller ones, given that our eyes only have a limited scope. Therefore we decided to use a subtler technique. This time we asked subjects to image and then scan lines of different lengths. Some of the lines were imaged from drawings; others were formed by the subjects to be as long as possible without overflowing. We used scanning times for the lines whose length we knew to calculate how long the lines must be that subjects generated on their own. The angle we estimated in this way was virtually identical to the one estimated using our "mental walk" task with other subjects. Thus, because the scanning method was so indirect and difficult to second-guess, and because it produced the same estimate as the comparable "mental walk" task, we could confidently conclude that there is a mental medium that does in fact have a spatial extent.

Given that the mental medium has a definite extent (even if it blurs gradually at the edges), it must also have a shape. It did not take long to think of ways of modifying our earlier experiments to measure the shape of the medium. In one experiment, for example, we asked subjects to image walking toward a foot-long ruler. In some cases the ruler was horizontal, in some cases vertical, and in others diagonal. By looking at the relative distances at which the imaged rulers seemed to overflow, we reasoned, we could infer the shape of the mental medium. For example, if the vertical ruler seemed to overflow before the horizontal one, the medium must be wider than it is high; and if the diagonal ruler overflowed at a distance between the horizontal and vertical rulers, the medium must be oval, whereas if the diagonal ruler overflowed at a farther distance than either the horizontal or the vertical one, the medium must be rectangular; and so on.[2]

What we discovered was that at the highest degree of acuity, the medium is circular. At the lower degrees of acuity (that is, around the edges), it gradually flattens out into an ellipse that is wider than it is tall.[3]

STABILIZED IMAGES

Perhaps the most direct demonstration that a functional spatial medium is used in imagery comes from studies of a specific kind of *adaptation*. This phenomenon has been known for some time in visual perception. Our eyes are continually moving, even when we try to keep them still. Paradoxically, this movement allows us to remain aware of an object: If you can rivet your gaze onto a single point on an object, after a while the edges of the object will seem to fade in and out. If the object is fixed on one spot on your retina with a special kind of contact lens, then the entire object will seem to fade after a while.

If stabilized patterns on the retina fade because neural mechanisms adapt (that is, because neurons stop firing), then we might expect to find similar effects when a mental image is stabilized: We may be able to adapt cells in the brain that actually embody the matrix (which is defined by what these brain cells accomplish, in this case mimicking a matrix), even though those brain cells are not arranged in an actual matrix. Close your eyes, image a capital letter *A*, and "stare" at a point midway across the horizontal bar in the middle. After a short time the letter should fade, and if you are careful not to move it or scan around it, the image should be very difficult to maintain. If you do move the image around or scan around it, you should be able to hold it much longer. This is exactly what we would expect if the brain cells that function as the medium became fatigued or stopped being activated where the letter is. This result is analogous to the original experiments done on perception.

The idea that holding a stabilized mental image can "adapt out" a given part of the medium leads us to make a simple prediction: The greater the overlap between the area occupied by a fixed first image and that of a second image that replaces it, the more difficult it is to form and use the second image. We tested this prediction in one experiment with the blobs illustrated in Fig. 4.5. These blobs were designed so that the medium-sized one could fit inside the area of the large one, and the small one could fit inside the area of the medium one. Each blob was constructed so that its rim was more jagged at some points than at others, the distance of the rim from the center dot varied, the inside of the blob was darker in some places than in others, and the internal rings were different distances apart.

Our subjects began by memorizing these three blobs. They also memorized four intersecting axes pointing in four different directions. Subjects were asked to image one of the blobs; then they were given the number of one of the axes, whereupon they imaged that axis laid across the blob. Finally, the subjects were given the name of one of the four features of the blob (rim, darkness, and so on). They decided as quickly as they could which end of the axis pointed to the part of the blob with more of that feature. For example, if a subject heard "A, 1, rim," he or she decided whether the dotted or undotted end of axis 1 would cover the more jagged part of the rim of blob A. This task was especially suited for our purposes because it is almost impossible to do without imagery.

The trick of this experiment was that on half the trials a subject would begin by imaging one blob, but then would be asked about one of the other two. We were interested primarily in the case where subjects began by imaging the big or little blob and then replaced it with the medium-sized one. As we expected, if subjects fixed their mental gaze on the large blob, it was harder for

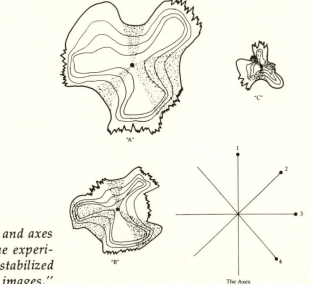

4.5. Blobs and axes used in the experiment on "stabilized mental images."

them to image and judge the medium one—which fit inside the area of the mental medium that was presumably "adapted"—than if they began with the small blob and the medium one extended outside of the adapted region.

In another variation we asked the subjects to scan back and forth over the blob while they were holding it in an image. Now there was no difference in how long it took them to replace the image of the big or little blob with that of the medium-sized blob, which is exactly what we would expect if fixing one's mental gaze on an imaged object keeps the representation in one location in the medium, and thus that part of the medium becomes "adapted out." When the imaged blob was being scanned, the representation was not in a single place in the medium—and therefore no part of the medium was adapted.

BRAIN DAMAGE: THE BLIND SIDE OF THE MIND'S EYE

The notion that the mental medium has spatial properties has received support from another source: data on the effects of brain damage due to stroke. A stroke is the result of a blocked blood vessel in the brain, which cuts off or reduces the flow of blood to the part of the brain normally supplied by that vessel. Starved for oxygen, the cells in the affected region cannot function and sometimes permanent damage results. Strokes often impair patients' vision, but only recently did it occur to anyone to investigate whether they also affect imagery.

One type of vision problem that can afflict stroke victims is *unilateral visual neglect*. People with this problem simply ignore half of their visual field—the left side if the damage is on the right side of the brain, and vice versa (each half of the brain controls the opposite half of the body). Patients with unilateral visual neglect do things like forget to put on clothing on one side, or forget to shave half their faces. They are not blind on one side, however; they merely ignore what they see there. Often these patients exhibit a form of "visual extinction": If you were to bend a finger held in front of the left side of such a patient's face, the person would report seeing it; if you held your finger to the right side, the person would also report seeing it. But if you were to hold up a finger on each side and bend them simultaneously, the person would report seeing only one of them. When the slightest effort is required to notice the affected side of the visual field, the patient simply ignores it.

Edoardo Bisiach and Claudio Luzzatti in Milan described the case of N. V., a lawyer who had a stroke at the age of 71. The stroke damaged primarily tissue in N. V.'s right parietal region, a part of the brain known to be involved in visual attention. N. V. demonstrated the typical symptoms of a patient with unilateral visual neglect. Not only did he ignore things on his left side, but he was completely unaware of his doing so. Bisiach and Luzzatti asked him to *image* a piazza he had seen many times before his stroke and describe what he "saw." N. V. rattled off a series of names—all features of the right side of the piazza. The doctors asked N. V. to change vantage points so that he was imaging the piazza from the opposite end of it. Again N. V. described only half of the piazza, but this time it was the other half, which was now on the right side of his image. Another victim of this kind of stroke, I. G., showed virtually identical behavior. In both cases, it was as if the mind's eye were examining only half the medium.

Even more striking is another set of findings reported by Bisiach, Luzzatti, and Daniela Perani. The researchers showed subjects cloudlike blobs moving behind a narrow slit so that only one part of the form at a time could be seen sliding past the slit. Normal people can easily identify the shape of the pattern after having seen it slide past the slit; most people claim they do this by building up an image of the whole pattern piece by piece. For patients with unilateral visual neglect, however, this task was not so easy. After they saw a pattern moving behind the slit, the patients were shown a second pattern moving behind the slit and were asked whether the two were the same. When the second pattern was different and the difference was on the neglected side of the two patterns, these subjects failed to recognize it. Again, it was as if they simply failed to "see" one side of their images.

This result also makes it clear that the effects of unilateral visual neglect on imagery are not just due to subjects' verbal reporting: Although a subject who describes only one side of a remembered piazza might be accused of seeing the whole thing but only talking about half of it, subjects' failure to "see" differences between a viewed pattern and an imaged one is unlikely to be a matter of reporting. There is also very little possibility that these results were produced by overly cooperative subjects who told the experimenter just what they thought he or she wanted to hear. Oddly enough, these patients usually do not realize that they are neglecting a side. They are not in a position to try to "fake it."

THE MESSAGE ABOUT THE MEDIUM

The mind evidently stores information in media, and properties of the medium affect how we can store and use information. In particular, from all the foregoing experiments we can infer that images are displayed in a functional spatial medium. Although it is not a literal screen, this medium nevertheless is capable of depicting visual information within certain limits of resolution, size, and shape. The evidence from brain damage not only supports this claim, but also tells us something about how that medium is actually embedded in the neural hardware.

Our conclusions about the medium follow from the research findings, but they also make sense for other reasons: For one thing, the medium's limited spatial extent fits in neatly with how we might expect visual perception and imagery to have developed over the course of human evolution. That is, the medium presumably evolved to process information from the sense organs, which means that it only needs to be large enough to handle the arc subtended by the eyes. And because the eyes are spread apart horizontally—as is, presumably, the spatial medium they feed— they have a greater horizontal scope. This connection between vision and imagery has other useful things to tell us about images and mental events in general, as will be evident in Chapter 5.

5

How Do We Know It's There When We Can't See It?

PART AND PARCEL of thinking is the ability to contemplate something in its absence. How is this done? Somehow we must represent the world to ourselves. Images seem to have this property because they resemble a percept (i.e., the representation of a perceived stimulus), allowing us to recognize what is being represented. Unlike words, images are not arbitrarily associated with what they stand for. Thus images provide a means for thinking about something when it is not there.

However, as was discussed in Chapter 1, a long-standing objection to the idea that images are basic to thought is the impossibility of finding an image that can represent a *class* of objects. If your concept of *shoe* were stored in your memory as an image of a brown loafer, for instance, where would that leave high heels, ballet slippers, and sneakers? Furthermore, even if you could come up with a shoe general enough to stand for all possible shoes, there would still be a problem: How would you store your concept of that particular individual shoe? If "brown loafer" stands for "shoe," then what image stands for "brown loafer"?

One way this problem might be solved is if people associate a word with multiple images. When a child learns a concept of some class of objects, such as dogs, he or she might encode the word *dog* into memory along with numerous images of different dogs. This way, the images would serve to depict the various objects within the class, and the word (or, more precisely, the symbol corresponding to it) would stand for a set that cannot be pictured as one single object. Once a set of words are so grounded, other words could then be defined in terms of them. This hypothesis is a nice way of having our cake and eating it too: We keep the flexibility of words and propositions, but also take advantage of the nonarbitrary connections between images and what they depict.[1]

But this neat solution depends on the actual existence of a resemblance between images and percepts, which is an empirical question. The mind's eye and the real eyes obviously appear to have something in common or they would not share a name. What else they share, however, is not obvious. The real eyes respond to light; there is no light inside the brain. The real eyes have lenses, retinas, and a host of other parts the mind's eye lacks. The two kinds of eyes, if they are similar at all, must resemble each other on the level of *function*. In Chapter 4 we discussed some evidence suggesting that the "mind's eye" processes operate on both images and percepts in similar ways. Let us now consider this possibility in more detail: Do images and percepts actually involve similar mental representations, and are these representations processed by the same mental mechanisms?

Nearly all philosophers and psychologists who have addressed this issue believed that vision and visual imagery are closely related. In 1651, Thomas Hobbes gave his view of the resemblance in his famous work *Leviathan:*

> And as wee see in the water, though the wind cease, the waves give not over rowling for a long time after; so also it happeneth in that motion, which is made in the internall parts of a man, then, when he Sees, Dreams, &c. For after the object is removed, or the eye shut, wee still retain an image of the thing seen.[2]

A century later, British philosopher David Hume put it more succinctly: "The idea of red, which we form in the dark, and that impression, which strikes our eyes in sun-shine, differ only in degree, not in nature." That is, "impressions" coming from the senses differ only in their intensity from the "ideas" arising from memory; "ideas" (images) and sensory impressions were assumed to be the same kind of thing.

If imagery and actual perception involve similar mental structures and processes, one might wonder how we tell them apart. The answer is that sometimes we do not. "Is this a dagger which

I see before me?" asked Shakespeare's Macbeth. "Or art thou but a dagger of the mind?" The Thane of Cawdor was not the only person ever to have trouble distinguishing an image from a percept. A classic study done at Cornell University by C. W. Perky in 1910 provided evidence that people can sometimes mistake an actual picture of an object for an image. Perky's subjects were seated before a screen in a well-lit room and asked to stare at the screen and image a common object, such as a banana. Unknown to them, behind the screen was a projector, which was casting a slide of the object to be imaged onto the back of the screen. As soon as the subjects said that they had mentally imaged the requested object on the screen, the illumination of the projector was slowly turned up. Eventually the slide was clear enough to be visible to anyone walking into the room. But none of Perky's twenty-four subjects ever noticed that they were looking at an actual picture. What they did notice was that the objects they were "imaging" were somewhat surprising. All the subjects, Perky reported, "noted that the banana was on end, and not as they had been supposing they thought of it; yet the circumstance aroused no suspicion."

Perky's experiment had two problems that prevent us from easily interpreting her findings. First, it could be that the subjects failed to notice the slide because they were concentrating on maintaining their images. That is, because they were busy with another task, they may have been distracted enough not to perceive the picture (it was, after all, quite faint). Second, the subjects were all inclined to be very cooperative; perhaps they were going along with what they thought the experimenter wanted. To be sure about the conclusions of Perky's experiment, then, we need an experimental design that will rule out the possibility that the simple effort of doing a second task was the reason subjects did not notice the picture. In addition, the experiment should have subtle enough predictions so that subjects will not be able to easily guess the expected outcome.

Sixty years elapsed before someone performed a revised version of Perky's experiment. As was mentioned in Chapter 1, behaviorism dominated most of psychology from about 1913 to 1960. Researchers were more concerned with overt behavior and external stimuli than with the mind in general or mental imagery in particular. When the high tide of behaviorism went out, it left behind a host of new experimental methodologies and an increased emphasis on conducting rigorous experiments. The "remake" of Perky's experiment done in 1970 by Sydney Segal and Vincent Fusella reflected the methodological legacy of the behaviorists.

If images and percepts really do arise through some of the same specialized mechanisms, Segal and Fusella reasoned, then confusions should be specialized as well. One should be more likely to mistake a visual stimulus for a mental image when one is simultaneously holding a visual image than when one is holding an auditory image (and vice versa for an auditory stimulus). In other words, because a visual image presumably "looks like" a visual percept, it is reasonable that people would have trouble telling them apart; but an auditory image and a visual percept are not very similar (partly because they rely on different processing mechanisms), so they should be easier to distinguish.

Segal and Fusella therefore asked subjects to form either visual images, such as of a flower, or auditory images, such as of a telephone ringing. Once the subjects had their images in mind, either a faint visual stimulus—a small blue arrow—was flashed in front of them, or a faint auditory stimulus—a harmonica chord—was played over headphones. The results confirmed the experimenters' hypothesis: When subjects imaged the flower and saw the arrow at the same time, they had trouble distinguishing between the stimulus they were perceiving and what they were imaging—more so than when they imaged the flower and heard the harmonica chord. Similarly, they confused their image of a ringing telephone with the auditory percept of the harmonica chord more than with the visual percept of the arrow. This result could not have been due to subjects' simply being distracted—if it were, one would not expect visual and auditory stimuli to have different effects. Furthermore, the prediction was subtle enough that it is unlikely subjects could have produced the results intentionally (the details of this claim depend partly on the data analysis, which is too complex to summarize here).

TANGLED UP IN IMAGES

If imagery and perception use some of the same mental mechanisms, then when a mechanism is tied up by imagery, subjects

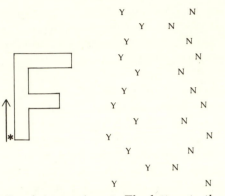

5.1. Stimuli for Brooks' experiment. The letters to the right are used to indicate properties of the corners of an imaged letter.

should have difficulty doing perceptual tasks that require that mechanism. Perceiving should *interfere* with the ability to image in the same modality at the same time. Canadian psychologist Lee Brooks investigated this notion in 1968. Brooks expected that it would prove difficult for people to use imagery and perception at the same time in the same modality (either vision or hearing), but that they might have an easier time handling, say, a visual percept and an auditory image. To find out, Brooks asked subjects to perform two tasks.

First, subjects were shown a block letter like the *F* illustrated in Fig. 5.1, which they were to memorize and then image. Then they were asked to classify each corner of the imaged letter, starting from the small star and working clockwise. One kind of classification was very simple: If a corner was at either the top or the bottom of the letter, they were to say yes, whereas if it was somewhere in the middle, they were to say no. So, for *F*, starting at the bottom left, the proper response would be, "Yes, yes, yes, no, no, no, no, no, no, yes." On some trials people spoke their responses out loud, which involved both talking and hearing while a visual image was being evaluated. On the other trials, they pointed to either a *Y* or an *N* on a page, for yes or no. Subjects were to work their way down a staggered column of *Y*'s and *N*'s on a page, pointing to a different *Y* or *N* for each corner they classified. This task required the subjects to search visually for the response at the same time the visual image was being evaluated.

The second task had nothing to do with letters or their corners. This time subjects were read a sentence, such as, "A bird in the hand is worth two in the bush," and asked to say immediately afterward whether each word in succession was a noun or not. So, for this sentence the correct response would be, "No, yes, no, no, yes, no, no, no, no, no, yes." The idea was that subjects had to use an auditory image of the sentence, perhaps maintained by "implicit speech" (talking to oneself), to make their choices. Here too they responded by either speaking the responses aloud or pointing to Y's and N's on a page.

The results were clearcut, as you should discover yourself if you try the task with the letter E (image it and start classifying the corners from the lower left) and the sentence, "Every good deed and thoughtful word deserves a just reward" (have someone read it aloud to you). What you should find is that it is harder to do the corner classification when you respond by pointing to letters on the response sheet than when you say yes or no aloud, but the reverse applies to the noun classification. Brooks concluded that having to search for the letters on the page (producing a visual percept) interfered considerably with his subjects' ability to hold and process a visual mental image, whereas speaking their responses did not interfere anywhere near as much. In contrast, when subjects imaged hearing a sentence (heard it in their mind's ear, so to speak), speaking the responses interfered more than visually searching out and pointing to letters. Speaking or hearing (or both) apparently uses some of the same structures and processes used in imaging sounds. This is presumably why it is so hard to remember one tune while another one is playing, or to memorize verbal material (by mentally repeating it to oneself) while listening to music; we are bound to "blot out" one when we really concentrate on the other.

WHERE DO VISION AND IMAGING OVERLAP?

From various experiments, then, it seems clear that some of the same mechanisms are involved in both vision and visual imagery. This idea gains additional support from studies such as the ones done by Bisiach and colleagues, described in Chapter 4, which show that brain damage can affect imaging in the same way it affects seeing. On the other hand, it seems very unlikely that *all* mechanisms used in seeing are used in visual imagery. Most people who are blinded after the age of seven, for example, report that they still have visual mental images. In recent years a number of researchers, led by Ronald Finke (who is now at SUNY at Stony Brook), Began trying to isolate the levels of the visual processing system that are shared by imagery and perception.

Visual perception is more accessible to observation than visual imagery, and it has been much more extensively studied and analyzed. We now know something about the neural mechanisms involved in transmitting visual information from the eyes: When we look at an object, light reflected off the object enters the eyes, where it strikes the light-sensitive retina at the back of each eye. There the physical pattern of light, dark, color, and so on, is translated into electrochemical impulses and transmitted via the optic nerve to the brain (Fig. 5.2). The optic nerves from the two eyes cross each other in such a way that information about the left half of what each eye sees goes along one nerve, whereas information about the right half of the view is carried by another nerve. Up to this crossover point (called the optic chiasma), impulses from each eye travel separately; after this point, impulses representing the left visual field travel separately from those representing the right visual field.

This rather odd setup is responsible for several interesting characteristics of human vision. For one thing, beyond the optic chiasma, interference with the visual system is likely to affect the left or right size of the image rather than what is viewed by the left or right eye. This separation of what we perceive into left and right visual fields is part of the explanation of unilateral visual neglect, described in Chapter 4. It is also the reason why our eyes need to (and usually do) move in exactly the same direction at the same time. The fact that human eyes both see the same scene is responsible, in addition, for our binocular vision, which contributes to our ability to perceive in three dimensions. Each eye takes in the world from a slightly different vantage point, owing to the two inches or so between their lenses, and the two views merge into one "stereo" picture.

Past the optic chiasma, information from the left visual field

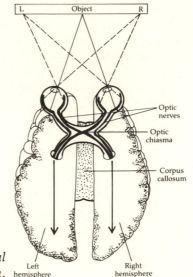

5.2. Transmission of visual information to the brain.

goes to the right half of the brain, and information from the right visual field goes to the left half. Processing is done all along the way, from the eyes to the cerebral cortex, the center of thought. When the nerve impulses reach the cortex they are interpreted as a visual pattern. The preliminary stages of vision—what goes on in the eyes, the optic nerve, and the more primitive parts of the brain—carry our what we can call *peripheral* processing. The cortical stage, where recognition of the input takes place, carries out what we can call *central* processing.

For imagery research, the usefulness of the distinction between peripheral and central levels of processing is that a number of perceptual phenomena have been localized at one general level or the other. People participating as subjects in experiments can be asked to perform a visual task using imagery instead of vision, and if the same perceptual phenomenon results from imagery as would happen with vision, it is reasonable to conclude that the specific mechanisms that produce the perceptual effect are also involved in processing images. To double-check, another group of subjects can be asked to guess what the result of the visual task would be. If they can figure it out, then it is possible that the original subjects may have been cooperating (perhaps unconsciously) with what they thought were the experimenter's desires. If the second group cannot guess the result, then it probably really does indicate that perceptual and imaginal processing make use of the designated level of the visual system.[3]

A good example of this kind of experiment is the one reported in 1976 by Ronald Finke and Martin Schmidt, who worked with a subtle type of afterimage that most people have never experienced. Ordinary afterimages occur whenever you look at a strong visual stimulus, such as a bright light: After you close your eyes or look away, a faint image of the stimulus persists for a few seconds. The afterimages studied by Finke and Schmidt are somewhat different. Called the McCollough effect (after their discoverer, Dorothy McCollough), they are associated with the *orientation* and color of the stimulus. To create the McCollough effect, subjects typically are shown black bars that alternate on either a red or a green background. If the black-on-green bars are presented vertically, then the black-on-red ones are presented horizontally (Fig. 5.3). Each pattern is shown to the subjects for a period of five seconds or so, followed by the other one. The patterns alternate back and forth for about five minutes and the subjects are asked simply to stare at them.

Next, the experimenter presents black bars on a white background. Amazingly, the subjects will now see a faint afterimage on the white bars in the color that is complementary to the one originally used for that orientation! For example, if the black-on-green bars had been vertical and the black-on-red ones horizontal, the vertical white bars would now appear tinged with red, whereas the horizontal white bars would appear tinged with green!

No one knows as yet what causes the McCollough effect. One of its remarkable aspects, though, is that it can persist for up to two weeks after the initial exposure period; that is, up to two weeks after studying the bars on the colored backgrounds, subjects will still see the black and white bars as tinged with red or green. This suggests that the effect is not peripheral—it is not like an ordinary afterimage, which fades in a matter of seconds. And if the McCollough effect in perception is caused by central mechanisms, there is every reason to believe that it should occur in imagery if the same mechanisms are used.

Finke and Schmidt tested this idea by showing people slides

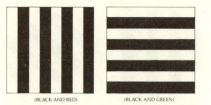

(BLACK AND RED)   (BLACK AND GREEN)

5.3. Patterns like those used to cereate the McCollough effect. Ordinarily the stripes are either black and red or black and green.

of colored patches, plain fields of green or red. Subjects were to project an image of black bars—vertical for one color, horizontal for the other—onto the patches. Sure enough, when later shown black and white stripes, the subjects apparently "saw" a faint tinge of red or green on the white bars. However, the experiment did not work when subjects were shown slides of black bars and asked to project an image of red or green in between them. Apparently color imagery, such as occurs in dreaming, takes place in some part of the brain other than that which underlies the McCollough effect.

Finke and Schmidt thus have narrowed down which mechanisms in the brain are used in imagery. When we understand more about the McCollough effect in perception, we will automatically inherit information about imagery. Moreover, because virtually nobody outside the field knows about the McCollough effect (and in fact, when it was first announced, many researchers refused to believe it), subjects could not have intentionally or unconsciously produced these results without using imagery.

Of course, the logic of the Finke–Schmidt study also works the other way. Given that imagery appears to occur mainly at the level of "central" processing, if we can show that a perceptual phenomenon also occurs in imagery we can then learn something new about it. Nancy Pennington and I conducted a study that not only tells us something about imagery, but reveals some characteristics of another peculiar perceptual phenomenon.

If you view a set of alternating black and white stripes, you can see them as distinct only if the stripes are thicker than a certain width. If the stripes are any narrower, they blur into a homogenous gray field. As it turns out, we can distinguish narrower stripes better if they are oriented either vertically or hori-

5.4 Stimuli used to measure the "oblique effect."

zontally than if they are oriented diagonally (Fig. 5.4). This phenomenon is known as the "oblique effect," and it is virtually unknown outside the laboratory.

Nancy Pennington and I asked a group of subjects to study stripes and then to image them. On half the trials the stripes were presented vertically, and on half they were presented diagonally (at an angle of forty-five degrees). After imaging the stripes, on half of the trials subjects "mentally rotated" the stripes into the other orientation and then worked with this image. This was to preclude effects due to problems in initially memorizing the stripes at the diagonal orientation. The subjects also were trained beforehand on how to estimate distances accurately. Once the subjects had formed the requested image, we asked them to image walking back from the stripes and to judge how far away the stripes appeared to be when they just began to blur. Another group of subjects actually observed a grid of stripes receding into the distance and reported when they were too far away to be seen distinctly.

Not only did we find that the diagonal imaged stripes seemed to blur at shorter distances than the vertical ones, but the difference in distances for the two conditions was the same for people imaging the stripes as for people actually seeing them. Thus we obtained the oblique effect in imagery, which suggests that the effect is not due to the architecture of the eye or the optic nerve (the peripheral level), but to higher brain processes (the central level). Somewhere in the visual cortex are cells that are less sensitive to diagonal lines, and these cells are recruited during both imagery and perception. Furthermore, another group of subjects, who did not participate in the task but only read descriptions of it, were unable to guess its outcome. This supports the notion that the imagery results really do tell us something about the actual mechanisms underlying imagery and perception.

The Medium and the Message Revisited

The experiment with diagonal stripes has some interesting implications for the question of how visual information from the outside world is represented in the mind. If our proposal is correct, and people use the same mental mechanisms to "recognize" objects in images as they use to recognize perceived objects, then we should find evidence that the mental matrix and mind's eye tests are used in both cases. The idea of a "mental matrix" is as plausible for vision as it is for imagery. When you look at, say, a dog, the light reflected off the dog strikes the retinas and is translated into electrochemical impulses; and once this happens, the question is the same as for imagery: How do those electrochemical impulses function to represent a visual pattern that can be identified as "dog"?

If our computer display metaphor is correct, then the "screen" that displays images is probably also used in perception. In imaging, we use the medium to replay stored information; in perception, we use it to view new information directly from the "camera" of the eyes. This idea gains support from the fact that patients who experience unilateral visual neglect in perception after brain damage also experience it in imagery. But more direct evidence comes from experiments that directly compare measures of the size and shape of the mental medium in imagery and perception.

In my original studies of the scope of the imagery field, a group of subjects was asked to perform the "mental walk" task with imaged rectangles of various sizes. These people studied a rectangle cut out of black cardboard, imaged it off in the distance, and envisioned walking toward it until it appeared to be so large that its edges began to blur. The rectangle's apparent distance at the point of overflow then was estimated, and we used these estimates to compute the angle subtended by the various-sized stimuli at their points of overflow. This angle averaged about twenty degrees. A second group of subjects performed the same task, but with the rectangles mounted on the wall; subjects literally stood far back and walked toward the rectangles (fixating on their centers) until the edges blurred. The actual distance at that point was measured, and we used these measures to compute the visual angle. This angle was also about twenty degrees! Furthermore, in both experiments all the rectangles seemed to overflow at the same angle, with bigger ones seeming to overflow at greater distances from the viewer.

I took this result to be good evidence that the same spatial medium is used in imagery and perception and that the scope of this medium imposes constraints on people's ability both to see and to image objects of various sizes. The only fly in the ointment was that other researchers had reported that people can see not just 20 degrees, but over 100 degrees. I was not too bothered by this, since we already knew that the angle subtended by an object at the overflow point varies according to the definition of *overflow*. It was clear that objects in images do not overflow all of a sudden but, rather, fade off gradually into the periphery of the "mental screen." But why such a large difference?

Ronald Finke suggested an answer. Perhaps in this experiment we were really measuring not the whole visual field, but how much of the field a person can attend to at once. That is, when we see, we normally take in more than what is directly in front of our eyes. Even when we are looking straight at something, we are aware of other objects to one side or another of our focus. But when we stare straight ahead and want to see everything equally far on both sides at once, we can only see objects a limited distance to each side. In contrast, if we just want to see an object on one side, it can be considerably farther to the side. The field of our simultaneous awareness, in other words, has a smaller scope than the field of awareness off to one side, out of the "corner of our eye," so to speak.

In the overflow experiments, subjects were asked to report about the range of simultaneous awareness—how far they could see to both sides at once. When the outlines of the rectangle or animal or other stimulus they were imaging passed beyond that region, it had "overflowed." However, the usual measure of the range of people's vision does not assess the range of simultaneous awareness but, rather, the maximum distance at which a person can see something out of the corner of either eye. This disparity seemed likely to explain the difference in the angles I had found and those reported elsewhere for vision.

If this hypothesis is true, then the mental medium should seem to have a larger scope when subjects can attend to an object toward one side of it than when they have to keep track of the whole field at once. Finke and I devised an experiment to test this idea. We asked some subjects to watch a pair of dots one centimeter in diameter moving toward the edge of their visual field, and other subjects to image the same thing. The subjects' job was to tell us when the two dots were so far toward the side that they seemed to blur together. We asked the subjects to watch or image the dots moving either horizontally (left or right) or vertically (up or down). Thus not only were we able to compare the angles obtained in imagery and perception, but we could compare the rough shapes of the visual fields as well.

As expected, we found much larger angles of vision when subjects had to attend to only one stimulus (the pair of dots) moving toward one edge of the field than I had found in my earlier experiments. The maximum angles were similar in perception and imagery (101 and 92 degrees, respectively) and were very close to the usual ones reported by other vision researchers. Furthermore, by varying the distance between the dots, we demonstrated that the shapes of the fields were also the same in imagery and perception—as expected if these shapes reflect the shape of the medium and the same medium is used in both tasks. At three centimeters apart, the dots could generally be seen or imaged farther to the side before they blurred together than when they were only one centimeter apart; in addition, these more widely separated dots could be imaged and seen farther toward the periphery when they were moving to the left or right than when they were moving up or down. Thus the medium seems to become elliptical as acuity decreases, although the region of highest acuity is circular.

This new technique resulted in larger estimates of the size of the medium in which images occur than were obtained originally. We still wondered about the reason for the size of the original estimate, however, and wished to show that we had really measured the size of the field the "mind's eye" could view at once. Thus Finke and I asked another group of subjects to image *two* pairs of dots moving in opposite directions from the middle of the visual field toward the edge. With the separation we used, the pairs blurred when the arc between the two pairs was about thirty degrees, in the neighborhood of the estimates I had previously obtained from the mental walk task.[4] Evidently the "mind's eye" can take in no more than about thirty degrees of arc at once, but the medium itself can store depictions that cover over 100 degrees.

THE MIND'S EYE IN IMAGERY AND PERCEPTION

If mental images and percepts are represented in the same spatial medium, it makes sense that people use the same "mind's eye" tests to interpret both types of stimuli. In either case, there is a pattern of electrochemical impulses that must be organized and "read" as a functional spatial pattern to become meaningful (see Chapter 2). If the same interpretive tests are used on both images and percepts, we should find evidence of the same mental processes in categorizing both perceived objects and imaged objects.

A particularly interesting demonstration of similar processing being used in both imagery and perception comes from a set of experiments carried out a few years ago by Peter Podgorny and Roger Shepard. Many of us sometimes have occasion to contemplate the tiled pattern on bathroom floors. When doing so, we may "see" the little squares as forming different patterns: a cross, letters of the alphabet, various geometric patterns, and so on. It is amazing how much one can do with only a field of little tiles. What Podgorny and Shepard discovered was that once such a pattern is imaged, it becomes almost as visible as if the pattern actually existed. Podgorny and Shepard showed subjects a matrix and asked them to imagine that a letter was formed by the blacking out of certain cells (Fig. 5.5). Following this, the subjects were shown the same matrix with a real dot or dots placed in one cell, and asked to determine whether or not the dots fell on the letter they had imaged. These subjects had no trouble answering quickly and accurately.

The results of this imagery task are especially interesting when compared to the results from a second experiment, in which subjects actually saw a letter in the matrix (as is illustrated in Fig.

5.5 Stimuli used in Podgorny and Shepard's experiment. Try to "see" the F in the right matrix by imaging the appropriate cells blacked out.

5.5). This time the subjects simply reported, as quickly as possible, whether dots actually fell on the figure. Not all of these decisions proved to be equally easy. For example, when a dot did not fall on the letter, the farther from the letter it was, the faster subjects reached their decision. Subjects also answered faster when a dot fell on an intersection, when more than one dot fell on the letter, and when the letter was small. The really striking finding was that the magnitude of the differences in reaction times were the same in the imagery experiment in the perception experiment. Furthermore, decision times did not vary systematically according to where the dots fell in the matrix; in other words, it seemed as though people did not perform a left–right search or the like, but rather could see the entire letter at one time, as we would expect if the area the mind's eye can inspect at once is about twenty or thirty degrees. The parallels between the imagery and perception data strongly suggest that information from the eyes and from visual memory is displayed in the same spatial medium, and that the same mental processes interpret both types of patterns.

CLASSIFYING IMAGES AND PERCEPTS

If we do indeed use the same mind's eye tests to "see" both percepts and images, an obvious question is, What are these tests? In terms of brain structures, this is impossible to say, at least for the present. We cannot take a functioning brain apart like a computer to watch its circuits in operation, nor would we be likely to learn much if we could. Again, the best way of understanding what the brain does is by analyzing its function, not its structure.

Stephen Reed of Florida Atlantic University has studied some aspects of visual processing that provide an interesting clue to the tests the mind's eye uses. Reed carried out a number of experiments in which subjects were briefly shown a pattern, such as a Star of David, and then asked to judge whether some simpler subpattern, such as a triangle, was a component of the first pattern. To do this, subjects presumably had to image the more complex pattern and inspect it for the subpattern. Reed found that certain subpatterns were recognized considerably faster and more accurately than others. For instance, you should have no trouble identifying a triangle as being part of a Star of David, but a parallelogram facing to the right should be harder to pick out (Fig. 5.6). If we can characterize what makes some subpatterns easy to "see" in an image and others more difficult, then we can say something about the tests that comprise the mind's eye.

As it turns out, the so-called Gestalt laws of organization offer an explanation. *Gestalt* is a German word referring to a whole that is more than the sum of its parts; in other words, the parts group to form an overall pattern that exists in its own right. A triangle, for instance, is more than just three lines touching end to end. The most basic Gestalt laws, which were formulated primarily in the 1930s by a group of German psychologists, can be summarized in terms of four general principles:

The *law of proximity* states that segments near each other will tend to be grouped together. Thus, XXX   XXX is seen as two units, whereas XX   XX   XX is seen as three.

The *law of similarity* states that similar segments will tend to be grouped together. Thus XXX000 will be seen as two units, whereas XX00++ will tend to be seen as three.

The *law of good continuation* states that points that can be described as forming a smooth, continuous line are seen as a single unit. So ⋯⋯ is seen as one unit, but ⋯… is seen as two.

The *law of good form* states that patterns that can be seen as forming symmetrical or regular figures will be seen as a unit. So () is seen as a unit but (⌣ is not.

Each of the parts that Reed's subjects had a hard time identifying was a pattern formed by cutting up or cutting across units that the Gestalt laws define as "good." For example, the parallelogram in the Star of David is made of segments from two "good," or more cohesive, units—the triangles. Evidently the tests that the mind's eye uses to interpret patterns break those patterns down into regular subpatterns and do not readily reinterpret them in other ways.

One of Reed's findings gives us reason to pause at this point,

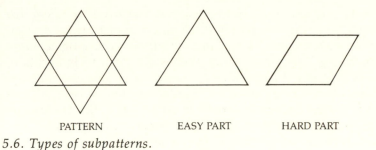

PATTERN   EASY PART   HARD PART

5.6. Types of subpatterns.

however. Although it is true that some subpatterns of images were harder to "see" than others, the difference was not as great as it was in perception. Furthermore, subjects took slightly longer in general to recognize both "good" and noncohesive subpatterns in an imaged pattern than in a perceived one. Apparently other factors in addition to the Gestalt principles affect difficulty in the case of imagery, factors that are not apparent in perception. One possibility is that it takes a certain effort just to maintain an image, making it harder to examine an·imaged pattern than one stored for us on a page. In fact, as will be discussed later, this is true; we are not very good at holding too much in an image at once.

Perhaps the most important thing about Reed's findings is that they help us to grapple with yet another of the problems that have vexed the philosophers. Recall that a mental representation cannot be ambiguous (as is the word *sage*); you are never puzzled about the meaning of a thought you just had (the implications, perhaps, but you never have had ambiguous thoughts per se). Thus, the argument went, how can images be used to store information in the mind, given that they are ambiguous? For example, a Star of David could be seen as a hexagon with six small triangles around it, two overlapping parallelograms with a small triangle at the top and bottom, and so on. But this concern is more theoretical than real: We do not see the star as being ambiguous; we see it as two large overlapping triangles. People usually see an object in a picture or an image as ambiguous only when they make an effort to do so. The Gestalt laws of organization and other perceptual laws (governing what you will see first, what you will see as more important, and so on) result in our habitually *organizing* a pattern in only one way. These laws may in part reflect the operation of the mind's eye tests used to categorize patterns, which are predisposed to work in specific ways. In fact, even very young infants organize patterns according to these kinds of laws, suggesting that the laws are inborn.[5] In addition, there is evidence that pictures are *identified* in a consistent way. A picture of a sitting man could be seen as "John's head," "bent knees," and so on, but it usually is only seen as illustrating one thing. Different pictures will be necessary to represent "bent knees" and the rest. Similarly, the same principles may apply to how images are interpreted, resulting in any given image usually standing for only one thing. If so, then images *can* be used to represent information unambiguously and provide a straightforward way of storing observed objects and events in the mind.[6]

MIND AND WORLD

In short, imagery allows us to solve at least part of the puzzle of how to put the world into the mind. Images are representations like those that arise during perception, and an object in an image can be examined and classified using at least some of the same (presumably "central") processes used to examine and classify objects perceptually. This discovery goes a long way toward explaining how mental representations can ultimately refer to things in the world. It also brings us closer to an understanding of imagery, but not close enough to provide a detailed theory. We need to know more about how the mind actually stores and uses information. More clues to this puzzle arise when we reflect on the *differences* between images and percepts. That is, although imagery and perceptions are similar in some respects, some of the most interesting properties of imagery are (fortunately!) utterly foreign to perception.

6

Private Creations

AN ELEPHANT WALKS into the candy store where you are buying a Mother's Day present. You notice that it is rather small, having just squeezed through the narrow door. But as you watch, the elephant starts to expand, like a balloon that is being pumped full of hot air. Suddenly the elephant has a crown on its head, and its tail is replaced by a yellow lion's tail with a thick furry tuft on the end. The elephant turns pink, turns to you with a wink, and then flickers out of existence altogether.

Was the elephant an image or a percept?

Although imagery and perception do operate in similar ways, they are far from identical. Visual percepts are stable, reflecting the reality around us, whereas visual mental images are mutable, at the mercy of the full range of our powers of fantasy. With mental images we can think about and transform what our eyes have told us. Sometimes these transformations are deliberate, as when you image how best to arrange luggage so it will fit into your car's trunk, or daydream about improbable events in a candy store. At other times, the transformations are not deliberate, as when you image the living room lamp to the left of the easy chair when it is really to the right. This is one of the hallmarks of mental events: The ease with which they can create scenes that never really existed or transform the commonplace into the extraordinary. If we are to solve the puzzle of how the mind stores and uses information, we must understand our ability to consider the hypothetical—to imagine the world not merely as it is, but as it could be.

The computer display metaphor of imagery suggests another way of looking at this basic difference between imagery and perception. We can think of percepts as being projected onto the mental matrix directly from the ocular camera; images, on the other hand, are formed from information already stored in the mind. Thus, the metaphor suggests that whereas percepts are essentially fixed by the input from the eyes, images can be altered at will. Once an image is formed, parts of it can be added, deleted, or modified, or it can be manipulated in any number of other useful ways, much as one might change the display on a cathode ray tube by manipulating information in the computer. These creative aspects of imagery are what make it such a valuable constituent of mental life. But the metaphor is only suggestive, and it is vague: There are a whole range of possible ways images might be stored and later formed in the matrix, and there are a whole range of possible ways they might be transformed. Thus, before we can carry out the task we outlined in Chapter 2—programming a computer to mimic human imagery—we need to know more about how images are created and transformed in the mind.

Given what we have established thus far about the properties of mental images, we are now in a position to probe into their origins. If we think of images as being formed from information stored in memory, two questions immediately arise: How are they stored? And how do we form them when we want them?

GENERATING IMAGES

One of the most striking facts about mental images is that we do not have them all the time. Thus images must be stored in long-term memory in some way that allows us to form them when we want them. In this regard, mental imagery is quite different from vision, which operates whenever our eyes are open and brings us a continuous stream of images whether we choose to concentrate on them or not. The voluntary quality of mental images, and our capacity to get rid of them when we do not want to look at them, is probably the main reason why they are frequently compared to photographs or slides.[1]

Analyzed introspectively, objects in images seem to materialize instantly out of nowhere, like the genie in Aladdin's lamp. This remarkable phenomenon was noted by Marcel Proust, the nineteenth century French writer who spent seven volumes and most of his life reflecting on the vicissitudes of memory. Proust compared memories to crumpled bits of paper which, when placed in a bowl of water, unfold as images into all the colors and shapes of flowers, houses, and people:

> And once I had recognized the taste of the crumb of madeleine soaked in her decoction of lime-flowers which my aunt used to give me . . . immediately the old grey house upon the street, where her room was, rose up like the scenery of a theatre . . . and with the house the town, . . . the Square where I was sent before luncheon, the streets along which I used to run errands, the country roads we took when it was fine. . . . All the flowers in our garden and in M. Swann's park, and the waterlilies on the Vivonne and the good folk of the village and their little dwellings and the parish church and the whole of Combray and of its surroundings, taking their proper shapes and growing solid, sprang into being, town and gardens alike, from my cup of tea.

Proust's idea of memories as unfolding bit by bit into an image may seem on the face of it to be sharply different from our computer display metaphor, which depicts images as constructed from data stored in the mental computer. In fact, however, Proust's conception is one way the computer could be programmed to operate. Perhaps one image, or one part of an image, gives rise to another, as one step in a program leads to another. But how do we actually form these individual images? Do they come into the mind full-blown or must each one be constructed? Whatever is going on here, it is happening awfully fast—so fast that simple introspection cannot tell us much.

The Matrix Hypothesis: Part I

The computer display metaphor suggests some possibilities about how the image storage and retrieval system might work. If the image itself is like a television picture, a functional matrix with dots in different cells depicting something, perhaps what is stored is another matrix, a sort of floor plan of where each dot goes. If this is true, then all we need to do to form an image is activate the second matrix. This model is roughly equivalent to saying that we have a set of neurons in the brain that store the information that goes into an image; to form the image, these neurons are simply activated, which directly results in a pattern of neural activity that is interpreted as a visual pattern in a matrix (i.e., a mental depiction).

How would one go about investigating this hypothesis? We decided again to use response time, given its usefulness in earlier experiments. This time, though, we did not measure the time it takes to *process* an image in some way ("scan" it, "inspect" it, and so on). Instead, we focused on the time it takes to bring an object to mind in an image (i.e., to picture it) after hearing its name.[2]

If the activation model just described is correct, we would expect it to work in one of two ways. First, the mental matrix might be turned on all at once, much as we turn on a television set. If so, then all images should take the same amount of time to form, regardless of their size or complexity. If every cell in the matrix is activated simultaneously, it does not matter what the pattern in the matrix is depicting. The alternative would be that individual cells are turned on one by one—more like coloring in a paint-by-numbers picture. If this is the case, then the larger and more complex the image, the longer it should take to form; that is, the more material in an image, the more cells it uses, and the more time is needed for all of them to be activated.

Several experiments were done to test these two possibilities. First we investigated the simpler form of the theory, that the whole matrix is turned on at once. We began by asking people to draw a set of squares, each one six times the area of the preceding one. Then we asked the subjects to image animals at the size of each square (Fig. 6.1). The largest square was the largest size each person could image an animal without it's overflowing, and the smaller sizes were scaled down proportionately. As soon as subjects had imaged the named animal at the indicated size, they were to push a button.

The results were simple: Subjects took longer to picture the animals when they were pictured at larger sizes. This happened even though each animal was imaged at each size, which eliminated the possibility that the nature or complexity of the object being imaged was a factor. We concluded, therefore, that the matrix is not turned on all at once: If images are formed from long-term memory all of a piece, it should not have taken any longer to image, say, a large kangaroo than a small one.

We also performed a variation of this experiment in which

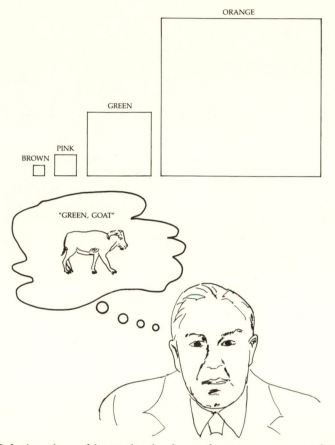

6.1. *Relative sizes of imaged animals; each square was one-sixth the area of the square to its right.*

subjects memorized and then imaged drawings of animals. There were two versions of each drawing: a simple outline and a fairly detailed picture (Fig. 6.2). Again, subjects were to push a button when they had imaged the requested drawing. Following this, they heard the name of a possible feature of the animal, which they were to look for on the animal. Finally, subjects were shown the drawing they had studied and one very similar to it and were asked which was the original. This sequence was repeated with numerous different drawings. We were in fact only interested in the subjects' first button push, telling us that the image was

6.2. Examples of undetailed and detailed versions of the drawings subjects were asked to image and recall.

completed, but by adding two more tasks, we could be fairly sure that (1) the subjects really were forming images of the drawings they studied and (2) they would not guess the purpose of the experiment, which was to see how long it took them to form the initial image. The results showed that subjects required more time to image the detailed drawings than the simple ones, confirming that images are not stored as a matrix that is activated all at once.

The Matrix Hypothesis: Part II

These experiments left us with a second possibility, that images are stored as a matrix that is activated cell by cell. If this is the case, then the time it takes to image a drawing should be directly related to the total amount of ink in the drawing, each speck of ink presumably being represented by a cell in the mental matrix. The nature of the image—what it depicts—should not matter. Whether it is a city skyline, a forest, a scene of people dancing, or the pattern of an oriental rug, the only critical factor should be the number of cells the image takes up in the matrix.

But images need not be stored using individual cells that correspond to dots or specks of ink. We suspected from the work with Gestalt principles that it was more likely that the mental matrix stores organized units, such as lines, enclosed areas, and so on. To examine this possibility, we needed to show subjects stimuli that contained the same amount of ink, but different numbers of organized units. What if we showed subjects not two drawings with the same amount of ink and different degrees of complexity, but one ambiguous drawing that subjects could see as either simple or complex?

We asked subjects to image the geometric figures shown in Fig. 6.3. Each of them could be perceived in two different ways—the one on the upper left, for instance, can be seen as either one

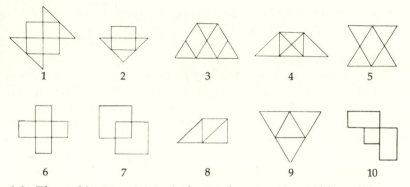

6.3. The ambiguous geometric forms that were imaged by subjects. Each pattern can be described in terms of either a set of contiguous forms or a set of overlapping forms.

square with two overlapping triangles or four smaller squares bordered by four smaller triangles. If the amount of ink, or the number of dots in the mental matrix, is indeed the crucial factor in imaging time, then the same figure should take subjects equally long to image, no matter which way they perceive it.

To set up the proper expectations in our subjects' minds, we told one group that they were about to see forms composed of rather large overlapping patterns. Under each figure was its description: For the upper leftmost figure described previously, this would be, One Square, Two Triangles. The other group was told that they were about to see forms composed of rather small patterns next to each other, each one again described in a caption, for example, Four Squares, Four Triangles for the preceding figure. After studying each figure, subjects were cued to picture the form and were to push a button when it was completely "visible."

When the experiment was finished, we found that the way subjects saw a figure did indeed affect the amount of time they took to image it. The figure described above, for example, required about 1.4 seconds on the average to image when it was seen as three parts, compared to almost 2.2 seconds when it was seen as eight parts. This is a very large difference for a processing system as swift as the mind's. In general, an increment of additional time was required for each additional part included in an image. Thus the possibility that images can only be stored as a simple pattern in a matrix that is turned on cell by cell proved to be just as wrong as the previous matrix hypothesis.

Assembling Parts

What appeared to be emerging from our experiments was the idea that people can store images in sections. It was clear that the form of storage was not the kind of mental matrix we had been considering, in which each point on the image is stored individually. Rather, the data suggest that the mind analyzes each image it stores and files it away in chunks: a triangle, a square, and so on. The result would be something like a model airplane or a bicycle or any other object you buy in parts and assemble yourself. That is, images might also be built out of separately stored parts, with some sort of mental instruction sheet specifying how they fit together.

But although we had ruled out the "simple activation" model of image storage, we had no positive evidence yet that the imagery system is set up so that the mind can store separate memories and amalgamate them into a single image. What if subjects in the previous experiment stored a matrix of the figure *and* the verbal description of each geometric figure, instead of just the figure itself, and used the description to turn on selected parts of the image from a matrix? This is very different from turning on the whole matrix either at once or point by point, but it still does not allow us to say much about the way images are stored. The only way to be sure that people are forming images from separately stored visual memories is to force them to store different parts of an object separately. So this is what we decided to do.

In this experiment, subjects studied drawings of animals that were presented either on a single page, on two pages, or on five separate pages. The drawings that were distributed across different pages each showed part of the animal, so that a whole animal would have appeared had the pages been held up together to the light. Subjects were allowed to study each page as long as they wanted, but they were never allowed to see more than one page at a time. As they progressed to each new page, the subjects were to "mentally glue" the new parts in the image to those from the previous pages. (You can try this by studying each picture at the bottom of the next five pages on the right, Fig. 6.4, as in a flipbook.) Finally, subjects were asked to image the whole drawing.

The more pages used to present a drawing, we found, the longer it took subjects to image the complete drawing. In fact, an additional increment of time was required for each additional page used to present the drawing. Once they imaged the drawing, however, subjects could answer questions about it equally well, regardless of the number of different memories they had "glued together." These results confirmed that people can in fact remember how something looks by storing its parts separately, and that images can be generated from multiple memories.

This was a satisfying result, not only in itself, but because it fit so neatly with other data on both memory and perception. The Gestalt laws of perception are derived from wide-ranging observations about people's tendencies to perceive visual information in coherent units, and investigations of verbal memory have demonstrated that much nonpictorial information is also processed and stored in chunks rather than either word by word or in whole passages. The mind evidently likes to organize information into relatively large chunks, which would save storage space and facilitate later searching through stored information for a specific memory.

"Mental Gluing"

Given the conclusion that the mind can construct mental images by assembling separate sections, a new question immediately arises: How does the mind put the sections together? Although objects in images seem to coalesce spontaneously, this does not mean that representations of parts really do come together all at once. The mind works so quickly that it could use any number of different processes to assemble an image without our being aware of them. This is, of course, one reason for doing reaction

6.4. *The first part of a drawing of a cougar. If you study this and the drawings on the following four pages, you should be able to "glue together" a composite of the entire animal in an image. In the experiment, the number of pages a drawing was presented on was varied to vary the number of units that were encoded. (Note: in the actual experiment the drawings were positioned so that they were in the correct corresponding parts of each page.)*

time experiments: Many of the time differences that reveal information about how the mind is evidently operating are too subtle to be picked up by introspection. For example, I am not aware of taking any longer to image my whole living room than one chair in the living room, but I know from the experiments that there is a difference. In fact, in all our studies where people were asked to image figures composed of a specifiable number of units, subjects required an additional increment of time to image each additional part. This result makes sense if a specific amount of time is required for each part, and we form images by adding parts sequentially rather than all at once.

There are two ways, however, that we might do this. On the one hand, assembling an image could be like fitting together the pieces of a jigsaw puzzle in which the pieces are cut along the shapes of the depicted objects and parts: The shape of each part could indicate how it matches up with other parts. In imaging a dog, for example, we might first image the body, then see that the neck matches up with a place on the body, then see that the ears fit onto the head, and so on. On the other hand, forming an image could be more like putting photographs on a tabletop in accordance with a description. In this case the instructions the brain follows in assembling an image are separate from the image itself, not contained in it.

It is easy to show that people can follow a verbal description to assemble different memories into a single imaged display. Virtually everybody claims to be able to envision George Washington riding a surfboard down a giant wave, although nobody has ever seen such a scene. In the laboratory, people showed the same capacity. We found that subjects had no trouble imaging items according to instructions that specified their positions. For instance, we asked subjects to picture a rabbit floating five feet above and five feet to the left of a teacup, and a violin six inches below the cup. Later, when they were asked questions about the scene, the subjects took more time to scan between objects that were supposed to be farther apart, showing that they had indeed placed the objects in the image as directed (Fig. 6.5).

These results do not tell us, however, *how* people use descriptive information to arrange separate images into a single scene. We considered two alternatives. On the one hand, the mind could use descriptive information much as you would if I asked you to

Cup Scene

The rabbit is floating five feet above and five feet left of
the cup.

Cup Scene

The rabbit is floating five feet above and five feet left of the
cup, and the violin is six inches below the cup.

*6.5. Examples of
stimuli used in an
experiment in which
descriptive informa-
tion was used to con-
struct images of
scenes.*

Cup Scene

The rabbit is floating five feet above and five feet left of the
cup. The radio is six inches below the cup, and the frying
pan is six inches right of the cup.

close your eyes and point straight ahead, and then point at something to your left side. You know where different locations are in
relation to a single standard—your body in this case or the center
of the spatial medium in the case of imagery. That is, the mind
might establish the locations of parts of an image by considering
their location relative to a single common origin in the medium.
On the other hand, the mind might place parts relative to each
other. This would be as if I asked you to point to a picture in
front of you, and then asked you to point to a spot on the wall
one foot to the left of the picture. You would have to find the
picture first and then use it as a reference point to locate the spot.
In imagery, there would be no single common reference point,
but parts would be placed by examining parts of the image already
formed before using a description to position another part.

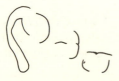

To distinguish between these two alternatives, we also performed a more direct test of the notion that the mind places parts of an image in relation to other parts. We asked subjects to image matrices made up of rows of alternating letters of the alphabet. Figure 6.6, for example, contains rows of *MNMNMN* or *MGMGMG*. The matrices differed in how confusable the letters were: *M* and *N*, for example, are more similar and therefore more confusable than *M* and *G*. Subjects took longer to image the matrices of confusable letters, as we would expect if they were constructing each image by inspecting it when it was partly formed to see where to place additional features. If each letter in the matrix was imaged independently, in reference to a central point rather than in relation to the other images of letters, the confusability of the letters should not have affected imaging time.

But what kind of descriptive information is used to coordinate parts of images? Perhaps people actually "talk to themselves," using verbal information, or perhaps they use abstract propositional information. Robert Weber and his colleagues at the University of Oklahoma showed that sometimes people *do* talk to themselves when forming multipart images. When asked to image each letter of the alphabet in sequence, people mentally "said" each letter prior to imaging it (Weber and Bach found this out by interfering with verbalization and showing that this selectively interfered with imaging in this task.) But the results of the matrix experiment could not have been produced by the kind of verbal prompting Weber discovered when we image in order letters of the alphabet: It takes people about 0.45 of a second to form an image of each letter, but only 0.1 of a second or so to image each part (column) of a matrix. Clearly, whatever it is that we are doing when we add parts to objects or patterns in an image, it need not involve saying the name of each part to ourselves and then imaging the part. Rather, nonverbal descriptive information (stored using propositional representations) apparently can be used here, which also explains why we have no awareness of using it (after all, if it is nonverbal we will not "hear it in our mind's ear," as it were).

More Guidelines for a Theory

It appears, then, that the mind uses some of the same processes to *generate* images as it does to *"inspect"* them. This is

M N M N M N   M G M G M G
M N M N M N   M G M G M G

6.6. Matrices of letters that vary in similarity.

somewhat surprising on the face of it: Picturing an object would seem to have very little in common with examining one for information. But image generation does not appear to be a single act; rather, it involves at least three distinct activities. First, information stored in long-term memory is translated into a spatial pattern in the mental medium. Second, separately encoded parts are arranged into a single amalgamated display, sometimes according to a description (verbal or propositional) of how they are to be arranged relative to each other. Third, in order to amalgamate individual images into a single composite the partially completed image is "inspected" and additional parts are placed in their proper locations. This last step is quite similar to "inspecting" an image once it is formed to evaluate the information it contains. The fact that all three processes are used to form an image makes it clear that imaging is considerably more complicated than simply activating a matrix or otherwise translating information point by point from memory into a visual display.

These conclusions add one more piece to an emerging theory of imaging. We can make a good case that images depict information and occur in a spatial medium that has a number of specifiable features, such as resolution limits (grain) and spatial extent (size and shape). Furthermore, it appears that images can be stored in parts, and we can form complex images by imaging each part individually and placing it relative to at least one other part; the partially completed image is inspected for the correct location of each new piece. The components of an image also can be used to create novel combinations or coordinated into particular spatial arrangements according to verbal directions.

The theory still has a number of holes, however, blanks we do not yet have enough information to fill in. For example, exactly how are the image segments stored? Is imaging a single part like activating a matrix, or is the part constructed from still smaller elements? Nobody has even begun to research these questions. And what else can we do with an image, once it is obtained? This question can be answered, at least in part, and the answers will allow us to fill a few of the gaps in our developing theory.

TRANSFORMING IMAGES

So far we have been considering how we can put a crown on an imaginary elephant's head, or switch tails in the daydream described at the beginning of this chapter. But what about imaging the elephant's growing larger or moving around? These kinds of transformations are a different breed of phenomenon. One point that keeps arising in investigations of imaging is that there is very little reason to *expect* objects in images to behave like real objects. That they often do so is actually quite remarkable, considering that images have none of the physical properties that limit what actual objects can do. If you envision yourself walking toward a distant ice-cream truck, the truck seems to get larger and larger as you get closer, but it could just as easily stay the same size or even shrink. As intangible as they are, however, images show a strong inclination to obey the laws of physics.

Roger Shepard at Stanford University was struck by this intriguing phenomenon early in his observations of imaging. Shepard noticed that when he mentally rotated an object in an image, for example, it moved through the points along the trajectory between its starting and stopping point, just as a real object would have done. If you imagine turning a globe from the Americas to Africa, won't you have to pass over the Atlantic Ocean to get there? It is possible to skip the trajectory—to picture the Americas, erase the scene, and then picture Africa—but isn't your natural inclination to mimic reality and go through a simulated rotation? Most people share these introspections. Although this kind of rotation might at first glance seem cumbersome, Shepard realized its obvious survival value: If a running animal is carrying a long bone in its mouth and approaches a narrow space between two trees, it is much better off imagining what will happen, and twisting the bone around, than waiting for the jolt of actual experience to teach it.

Shepard's curiosity about the way people manipulate images

led him and Jacky Metzler to do the experiment described in Chapter 3. Shepard and Metzler asked subjects to view two drawings of three-dimensional geometric forms (see Fig. 3.2) and then report whether both drawings represent the same form, irrespective of orientation. To do this, the subjects mentally rotated one figure in the image until it aligned (or did not) with the second one. Whether the second figure represented a rotation within the picture plane (that is, clockwise or counterclockwise) or in depth (left to right or up and down), subjects were usually able to tell if it matched. The farther they had to rotate the object, though, the longer it took them to answer.

But can we be sure from these findings that the subjects really were transforming their images through all the intermediate positions along the trajectory? It could be argued that no actual "rotation" process was taking place; rather, the subjects were making some kind of point-by-point comparison that became more difficult as the difference in alignment between the two drawings increased. This seemed unlikely, given subjects' introspective reports of rotating imaged objects, but it was a possibility. Lynn Cooper, who now teaches at the University of Pittsburgh, designed an ingenious way of finding this out.

Cooper's first step was to establish the rate at which her subjects normally "rotate" an image (i.e., transform the underlying representation so that the object is represented at progressively different orientations).[3] To do this, she had subjects first memorize a set of odd-shaped two-dimensional geometric forms. Then the subjects were shown the forms, one at a time, at different orientations and asked to decide if each form was normal or mirror reversed (Fig. 6.7). To do this task they imaged and then mentally rotated the form to the upright position. Such a rotation was necessary because it is difficult to discriminate between normal and mirror-reversed orientations and the subjects were unfamiliar with the forms at novel orientations. And in fact the subjects took increasingly more time to evaluate figures that were presented at increasingly greater rotations from the original upright orientation. Cooper was able to use these results to estimate the rate at which each subject rotated his or her image.

6.7. Geometric forms like those used by Cooper to study mental rotation. Are they same or different?

Armed with this information, Cooper proceeded with the next phase of the investigation. She now had the subjects rotate a geometric form around and around in the image. At some point a picture of the figure would suddenly be presented, and the subject was to compare the imaged form to this drawing. Using her estimates of each person's rotation rate, Cooper presented the drawing either in exactly the position the form should have been at that point or at some specified angle away from that estimated position. As predicted, the subjects' matching times were fastest when the drawing was oriented as the form should have been in the image. By itself, however, this result might just indicate that subjects learned to evaluate the drawing without comparing it to their images at all. Thus, it is critical that Cooper also found that matching times *increased* as the test stimulus was oriented at increasingly greater angles away from the imaged form, as would be expected if subjects had to rotate their images more to make the comparison. Cooper had succeeded in "catching the image on the fly" by computing where along its trajectory it should be at a given instant. This is very strong evidence that subjects really did rotate images through the intermediate points along a trajectory.

Rotating Images and the Computer Model
One question that remained was *how* people rotate images. As vivid as an object in an image may seem, it is not a real object obliged to follow the physical laws that govern a rotating globe or bowling ball. Steven Shwartz, then at Johns Hopkins, believed

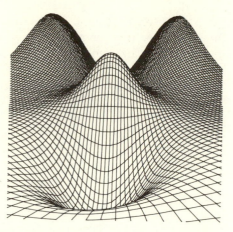

6.8. A computer graphics display of a three-dimensional surface.

that the best way to understand mental rotation was in terms of our computer display metaphor. Computers can be programmed to display rotating three-dimensional objects, even though the screen is actually only two dimensional (Fig. 6.8). Thinking about how one would program a computer to carry out a rotation, Shwartz considered two processes that might be used to rotate images. First, the image could be allowed to fade and then be regenerated in a new orientation; and second, the image itself could be manipulated, much the same way a computer shifts the dots in a matrix to show one shape gradually changing to another. The findings of experiments like Lynn Cooper's favored the second alternative. For that matter, so did logic: If people rotate images by regenerating them in new positions, why imagine going through a whole trajectory? But people's minds are not always so logical, and introspection alone cannot tell us whether we are "seeing" a series of separate images (a kind of mental movie) or a continuous shift (a kind of mental videotape).

If images really are shifted incrementally and not replaced by a series of other images, Shwartz reasoned, then it should take longer to rotate a large image than a small one. This prediction hinges on the idea that we only process the portion of the medium where the image is displayed. The larger the image, the greater the portion of the spatial medium that must be processed, and thus the more time should be needed to shift the pattern. Furthermore, the difference in time to rotate a larger image should be amplified when the image is rotated further: For each degree of rotation, more time will be required for the larger image, and this difference will be compounded as more increments of rotation are completed by the image. For example, if a large image requires one-tenth of a second longer to rotate ten degrees than a small one does, the large image will require two-tenths of a second more to rotate twenty degrees, four-tenths of a second more to "rotate" forty degrees, and so on, the difference increasing with the amount of rotation. Measuring how much time it takes subjects to rotate large and small patterns in images, however, would not necessarily reveal whether they are actually manipulating the images or regenerating them. Generating a large image, remember, is also more time-consuming than generating a small one.

Fortunately, Shwartz used forms of two different levels of complexity as the patterns subjects were required to image. If subjects were generating new images in sequence, the more complex images should require more time to rotate, and the difference in time should increase as the images were rotated more (because the difference would be compounded as the images were generated an increasing number of times).

Shwartz's experiment was based on a technique developed by Lynn Cooper. Subjects saw a pattern and memorized it; then the pattern was turned off and a small arc was presented. This arc cued the subjects to rotate the imaged pattern until its top aligned with the arc (Fig. 6.9). As soon as the pattern lined up, the subjects pushed a button. Shortly thereafter, a second figure was presented. This figure was either at the same orientation as the pattern in the image or slightly off, and was either identical to the original pattern or different. Subjects were to decide as quickly as possible whether this second stimulus had the same shape as the first.

The most interesting result of Shwartz's experiment was the amount of time subjects took to rotate the patterns by various amounts. The greater the rotation, the longer subjects took to carry it out, as previous experiments had established. In addition, with increasingly larger angles of rotation, large patterns

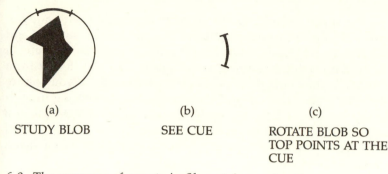

(a) (b) (c)

STUDY BLOB SEE CUE ROTATE BLOB SO
TOP POINTS AT THE
CUE

6.9. The sequence of events in Shwartz' experiment.

required increasingly more time to rotate in the image than small ones. However, it did not take subjects any longer to rotate complex patterns than to rotate simpler ones. These two findings together suggest that the images were not fading and being regenerated in different positions, but that subjects were rotating them by shifting them through the medium. Complex patterns, you will remember, take more time to image than simple ones. If subjects had generated a new image to align with the arc rather than shift the existing one through a trajectory until it matched, then complex patterns would have taken longer to rotate than simple ones. (The supposition that subjects did actually orient their images was supported by another finding: Subjects could identify a match between an imaged pattern and a drawing fastest when the two were in the same position. The greater the difference between the angle of the imaged pattern and that of the drawn one, the longer subjects took to compare them.) It appears, then, that we work directly on our images when we rotate them, much as a computer does when it rotates a pattern through a matrix (which can be displayed on a CRT screen as it is happening).

Experiments with other ways of manipulating patterns in images have turned up information about how people perform transformations other than rotation. Size transformations, for instance, seem to operate similarly to changes in orientation. When we compare two similar shapes of different sizes, we image one shape expanding or contracting until it matches the other.

The greater the size discrepancy, the longer it takes to make the comparison. We also can change *both* the orientation and the size of a shape in an image in order to compare it with another figure. The evidence so far indicates that the size adjustment and the rotation are done in succession rather than simultaneously, which suggests that imaging a change in size is different from zooming in on an object or panning back from it.[4] If you picture a rotating rectangle, you probably can imagine zooming in on it as it turns; but is it as easy to imagine a rotating rectangle at a constant distance and expanding in size? This is another one of those areas of imagery research where much interesting work remains to be done.[5]

A Fantasy Revisited

Remember the expanding elephant fantasy that opened this chapter? When we began we had a good idea of what images proper are like, but very little sense of how they are created and transformed. We now have some insight into how these processes work, and in fact know almost enough to program a computer to image a crown on an elephant's head and make a tiny elephant expand or rotate around in an image. Knowing roughly what the pieces of the imagery system look like, we are in a position to learn more about the system by trying to program a computer to mimic human processing.

7

Computer Model
of Mental Imagery

CONSTRUCTING A THEORY is a little like fitting together the pieces of a puzzle. In the mature sciences, such as physics and biochemistry, enough pieces are known, and their shapes are distinct enough, that there often seems to be only one possible way to fit them into a coherent pattern. Sometimes, in fact, there appear to be so many pieces that one pattern is hardly enough to accommodate them all. With visual imagery, the situation is different: Not only are we missing numerous pieces, but the shapes of some of the pieces are still uncertain. This leaves us with more than one way to put the puzzle together—and hot debate about which way is correct, as should be evident from the recurring references to propositionalist counterexplanations for experimental results.

How can we determine the best way to fit together the various pieces of data on imagery? There is no simple answer to this question, partly because it is really two questions. First, how does one go about constructing a theory of imaging? As the preceding chapters imply, no simple recipe is available. Theory building is largely an art form, a mixture of logic, intuition, and trial and error. Second, how does one decide whether a theory is any good? This too can be done in many ways. There are, however, three rules of thumb for judging a theory: It should explain the existing data, predict new data, and provide guidelines for future research. Each of these criteria is worth a brief examination before we go on to apply them to imaging.

THE COMPLEAT THEORY

The first thing a good theory should do is explain existing data. This seems obvious until we think about what *explain* means. It would be possible, for instance, to explain why airplanes fly by saying that invisible demons hold them up. Aside from the issue of its accuracy, this explanation is unsatisfying because it does not get us anywhere: We still need a further explanation of how the demons operate. A good explanation should reduce the number of unanswered questions we have; it should boil down a diverse set of phenomena to a single set of simplifying principles.

Second, a good explanation should be susceptible to testing. The philosopher Karl Popper said that good theories are in principle *falsifiable;* that is, we should be able to tell if it is wrong. If there is no way, in principle, of showing that a theory is *wrong,* we can never be sure if it is *right.* The theory that flying airplanes are held up by invisible demons is hard to test: There is no easy way to prove that such demons do not exist. Physical laws, on the other hand, can be tried out in various situations: If a proposed law is false, its predictions will not work out and it can be discarded.

Often this need for an explanation to be testable comes down to saying that a good explanation is a *mechanistic* one. That is, the best way to understand how something works is often to treat it as a machine, breaking it down into a set of component parts, properties, and interactions among them. For example, the hands of a watch move because a set of elastic metal springs straining to straighten out causes a set of rigid metal cogs to push each other around. Knowing the parts of the watch, their composition (what metal, how thick), and the physical laws that govern the operation of each part of the watch, we can construct an explanation of the whole. If the explanation fails to fit all the watches to which we apply it, we can examine the individual components of the theory for flaws, just as we might take a machine apart if it failed to work.

The criterion of testability is usually couched in terms of prediction: A good theory should not only explain data, but should successfully predict new data. From the theory it should be possible to predict what will happen in new situations. When Sigmund Freud introduced psychoanalytic theory, his ideas upset many people because of their implication that sex is at the root of nearly all human actions; but the theory upset scientists mainly because it does not generate predictions. To take a simple example, Freud was fond of finding symbols everywhere. Long tubular objects were usually considered phallic symbols, and a patient's relation to them was taken to be revealing of his or her deep underlying conflicts and desires. But when asked about his own fondness for cigars, Freud is reputed to have said, "Sometimes a cigar is only a cigar." It is hard to argue with this, but it raises a problem: How do we know when a cigar is only a cigar and when it is a phallic symbol? Unless the theory tells us this, we cannot use it to make predictions: If the theory tells us that Freud's fondness for cigars may reflect latent homosexuality, or that it may just as likely not mean a thing about his feelings toward other men, it does not add much to our understanding.

The third criterion for a good theory is a little harder to state. A theory should be *vital:* In addition to explaining and predicting data, a theory should help structure the issues in a field in a useful way. This structuring results in an orderly program of new investigation, which in turn results in new data to be explained. In fact, the best theory usually has its own demise built into it—it leads researchers to collect data that eventually put a strain on it, breaking ground for a new, more sophisticated theory. This criterion is especially important for a theory in cognitive science. We have only a few of the puzzle pieces, and we need to collect more to discover whether we have fitted them together correctly. Thus, we want the theory to provide guidelines that will lead us into new classes of open questions, where we can collect data that will lead to further development of the theory.

A THEORY OF IMAGING

Given these criteria, we can return to the task of building a theory of imagery begun in Chapter 2. In explaining imaging, you will recall, the goal we set was not to trace the operation of neurons in the brain, but to describe the steps the brain goes through in terms of the symbols and processes that handle them. Our concern is with mental activity, not with the biochemistry that makes it possible. These functions of the brain in imaging can be divided into two classes: structures and processes. *Structures* are used to represent information. They include both the *media* in or on which the mind's activities occur and the *data* those media store—much like a blackboard and the pattern of chalk marks that appears on it. *Processes* operate on or through the media structures to interpret or transform the data structures, like the process of reading chalk marks or drawing new ones on a blackboard.

The experiments revealed many systematic properties of imagery, and any correct theory must explain these findings. For example, we discovered a systematic relationship between the time it takes subjects to scan an object in an image (T), the rate of scanning (R), and the distance scanned (D). We can summarize this relationship as $T = RD$. If a person scans 10 degrees of visual arc at a rate of 20 milliseconds per degree, the scan time will be 200 milliseconds, which is roughly correct. But this description does not tell us how scanning *works*; it just describes the input–output relations of the processing involved.

It is now our task to try to explain the finding by figuring out how processing is actually carried out in the mind. Using our computer display metaphor, we could hypothesize that the image moves across the spatial medium in small increments until the sought part falls in the center of the medium (which is most resolved and in focus). If this is so, then $T = RD$ describes image scanning because more time is required to move the target part of the image further to reach the focal point of the medium. However, for any given finding, there are many ways of imagining how processing is carried out. We could also hypothesize that the point of focus shifts over the image, like a spotlight shifting over a billboard, till it reaches the target of the scan. In this case, $T = RD$ describes the amount of time needed for the focus point to move. It is easy to come up with many alternative theories when only a single finding is considered, but much harder when numerous different findings are considered at once. In specifying the underlying structures and processes used to accomplish one task, we are then stuck with assumptions that will be used in explaining how other tasks are performed. Thus our explanations for different tasks will interlock under the umbrella of a single theory, which will specify the structures and processes of the mind.

Theories and Models

Because most theories are incomplete, they often cannot be used directly to study a phenomenon; rather, we ordinarily fill in

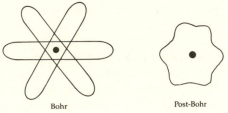

7.1. *The Bohr atom and its modern counterpart.*

Bohr   Post-Bohr

details by creating a model. The kind of model we are interested in here is a sort of extended metaphor, a concrete representation of our ideas about something. A correct model will behave like the thing being modeled in the relevant respects. For example, a model of an airplane might be put in a wind tunnel to tell you how the plane itself will handle in a storm. We must be careful when working with models, however; for one thing, a model usually can be interpreted in more than one way and must be construed correctly if it is to be useful. Niels Bohr's famous model of the atom as a miniature solar system (devised in Denmark in 1913) is a good example (Fig. 7.1). The rings in the model do not stand for any physical structure, but for the orbits of moving particles. A more recent model of the atom conveys the same idea by depicting these particles as a cloud, to indicate that the electrons' charges may be anywhere around the nucleus at any given instant.

In addition, models, unlike theories, include features that are not to be taken seriously. For example, the relative sizes of the drawings of the electrons and protons may be meaningless. In fact, models can be thought of as having three kinds of features: those that are relevant to the theory embodied in the model, those that are not, and those whose relevance is uncertain. In models of the atom, the relation between orbiting particles and the central nucleus is clearly relevant to the theory; many properties of atoms derive from this organization. The width of the lines used to draw the orbits is not relevant; but what about the shape of the particles' orbits? This is not so apparent. The Oxford philosopher Mary Hesse claims that a primary role of models is to lead one to figure out what to do about this third class of features. That is, one of the things that makes a model vital is the inducement it gives researchers to collect new data that will help build a better theory.

The model of imaging that forms the core of this book consists of a matrix processed in a computer (connected to a CRT so we can see what is going on). So far, we have used the model as a loose analogy. But the proof of the pudding for imagery research is in how well the model works in practice. Beginning in the spring of 1977, and for three years thereafter, Steven Shwartz and I filled in the details of the metaphor and created a computer program to simulate human imaging. The goal was to mimic as closely as possible the mental events that occur when a person generates and uses mental images.

Being a model, our computer program contains some features that are not to be taken seriously, that is, that do not embody features of the underlying theory. For instance, the programming language we used forced us to do things in a way that would be convenient for the computer, which clearly is not necessarily the way that would be most convenient for the brain. Insofar as possible, however, the properties we programmed into the computer duplicated what we had ascertained about the structures and processes that underlie human imaging. Most of these you will recognize from the research described earlier in this book. Our reasoning was that if we really did understand how people image, we should be able to program the computer to carry out the same sequence of events. Once we had the model, we could play with it: We could put in an input and see what it did, and then compare this behavior with that of people in similar circumstances. To the extent that the program did mimic human behavior, the principles that govern its operation (i.e., the theory it embodies) would comprise an explanation of the existing data. Furthermore, we could put in new input and use the program's behavior to predict what people would do in novel situations. This use of a computer model is especially important when a theory is very detailed and complicated. As mentioned earlier (in Chapter 2), the computer model serves the function of a note pad when one is doing arithmetic: It helps keep track of everything so that you don't get a headache trying to mentally juggle everything at once. Sometimes the predictions obtained in this way are surprising, which often points out an error in your thinking or an unexpected prediction, as we shall see shortly.

STRUCTURES IN ACTIVE MEMORY

To start off with, we needed to give the computer a set of structures comparable to those apparently used in human imaging. The fact that people do not image all the time—sometimes we are conscious of having an image, sometimes we are not—suggested two groups of structures: those in active memory, which occur only when we are actually imaging, and those in long-term memory, which store images when we are not experiencing them.

From the research it seemed fairly clear that there are two kinds of active memory structures: One is the mental medium in which images occur; the other is the data displayed there. As was noted in Chapter 4, the properties of the medium will affect all data present in it. So, for example, if the medium has only a limited resolution, no "picture" within it can have details finer than this limit. The data were most easily interpreted as showing that the medium acted like a space, with data structures depicting information within it. (This notion is valuable for explaining findings such as the fact that people require more time to scan greater distances across objects in images.) In our computer model we therefore included a matrix of cells that can function like a space (see p. 221), carrying information that can be converted to a visual display on a screen or in a printout. In their visual form, the computer's images consist of patterns of points, each point represented in a printout by a letter of the alphabet (Fig. 7.2). These letters could just as well be dots, but using letters enabled us to do certain things with the images that dots would not have conveyed, as will become evident shortly.

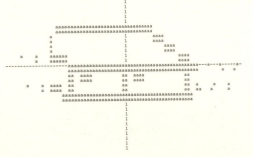

7.2. A simulated image of a car that has overflowed the spatial medium.

7.3. A simulated image
of a car imaged at a
small size. Notice that
the grain of the medium
has obscured the door
handles and wheel wells.

The matrix representing the mind's spatial medium has several properties that were dictated by our experimental findings. First, the mental medium has a limited spatial extent, which we knew from studies aimed at measuring the scope of the medium. The "edges" are not cut and dried, however. Resolution gradually drops off with distance from the center; images beyond a certain size will blur around the edges and then gradually overflow the medium altogether, as the printout of an image of a car in Fig. 7.2 shows. Although the region of greatest resolution appears to be circular, the medium is distinctly oblong as one moves toward the periphery.

Second, the medium has a grain. If an object is imaged too small, parts of it become impossible to make out. This finding was relatively easy to mimic on the computer (Fig. 7.3). When the car is imaged at a small size, the door handles and the "wheel wells" (where the wheels go on the bottom) are not visible. This is because the matrix contains only a limited number of cells in which to put points. When points are crowded close together, they overlap—two or more points fall into the same cell. On the printout, overlap is shown by capital letters, signifying that the cells contain more data than is actually visible in the image. Lowercase letters indicate cells containing only one point each. We do not claim in our theory that the human brain has a literal matrix like the one used in this model, with distinct cells in which points are placed to compose an image, but we do know that the mental medium has a grain, and this seemed to be the best way to simulate it.

Finally, as soon as an image is generated in the medium, it begins to fade. Various research findings (summarized in Chapter 10) suggest that images do not fade all at once, but in parts (they are also generated in parts, a point we will return to in a moment). We therefore needed to give the medium the capacity to show some parts of an image as clearer—less faded—than others. Given that people hold onto an image by refreshing the fading sections, we also wanted the computer to be able to do this. Maintaining images is a matter that goes beyond the nature of the medium, though, so let us defer the details of this aspect of imaging for the present.

Our computer model, then, embodies four important properties of the human imagery medium: First, the medium functions as a space, with a limited extent, a specified shape, and the capacity to depict spatial relations, although it is not a literal physical space. Second, its area of highest resolution is at the center; around the edges of the medium, things get fuzzy. Third, the medium has a grain that obscures details on "small" (relative to the "space" available in the medium) images. And fourth, once an image is generated in the medium, it begins to fade.

The data depicted within the medium consist of regions of activation, that is, arrays of points that actually comprise the image. Each point in the array corresponds to a specific point on the imaged object, and spatial relations between the points on the object (as seen from a particular point of view) are preserved in the relations among points in the array. The data structures, in other words, exhibit what I have called the privileged properties of imagery (see p. 32).

STRUCTURES IN LONG-TERM MEMORY

In long-term memory, things are more complicated. Here the structures are storage rather than display facilities, which means that a whole different set of structures must be involved. We know very little about the medium or media in which images are stored. At least two types of data are stored in long-term memory, consisting of information about visual and nonvisual properties. Some visual information produces a depictive pattern in the spatial medium when it is activated. We do not know the format used to store this information in human long-term memory. In the computer model, each point on an image is stored as a pair of coordinates, numbers that indicate where each point should be placed in the matrix to depict the imaged object. The nonvisual information probably is stored propositionally and must be organized in a way that will allow us to explain why some of the nonvisually stored features of an object are more strongly associated with the object than others. When people search their mental file for the features of a cat, as you may remember from Chapter 4, they identify *claws* as being on the list more quickly than *head*, though a cat's head is usually more visible than its claws on the animal in an image. The visual data stored in a long-term memory, on the other hand, must be in the form of little packets of information labeled by a name or phrase (e.g., "thing I saw under the hood"), with each packet representing part of a whole object. In our model each packet is a separate file of coordinates specifying where points should be placed in the matrix to depict a part. The packets are named, which makes it possible to find a particular image when it is wanted.

In designing the long-term memory component of our computer model, again we were concerned not with duplicating the details of neural activity during imaging, but with simulating the mental events that occur when a person has an image. We stored propositional information in the form of lists, with strongly associated features at the top of each list. Each list has a name by which it is accessed: The propositionally stored information about cats, for instance, is called up under the name CAT.PRP. These lists contain many different kinds of information. One thing we store propositionally is information about an object's component parts. In our model a notation that an object has a part is indexed by the relation HASA (for example, HASA.TAIL). The location of each part on the object is also specified, indicated by a relation and a "foundation part" that provides the reference point for positioning the part. In the file CHAIR.PRP, the location entry for "cushion" is LOCATION FLUSHON SEAT (FLUSHON is the relation, SEAT the foundation part). Elsewhere in the computer's memory is the definition of FLUSHON, which corresponds to "covering the foundation part with no material overhanging or not covering." In addition, the propositional file includes an abstract description of the critical aspects of an object's or part's appearance; we need to store some sort of general description of a thing or parts of it if we are to recognize it (or parts of it).

The propositional file for each object or part also includes its rough size category. It appears that all objects and parts are categorized either directly in relation to some universal standard (such as the size of a human being) or in relation to different standards (such as, for parts, the size of the object to which they belong), which in turn are categorized in relation to a universal standard. (People know that a Honda is bigger than a Great Dane, even though a Honda is small for a car and a Great Dane is big for a dog; we know that dogs are generally smaller than cars.) Current evidence does not strongly favor either alternative, so we directly related each object and part to a single standard as the basis for assigning sizes in our model, labeling each object and part as one of five sizes (huge, large, very small, and so on).

Another feature of the file is the name of the object's superordinate category. For "chair," the listing would be SUPERORD. FURNITURE. This feature reflects people's ability to make deductions from superordinates, as when we deduce that a Basenji must have four feet because we are told that it is a dog and we know that dogs have four feet.

Finally, each object's propositional file includes the names of the various image files storing representations of the object's appearance in long-term memory.

We theorized that every image has two aspects: a skeleton, which depicts just the rudiments or the basic shape of the object,

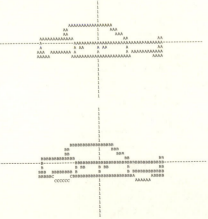

7.4. Two simulated images of a car: a "skeletal image" without added details (top) and an elaborated image (bottom). Points imaged at the same time are printed with the same letter; these points also fade at the same time.

and possibly ancillary parts, which are details placed on the skeleton once it is generated (Fig. 7.4). (*Skeleton* in this sense does not mean an internal framework, like the skeleton of an animal or a building, but rather a sketchy representation of an object.) We needed to posit skeletal images in order to have some foundation parts, some "hooks" on which to hang the details. Our hypothesis was that people always encode a skeletal image of an object (or pattern), but how many additional features they encode varies. The idea that we do not always encode all the possible features of an object into long-term memory would explain why we often can image an object (such as a frog) yet not be able to "see" all its details (such as whether it has a stubby tail). The contents of these ancillary files are determined by what you notice when you see an object or scene.

GENERATING AN IMAGE

Positing a set of structures that make imaging possible is a little like designing a set of instruments for an orchestra. We now have to specify how they should be used. Thus we theorized that there was a set of processes that operate on the structures in distinct ways, depending on what one is trying to do in imagery. Structures without processes are like instruments without musicians: They just sit there. We needed musicians to play the instruments.[1] Our computer model includes a library of processes designed to parallel the various operations the mind carries out when a person generates, "inspects," transforms, and maintains an image. These are easiest to describe in terms of how individual processes work together in accomplishing different things with imagery.

Before you can do anything with an image, you must form it, which requires looking up the necessary information in long-term memory and producing a pattern in the image medium. We named the basic processes used in generating images PICTURE, FIND, and PUT, all of which are coordinated by the IMAGE process. When the computer is called on to generate an image, the IMAGE process is immediately engaged. Its first act is to check the propositional file of the object to be imaged and see whether it contains the name of a skeletal image file, which contains an encoding of the general appearance of the object. If so, the IMAGE process uses the PICTURE process to form the image. The PICTURE process activates a set of coordinates stored in long-term memory, creating a pattern (a skeletal image) in the image medium. Unless a size or location is specified, the image is generated at a standard location in the spatial medium and at a size that just fills the regions of highest resolution in the medium (this is in fact what people do). The PICTURE process can, however, form the image at any requested size and location, just as a person can.

The PUT process adjusts the PICTURE process so that parts are placed correctly relative to the skeletal image. But before doing so, the PUT process must first figure out where a part goes. Thus the PUT process first searches through the list of propositions associated with an object, looking for the name of one of the object's parts (such as "cushion" in the CHAIR file). If the PUT process finds the name of a part (e.g., HASA.CUSHION), it now looks up the propositional file for that part and finds its location (for "cushion," this would be LOCATION FLUSHON SEAT). The PUT process next finds out what the location word means by looking up its description (the description is expressed mathematically); it then calls on the FIND process. The FIND process takes the name of the foundation part (SEAT) and locates that part on the imaged object, if it is visible. In order to do so, the FIND process first looks up the description of the part (expressed mathematically); then it uses that description to search for a particular spatial pattern in the skeletal image that has been generated in the spatial medium, along with any additional parts that may already have been placed on the skeleton. The pattern it looks for depicts the foundation part, that is, the section of the available image where the part to be added should be attached. If the foundation part is visible on the image, the FIND process conveys its size and location to the PUT process. From these data, the PUT process then calculates how big the new part ("cushion") should be and where in the medium it should be placed. This information is then used to adjust the PICTURE process so that an image of the new part is generated correctly in relation to the existing image (Fig. 7.5).

To summarize, the PICTURE process actually makes images, in the sense of transforming stored data into a depictive pattern in active memory. The PUT process directs where the PICTURE process should place ancillary parts in relation to an existing image,

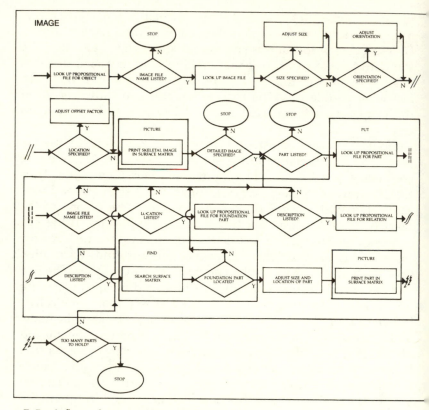

7.5. A flow chart outlining how images are generated. The large boxes indicate which process is operating and the small ones indicate specific acts carried out; Y stands for yes, and N for no.

based on information about the relation and location of the foundation part (provided by the FIND process). Finally, the IMAGE process supervises the work of all three; it decides whether a skeleton or a detailed image will be generated, for instance, depending on such factors as whether the ultimate task is to compare the general sizes of two objects or to scan an image for a particular feature. In theory, the IMAGE process bases its decisions on input from the rest of the cognitive system; in the computer model, most of this input comes from the person using the program. This process is also responsible for producing images in novel combinations, which it does by feeding new relations to the PUT process: For instance, it can generate an image of a horse with its tail coming out of its forehead if so instructed.

The IMAGE, PICTURE, PUT, and FIND processes enable our computer model to carry out many of the same functions the human mind performs in generating images. The theory posits that the mind has these processes, which function in roughly the same way as those in the computer. Compared with the mind, however, the model is primitive. Placing a cushion on the seat of an imaged chair is an achievement for a computer, but the task is considerably more complicated in the larger world, where chairs range from thrones to stools and may not have even such universal features as legs and a seat. We do not claim that the model solves the entire question of how people generate images—only that the series of processes we have postulated must be centrally involved in image generation. This kind of idealization, dealing with the major phenomena and setting aside the "glitches" for now, has proved very useful in other sciences.

INSPECTING AN IMAGE

Other processes in the computer's library come into play when we simulate "inspecting" an image. The LOOKFOR process coordinates the PICTURE, PUT, and FIND processes when the computer is instructed to "see" whether an object has a specified property. Suppose, for instance, the computer were asked to image a rabbit and then to examine it to find out whether a rabbit has a pointed nose. First, an image of a rabbit must be generated. In preparation for inspection of the image, the LOOKFOR process then directs a process called REGENERATE to make sure the image is as clear as possible (the function of the REGENERATE process is to refresh images that have begun to fade).

The LOOKFOR process also summons a process we call RESOLUTION to gauge the density of points in the image. This is the computer's way of judging image size: Small images occupy only a small part of the matrix and hence have a relatively high density, with a high proportion of cells in the matrix containing more than one point, whereas large images are sparser and have few points overlapping. From the size label in the propositional file of the sought part, the LOOKFOR process can tell whether the image is at the optimum density for that part to be visible. A rabbit's nose, being "very small," would be judged as unlikely to be visible in a small image of a rabbit. Given this cue from the RESO-LUTION process, the LOOKFOR process would adjust the size of the image, using the ZOOM process to enlarge it so that the grain of the medium will not obscure the rabbit's nose. If the image was too large, so that its edges might have overflowed the medium and the part might therefore not be in the area of greatest resolution (or might be completely out of view), the PAN process would be used to shrink it.

The LOOKFOR process also looks up the description and location of the sought part to see whether it falls at one end of the object being imaged. A rabbit's nose would be described as located at the front end of the rabbit; so the LOOKFOR process would next check whether that end has overflowed the medium. If it has, the LOOKFOR process calls the SCAN process to shift the image through the medium, filling in new material at the leading edge as it goes, until the relevant end of the image is in the area of highest resolution.

Once the image is ready to be inspected, the LOOKFOR process searches for the named part ("nose") by calling on the FIND process. This process acts now just as it did when it was used in generating images. But instead of searching for a foundation part, so that another part can be correctly placed, it simply searches to see whether the part is there or not. If the FIND process fails to locate the part in the image, the LOOKFOR process goes through the object's propositional file checking for other HASA entries that belong in the appropriate region of the object (e.g., the front or back end) and directs the PUT process to integrate those parts into the image. After a new part is filled in, the FIND process again searches for the sought part. The hope is that one of the new parts (such as "head") will include the sought part (the nose), and the part will then be visible. If so, the LOOKFOR process continues; if not, it responds with a statement saying that the part is not there. If the nose is found, the FIND process is then used to compare its shape to the description of "pointed." If this description fits the pattern identified as the nose, the LOOKFOR process (finally!) answers yes; otherwise it answers no.

If this all seems like a lot of work for such a simple question, you should appreciate what this tells us about the human mind. Thinking of mental imagery at the level of detail necessary to

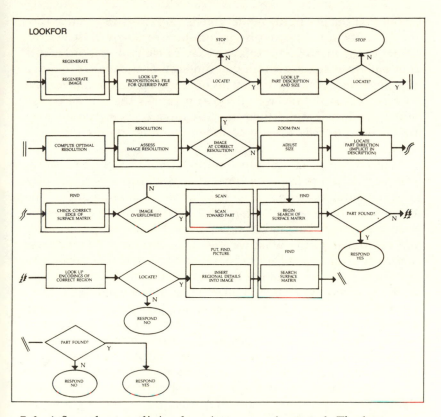

7.6. A flow chart outlining how images are inspected. The large boxes indicate which process is operating and the small ones indicate specific acts carried out; Y stands for yes, N for no.

program a computer, we discover just how complicated the mind's workings really are (Fig. 7.6). Who would have guessed introspectively that so much would be required for something that seems so simple?

TRANSFORMING AN IMAGE

Three of the processes used in transforming images have already been mentioned—ZOOM, PAN, and SCAN. The ZOOM and PAN processes change the size of an existing image.

When the ZOOM process enlarges the image, the outer points

(recall that images in the model consist of points in a matrix) are moved outward, followed by points progressively closer to the center of the matrix. This dilation may cause two or more points that had been squeezed into the same cell of the matrix to move into separate cells, where they become visible in the image. The PAN process is the reverse of ZOOM; it causes the central points and then those around them to shift inward. Some points may be forced into cells already occupied by other points, with the result that details of the image are lost from view.

Scanning an image appears, on the face of things, to be a process very different from the ZOOM and PAN processes. Introspectively, scanning does not seem to be a transformation undergone by images, but a way of interpreting imaged objects. When we scan the view from a mountaintop or a skyscraper, we certainly are not transforming what we see; why should it be otherwise when we scan an image? One obvious answer is that the mind's eye, being a structure in the brain, does not move across images in the way our eyes move to take in a scene. Indeed, the mind's eye (the FIND process in our theory and model) does not deal with actual physical pictures at all. Given this fact, the analogy to a real eye falls flat and provides no insights into how the mind's eye scans images. In our model, instead of moving the center of focus across the image, the image is moved across the center of focus. That is, the mind's eye does not shift over the medium like a spotlight so as to enable the area of greatest resolution to fall on the desired part of an image; instead, the points that comprise the image shift left or right, up or down, until the target region falls in the focal area (the central, most highly resolved part of the spatial medium). When called on to scan something, the computer keeps track of the coordinates representing points just off the edge of the medium and brings these points into the matrix as the image moves.

When you think about how imagery and perception relate to each other, it makes sense that scanning an image should work in this way rather than in the way it does in actual visual perception. It appears that vision and imagery use many of the same neural structures in the brain. For vision, these structures need to handle only the limited arc the eyes can take in. Yet most of us claim to be able to scan an object or scene in an image—such as the inside of a living room—a full 360 degrees around. Given a medium of limited extent and a moving focal point, our mind's eye should bump into the edges when we try to scan a full circle. The fact that it does not suggests that it is the image, and not the area of resolution, that changes position, with new parts of the image being generated continuously as we scan in a given direction.

This idea also allows us to explain why we scan at the same rate within the "visible" parts of an image as we do to a part "off screen" (as has been found repeatedly in the laboratory): In both cases, we are in effect moving a pattern through the mental medium, adding new material at the leading edge as appropriate.

In addition to the ZOOM, PAN, and SCAN processes, a ROTATE process participates in transforming images. This process rotates an image around a pivot point, shifting the points of the image through the medium. Like the ZOOM, PAN, and SCAN processes, the ROTATE process is limited in the model to transformations in two dimensions, rather than the full three dimensions of human imagery. However, the ROTATE process differs from the other three in a significant way: Whereas the other processes transform the entire contents of the medium uniformly, the ROTATE process operates only on a specific region of the medium, usually those cells occupied by a particular set of points. This is necessary because people can imagine a single item in a scene rotating, without having to rotate the entire scene. The other three processes shift everything in the image in a given way; this kind of general operation is called a *field-general* transformation. The ROTATE process, in contrast, performs *region-bounded* transformations, altering only material in a specific portion of the spatial medium. The importance of this distinction will become evident when we turn to generating predictions from this theory of imaging in Chapter 8.

All of the processes described thus far must work in conjunction with either the FIND or RESOLUTION process. One of these processes is necessary to monitor the transformation, providing feedback about its progress. When the image has been transformed far enough (e.g., so that the sought part is visible or the correct resolution has been achieved), the transformation process is stopped. In addition, some other process (such as LOOKFOR) must set the direction and rate of the transformation.

The final transformation we built into the model differs from the rest in that it alters the activation of the image, not the pattern itself. The REGENERATE process, as was already mentioned, prevents the images from fading away immediately after they are generated. As you may have noticed, the letters of the alphabet comprising printed out images from the model range from *A* to *C*. This is because the REGENERATE process refreshes images one part at a time, just as we claim the mind does. In the model, parts of an image fade in the order they were generated. The REGENERATE process follows this same order, sharpening one part after another. When a part has just been generated or refreshed, it is printed out as *A*'s. As it fades, it shifts to *B*'s and finally to *C*'s.

This concludes our overview of the theory. What we have done is a little like preparing the way for a language by specifying the letters of its alphabet. Just as all words are formed by combining the letters in different ways, the theory posits that all imagery tasks are performed by combining structures and processes in different ways. In Chapter 8 we will see how this is done and how the theory leads to predictions and new, unanswered questions.

8

The Computer Model in Action

TO SOME EXTENT, a computer that can image is like a dog that can walk on its hind legs: We are impressed not so much by how well it does it as by the fact that it can do it at all. In creating an imagery program, however, our interest was not solely the challenge of getting a computer to mimic human behavior. Rather, we wanted a concrete model of our theory of what the mind does during imagery. The value of the model, in turn, lies in its ability to help us explain the research findings, make new predictions, and lead us to ask further interesting questions about mental imagery. If the theory cannot explain the existing results, there is no point in going any further; so let us start by considering some representative findings and the explanations the model gives us for them.

EXPLANATIONS

So far, we have been concerned with what goes into the computer. Now we are ready to see what comes out. Given structures and processes designed to parallel those of the human mind, can the computer in fact simulate imaging? We can answer this question by following the computer through a task, watching what it does at each step, and seeing where it ends up.

In the course of this book, we have discussed a wealth of data on visual mental imagery. These data fall roughly into three general classes: generating images, inspecting images, and transforming images. By examining how the model explains key findings about each type of task, we can see what it tells us about how the mind performs the same function.

Image Generation in People and Program

We have four things to explain about how images are generated: Why does it take more time to form images of more detailed objects? Why is an additional increment of time required to image an object for each additional part it contains? How can verbal and propositional information be used to coordinate parts of images into a single entity? Why do large images normally take more time to form than small ones?

As an example, let us trace through how the program images a car. Observing its progress is made easier by the printed tracing the computer produces as it performs the task (see Table 8.1). Each time the computer calls up one of the processes in its repertoire, it prints out three asterisks, the name of the process, BEGINS, and three more asterisks. When a process finishes its part of the task, the computer prints out a similar notice that the process has ended.

As the tracing from the computer shows, generating the image begins when we command the computer to image a detailed car (a single asterisk at the far left of the tracing indicates a command from the outside). The IMAGE process is called up at this point and begins looking for a propositional list containing facts about cars. It finds one (CAR.PRP) and enters it. IMAGE then looks in the propositional file to see if the computer knows what the object looks like. When it discovers the name of the skeletal image encoding (CAR.IMG), it looks for the file with that name and then calls the PICTURE process to begin using what is in the file to generate an image.

Because our command did not specify a size or location, PICTURE forms a skeletal image of the stored car so it just fills the most resolved center part of the matrix. Because we asked for a detailed image, IMAGE then checks the propositional file to check if any parts are stored. It finds one: HASA.REARTIRE. PUT is called to integrate the image of the rear tire onto the skeletal image at the appropriate size and location. To do this, PUT looks up the location of the part and a description of what that location looks like; it then looks up the name of the relation and its definition. Having both these pieces of information—"rear wheel base" (where the rear tire goes) and "under" (how it goes there)—PUT calls FIND to locate the rear wheel base. FIND searches the image, looking for the particular pattern of points in the matrix that depicts the car's rear wheel base. Having located it, FIND ends and PUT continues (notice that one process can "wait in the wings" for another to carry out its part of the job before proceeding).

Table 8.1   Trace of the simulation generating an elaborated image of a car at the default size and location.

---

*IMAGE FULL CAR

IMAGE BEGINS
LOOKING FOR PROPOSITIONAL FILE FOR CAR
CAR.PRP OPENED

CHECKING PROPOSITIONAL FILE FOR NAME OF IMAGE FILE
NAME OF IMAGE FOUND: CAR.IMG

LOOKING FOR IMAGE FILE CAR.IMG
CAR.IMG OPENED

PICTURE BEGINS
TURNING ON POINTS IN SURFACE MATRIX WITH SIZE
    FACTOR = 1.0
PICTURE ENDS

CHECKING PROPOSITIONAL FILE FOR NAMES OF PARTS
PART FOUND: HASA REARTIRE

PUT BEGINS
LOOKING FOR PROPOSITIONAL FILE FOR REARTIRE
REARTIRE.PRP OPENED

CHECKING PROPOSITIONAL FILE FOR NAME OF IMAGE FILE
NAME OF IMAGE FILE STORED: TIRE.IMG

CHECKING PROPOSITIONAL FILE FOR LOCATION OF REARTIRE
LOCATION FOUND: UNDER REARWHEELBASE

LOOKING FOR PROPOSITIONAL FILE FOR REARWHEELBASE
REARWHEELBASE.PRP OPENED

CHECKING PROPOSITIONAL FILE FOR DESCRIPTION OF
    REARWHEELBASE
DESCRIPTION FOUND

LOOKING FOR PROPOSITIONAL FILE FOR UNDER
UNDER.PRP OPENED

CHECKING PROPOSITIONAL FILE FOR DESCRIPTION OF UNDER
DESCRIPTION FOUND

FIND BEGINS
BEGIN SEARCHING SURFACE MATRIX FOR REARWHEELBASE

Table 8.1 Trace of the simulation generating an elaborated image of a car at the default size and location. (*Continued*)

SEARCHING FOR LOWEST POINT LEFT
FOUND AT   −23   −3

FOLLOWING HORIZONTAL RIGHT TO END
FOUND AT   −19   −3

SEARCHING FOR NEXT HORIZONTAL POINT RIGHT
FOUND AT   −10   −3
FIND ENDS

BEGIN TO PUT ON PART: REARTIRE

PICTURE BEGINS
TURNING ON POINTS IN SURFACE MATRIX WITH SIZE
  FACTOR = 0.9
PICTURE ENDS
PUT ENDS

CHECKING PROPOSITIONAL FILE FOR NAMES OF PARTS
PART FOUND: HASA FRONTTIRE

PUT BEGINS
LOOKING FOR PROPOSITIONAL FILE FOR FRONTTIRE
FRONTTIRE.PRP OPENED

CHECKING PROPOSITIONAL FILE FOR NAME OF IMAGE FILE
NAME OF IMAGE FILE STORED: TIRE.IMG

CHECKING PROPOSITIONAL FILE FOR LOCATION OF FRONTTIRE
LOCATION FOUND: UNDER FRONTWHEELBASE

LOOKING FOR PROPOSITIONAL FILE FOR FRONTWHEELBASE
FRONTWHEELBASE.PRP OPENED

CHECKING PROPOSITIONAL FILE FOR DESCRIPTION OF
  FRONTWHEELBASE
DESCRIPTION FOUND

LOOKING FOR PROPOSITIONAL FILE FOR UNDER
UNDER.PRP OPENED

CHECKING PROPOSITIONAL FILE FOR DESCRIPTION OF UNDER
DESCRIPTION FOUND

FIND BEGINS
BEGIN SEARCHING SURFACE MATRIX FOR FRONTWHEELBASE

SEARCHING FOR LOWEST POINT RIGHT
FOUND AT   24   −3

FOLLOWING HORIZONTAL LEFT TO END
FOUND AT   21   −3

SEARCHING FOR NEXT HORIZONTAL POINT LEFT
FOUND AT   12   −3
FIND ENDS

BEGIN TO PUT ON PART: FRONTTIRE

PICTURE BEGINS
TURNING ON POINTS IN SURFACE MATRIX WITH SIZE
   FACTOR = 0.9
PICTURE ENDS
PUT ENDS

CHECKING PROPOSITIONAL FILE FOR NAMES OF PARTS
CAN'T FIND ANY MORE PARTS
IMAGE ENDS

IMAGE COMPLETED

PUT now has the necessary information about how to adjust the PICTURE process so that an image of the part (REARTIRE) will be placed at the correct location (UNDER REARWHEELBASE) at the correct size. PUT therefore uses the information to adjust PICTURE, which images the tire in place. At this point, both PICTURE and PUT end. IMAGE takes over again and checks for the name of another part, repeating the entire process until all the parts are imaged (two, in this case) or until so many parts have been placed on the image that no more can be held up.

From observing the model as it generates an image, we can offer an answer for each of the four questions posed earlier. It is clear why a more detailed image takes longer to form: The mind, like the computer program, must have to locate each part in memory and image it separately. Similarly, the reason each additional part requires an additional amount of time to image is that for each one, the same process is repeated. This gives us an explanation of another finding as well, that different kinds of parts may take different amounts of time to image. As you may recall, people take longer to image the columns of a matrix composed of alternating similar letters (for instance, *MNMN*) than those of a matrix composed of dissimilar letters (such as *MGMG*). This result makes sense if FIND has to go through more exacting tests to distinguish an *M* from an *N* as the foundation part for the next letter than to distinguish an *M* from a *G*. That is, as FIND examines the image to spot the location where the next letter should go, it can tell an *M* from a *G* by looking for a straight vertical line, but telling *M* from *N* requires additional time-consuming tests.

The theory also helps us answer the third question, about how people use verbal and other propositional information to coordinate the parts of an image: Stored information about how various parts look (simulated by coordinates in the object's IMG file) is linked together by propositional descriptions (such as UNDER REARWHEELBASE). Suppose, for example, that someone gives you the verbal instruction, "Picture yourself in a boat on a river with tangerine trees and marmalade skies." You can use the names of things in the instruction as the basis for pulling images of various parts and properties out of storage in memory, and the relations can be used to arrange them into a novel image. That is, from one image file your mind draws an image of yourself, from another it draws a river, from another a boat, and it combines them using the propositional relations "in a," "on a," and "with." (How colors are handled is an open question at the moment.)

Finally, the theory explains why large images take longer to form than small ones. In a large image, FIND can locate most of the places where parts belong, so IMAGE can keep on going through the list of propositions for more and more parts to add. In a small image, some features are obscured by the grain of the medium, causing FIND to fail to locate the foundation parts and IMAGE to give up. You can see on the printout of a car imaged at a small size (Fig. 7.3) that the rear wheel base is not visible, so the computer has not been able to integrate the rear tire onto the image.

Image Inspection in People and Program

With regard to image inspection, we have three general findings to explain: Why does it take longer to "see" small parts of images, or parts of small images, than large ones? Why does it take longer to find parts in detailed images than in simple ones? And why are people faster at recognizing parts that conform to the Gestalt laws of organization (see Chapter 5) than other kinds of parts?

We can see how the model and the theory offer explanations for these questions without going through a computer tracing step by step. You recall that to "inspect" an image, LOOKFOR is invoked. LOOKFOR first takes any necessary steps to adjust the size and location of the image so that the region depicting the sought part is clearly in view and focused. To do this may require the assistance of the ZOOM or PAN processes, to enlarge or shrink the image, or SCAN, to move it into the center of the medium. Once the image is ready, LOOKFOR calls FIND to do the actual inspecting.

This sequence explains why small parts of images, or parts of small images, take longer to "see" than large ones. If the image is at a small size initially, the grain of the medium obscures its features; adjusting the size of the image requires time, in both the computer model and the mind. Notice that the grain of the medium is instrumental in explaining two different findings: why the mind is usually faster at forming small images than large ones and why it takes more time to see parts of smaller images. This is one of the criteria of a good theory, that apparently disparate phenomena can be explained in terms of the same underlying principles.

What about the next finding, that it generally takes longer to find parts on complex images than simple ones?[1] If you are asked to scan an undetailed car in an image until you see the hood, you can spot it quickly; but if the car is detailed, finding the hood will take slightly longer. One reason for this, as was noted in Chapter 3, is that on a detailed image, more parts have to be scanned over; that is, as SCAN shifts the car image across the medium so that the hood will be in the region of sharpest focus, FIND is busy checking each part that crosses the center of the medium to see if it is a hood.

But there is a second possible explanation for this finding as well, one that relates to the way we hold images in mind. Maintaining an image is a lot like juggling: Each piece is tossed into the air separately and must be caught and retossed continually if it is to stay up there. The parts of an image fade at a specific rate once they are generated. The REGENERATE process keeps catching

8.1. How parts are preserved in images. Different letters indicate different amounts of fading.

them, refreshing them, and tossing them back into the image, but it cannot move fast enough to keep more than about four units in sharp focus at once. Thus the more parts an imaged object contains, the more likely it is that the part being looked for is not visible at the moment the image is inspected. To find it may take a "second glance," and may even require invoking the PICTURE and PUT processes to generate an image of the part anew.

The third finding to be explained is that "good" parts (defined by the Gestalt principles) are easier to access in an image than other parts. If you picture a Star of David, you can easily see a triangle in it, but a parallelogram is harder to make out—so much harder that many people deny there is one. Why? The answer probably has two parts, both reflecting the fact that the Gestalt laws represent the rules the brain follows in dividing images (and percepts) into parts so that they can be stored in memory. On the one hand, images are generated in parts, and they fade in parts. (These parts are determined by how you see an object in the first place.) The computer model shows this by printing out the two triangles in Fig. 8.1 in different letters, indicating that one triangle has begun to fade while the other is still fresh. Not only does each triangle have a built-in tendency to "stick together," then, but the two may not even be equally visible in the image at any given moment. This makes patterns that consist of segments from different parts, such as parallelogram, difficult to see. On the other hand, the tests used by the FIND process are themselves molded by the Gestalt laws. The FIND process seeks out continuous lines, sees parts close together as composing a group, and so on. Thus if a part is made up of segments that are not organized into a "good" part, more tests will be required to see it.

Image Transformation in People and Program

The major finding about image transformations is very puzzling. Images seem to be transformed gradually, depicting the intermediate points along a trajectory. But why? They are not constrained by the laws of physics that govern the behavior of real objects, so what makes them follow this particular law? A common explanation is that it is just habit: We are used to seeing objects move through all the intermediate locations along their path, so we force objects in our images to do the same. Some advocates of this view throw in an evolutionary component: Rotating images has adaptive value—over the eons, those of our ancestors who imaged things this way had a higher survival rate than others.

I do not like this kind of theory myself, for two reasons: First, it is unclear what makes such behavior pattern "adaptive." Take the case of the animal carrying a bone in its mouth as it is running toward a narrow opening between two trees. It clearly is useful for the animal to be able to image turning the bone before reaching the opening, but it seems unlikely that there is any adaptive advantage for the animal in imaging the bone going through a whole trajectory. In fact, the added time might be just enough to prevent the animal from realizing that it needs to rotate the bone to make it through. Depending on what was following up the rear, the crunch into the trees could put this animal out of the picture as a potential ancestor. Second, both habit and evolutionary advantage are difficult theories to test and therefore to disprove if they are wrong. I prefer to work with mechanistic explanations that are potentially disprovable and useful, in addition, as a basis for further exploration.

The computer model suggests that the reason we rotate images (or scan, expand, or otherwise transform them) in small increments is a consequence of three principles. First, moving a point in the medium presumably is easier than generating a new one. To let an image fade and then go back into storage and then pull it out again (in a new position) takes not only the PICTURE process, but also considerable involvement of the PUT and FIND processes. Second, the brain, like all physical systems, is prey to noise—random events that interfere with the phenomenon of interest. Thus if 100 points are moved by one degree, they will not all end up perfectly aligned; some will have moved a little farther than others. If the error due to noise is some small but constant percentage, then the actual size of the error will increase with the size of the transformation. The farther the points are moved, the greater the disarray at the end of the shift. You can "see" the consequences of this if you try imaging the face of someone you know well and then rotating it. I find that after about 100 degrees the face starts looking mangled, with the eyes twisted off center and the mouth crooked. Most people I have asked have reported similar introspections. (An experiment could be done to show that this happens, but no one has yet performed it.)

As an image is transformed, then, it gets scrambled, which means it must be realigned for the transformation to be successful. This brings us to the third principle suggested by the theory: The processes that realign the scrambled parts can only work if the deformation is relatively minor. If the image becomes too distorted, then the FIND process must be used to locate where parts are and where they go, and this process has trouble identifying and relating parts when they are in nonstandard orientations. (It is well known that people have trouble identifying faces perceptually when these are tilted too far around, suggesting that the FIND processes used here are especially sensitive to orientation. If this is the case, we would expect it to be difficult to keep a face intact as its image is rotated—as is reported by most people.)

Therefore, the most efficient way to transform an image is to move it a few degrees at a time. In this way we take advantage of the fact that parts of images are easier to move than to generate anew; and we also hold the amount of image scrambling due to noise in the system down to a manageable level. Presumably each time the image moves far enough to begin losing its shape some process in the system realigns the points so that the transformation can continue. These principles allow us to explain why images are transformed a small increment at a time; and because each increment takes time, the larger the transformation the more time is required.

These explanations of various basic findings about how images are generated, inspected, maintained, and transformed can be extended to most of the experimental results described in earlier chapters. The theory is weak, however, in providing explanations for the data showing similarities between imagery and perception (Chapter 5). Most of the findings showing similarities between these two activities can be explained if we assume that the spatial medium and the FIND process are used in both cases. However, the really striking results—such as the McCollough effect (see Chapter 5)—depend on details of the FIND process that have yet to be understood.

PREDICTIONS

Einstein's general theory of relativity was impressive in that it not only explained a host of seemingly disparate phenomena in physics, but made striking predictions about a number of them. In one case, Einstein used the theory to predict to multiple-decimal-point accuracy how much the sun's gravity should bend light waves passing by it. This kind of quantitative precision is particularly impressive because it is unlikely that any other theory would have come up with the same prediction. There is a lesson here for all theories, great or small: One property of a good theory is that it generates predictions that would not follow from other theories. Testing these predictions is therefore an important test of the theory, for if they are confirmed, the theory gains support while rival theories lose credibility.[2]

When we created our computer model of imaging, our first test of the theory behind it was to see whether the model could explain existing data. For the most part, it did.[3] The second test is to use the model to make predictions about how people use visual imagery. If experiments with human subjects bear out our predictions, we can begin to take the theory seriously.

The predictions we decided to test fell into four general categories. The first three are probably familiar by now: We wanted to investigate how images are generated, inspected, and transformed. The fourth category, which will be explored in later chapters, involves the spontaneous use of imagery to answer questions or solve problems. Rather than catalog all of the predictions we made, let us just consider a typical example for each of the first three topics so you can see how the model and theory can be tested.

Generating Images: FINDing Foundation Parts

Let us begin by considering an initial prediction that failed. failed. One of the central claims of our imagery theory is that the image inspection process is also used in generating images. When a new part is placed in an image, the place where it belongs (the "foundation part") is first located by the FIND process, and only thereafter can the PUT process arrange for the part to be integrated into the image. This idea allowed us to explain the previous finding that smaller images are generated faster than larger ones. Recall that with smaller images many potential locations where parts belong simply will not be visible—the "grain" of the medium obscures them. A larger image, on the other hand, will allow one to place more parts in it. Hence, a person completes smaller images sooner because he or she is forced to stop adding parts into the smaller image sooner, being unable to "see" where to put any more details. This explanation leads to the following prediction: Subjects should take much more time to image complex objects at a large size than at a small size. On the other hand, simple objects—that is, objects with few parts—should take about the same amount of time to image at either a small or a large size. The limitations imposed by the grain of the medium should get in the way when subjects try to add parts into the small images of complex objects, but the medium's grain should not affect the images of simple objects.

Martha Farah and I tested this hypothesis by asking subjects to memorize visually simple objects, such as a bar of soap or a blank box, and visually complex objects, such as a calculator or a typewriter. We asked subjects to memorize the appearance of the objects, picture them at large and small sizes, and then answer questions about their features. Again, our measure of interest was the time subjects took to construct the initial image.

The results came out exactly the opposite of what we expected. People took the most time imaging the complex objects at a small size, substantially longer even than they took to image those objects at a large size.

What had happened? One subject's remarks after the experiment gave us a clue. She said it was harder to see where parts should go on small objects than where they should go on large ones, so she had struggled longer to fill in the small ones. Knowing she would later have to answer questions about the features of the objects in her images, she wanted to be sure not to leave out any of the parts.

From this comment we realize that including the questions about features was our undoing. In the first experiment, where we measured how long people took to form images of animals at different sizes, we had not asked questions about each animal after subjects imaged it; they were simply to push a button when the animal was complete. And large images had taken them longer to form than small ones. So we repeated the present experiment without the questions. This time, the results matched our predictions exactly! Subjects took longer to form a large image of a calculator than a small one, and needed less time in general for the simple objects and about the same amount of time to form either a small or large image of a bar of soap.

Taken together, the results provide support for the view that the mind forms images by "looking" for where each part belongs and then placing the part at the correct location. Our findings also indicate that motivation plays a role in how someone images a thing, which is not really surprising. No matter how motivated people were, though, they still were constrained by the limited resolution of the mental medium. That is, the grain of the medium made it difficult and time-consuming to locate "foundation parts" in smaller images, however hard the subjects tried. If they tried hard, they took longer with small images of complex objects; if they did not struggle to add parts, they took less time. Thus these results confirm the underlying principles that provided the basis of the prediction in the first place—even though the theory was silent on an important contributing factor. This means that we have gained not only support for the key claims of the theory, but guidance for its further development.

Inspecting Images: A Potential Embarrassment

Although images are pictorial, they are not pictures. One prediction about image inspection derived from a critical difference between images and pictures: Specifically, the parts of an image are generated sequentially and an image begins to fade as soon as it is formed. If too many parts are included in an image, it follows that not all of them will be displayed at once: Some will always be fading out of the visual medium as others are being refreshed. Because only a few parts can be held in an image at once, we would expect that people frequently should have to generate a part of an image anew in order to see that part sharply when they "inspect" the image.

For example, picture a lion. Is the tuft on its tail larger than its front paws? As soon as you focus your mind's eye on the two parts in question, they both show up clearly, though they may not have been vivid enough to compare when you first pictured the animal. Compare this to what happens when you decide whether the front or back of a lion is higher off the ground when it walks. Now the general "skeletal" shape is all you need to make the judgment, and you do not need to add in more details. The skeletal image is always present if you have an image, whereas the parts usually must be added if they need to be seen in detail.

As it turns out, images of more strongly associated parts are formed more quickly than images of less associated parts (e.g., people can evoke the image of a lion's mane more quickly than that of a lion's back). This finding was predicted by the theory because we claim that the HASA entries are ordered in terms of association strength, and a HASA entry is looked up when one begins to generate an image of a part (see Table 8.1 for an example with an image of a car with tires on the front and rear). Thus we are led to the following prediction: If images of many parts must be generated only when one is asked about them, then more strongly associated parts should tend to take less time to *see* when a person inspects an object in an image.

When we first discovered this prediction, we took it as an embarrassment. At first glance, the idea that people take longer to "see" less highly associated parts in an image seems to conflict with some previous findings about image inspection described in Chapter 4. You will recall that in trying to rule out a propositional explanation for the effects of size on the time subjects took to find parts in an image, we had varied the size and the association strength of parts. For "mouse," for instance, "whiskers" is more strongly associated than "back," but "back" is larger and more clearly evident in an image. In that experiment we found that when subjects were asked to use imagery, they needed less time to see the larger features, even though those were less associated with the animal. When subjects did not use imagery, however, they verified the smaller, more strongly associated features more quickly. But this contradiction is more apparent than real: The earlier results do not mean that association strength has no effect at all when subjects inspect images; rather, they show that the effects of size were great enough to overwhelm those of association strength (if any). With this in mind, we designed a new experiment that would allow us to judge the influence of association strength independently of the effects of size. We made up a list of four kinds of features, balancing high and low association strengths with large and small sizes (see Table 8.2). Subjects were asked to image an animal and examine it to decide whether a named feature of the animal was true or false: for example, "alligator—belly." True and false features were each presented on half the trials, randomly mixed.

Table 8.2. Trace of the simulation inspecting an impoverished image of a car, which requires filling in a region.

---

*LOOKFOR REARTIRE

LOOKFOR BEGINS
REGENERATE BEGINS
REGENERATING IMAGE
REGENERATE ENDS

LOOKING FOR PROPOSITIONAL FILE FOR REARTIRE
REARTIRE.PRP OPENED

CHECKING PROPOSITIONAL FILE FOR DESCRIPTION OF REARTIRE
DESCRIPTION FOUND

CHECKING PROPOSITIONAL FILE FOR SIZE TAG
SIZE TAG FOUND: MEDIUM   OPTIMAL RESOLUTION = 85.0

RESOLUTION BEGINS
CHECKING CURRENT RESOLUTION OF IMAGE
CURRENT RESOLUTION= 89.4
***RESOLUTION ENDS**

IMAGE AT CORRECT RESOLUTION—NO NEED TO ZOOM OR PAN

CHECKING PROPOSITIONAL FILE FOR DIRECTION OF PART
DIRECTION FOUND: LEFT

Table 8.2. Trace of the simulation inspecting an impoverished image of a car, which requires filling in a region. (*Continued*)

FIND BEGINS
BEGIN SEARCHING SURFACE MATRIX FOR REARTIRE

SEARCHING FOR LOWEST POINT LEFT
FOUND AT   −23   −3

FOLLOWING HORIZONTAL RIGHT TO END
FOUND AT   −19   −3

SEARCHING NEXT HORIZONTAL POINT RIGHT
FOUND AT   −10   −3

LOOKING FOR PART BELOW
PROCEDURE FAILED
FIND ENDS

CAN'T FIND REARTIRE

LOOKING FOR PROPOSITIONAL FILE FOR CAR
CAR.PRP OPENED

CHECKING PROPOSITIONAL FILE FOR REGIONAL DETAILS
REGION FOUND: HASA.REARREGION

PUT BEGINS
LOOKING FOR PROPOSITIONAL FILE FOR REARREGION
REARREGION.PRP OPENED

CHECKING PROPOSITIONAL FILE FOR NAME OF IMAGE FILE
NAME OF IMAGE FILE STORED: REARREGION.IMG

CHECKING PROPOSITIONAL FILE FOR LOCATION OF
    REARREGION
LOCATION FOUND: UNDER REARWHEELBASE

LOOKING FOR PROPOSITIONAL FILE FOR REARWHEELBASE
REARWHEELBASE.PRP OPENED

CHECKING PROPOSITIONAL FILE FOR DESCRIPTION OF
    REARWHEELBASE
DESCRIPTION FOUND

LOOKING FOR PROPOSITIONAL FILE FOR UNDER
UNDER.PRP OPENED

CHECKING PROPOSITIONAL FILE FOR DESCRIPTION OF UNDER
DESCRIPTION FOUND

FIND BEGINS
BEGIN SEARCHING SURFACE MATRIX FOR REARWHEELBASE

SEARCHING FOR LOWEST POINT LEFT
FOUND AT -23 -3

FOLLOWING HORIZONTAL RIGHT TO END
FOUND AT -19 -3

SEARCHING FOR NEXT HORIZONTAL POINT RIGHT
FOUND AT -10 -3
FIND ENDS

BEGIN TO PUT ON PART: REARREGION

PICTURE BEGINS
TURNING ON POINTS IN SURFACE MATRIX WITH SIZE
   FACTOR = 1.0
PICTURE ENDS

PUT ENDS

FIND BEGINS
BEGIN SEARCHING SURFACE MATRIX FOR REARTIRE

SEARCHING FOR LOWEST POINT LEFT
FOUND AT -23 -3

FOLLOWING HORIZONTAL RIGHT TO END
FOUND AT -17 -3

SEARCHING FOR NEXT HORIZONTAL POINT RIGHT
FOUND AT -11 -3

LOOKING FOR PART BELOW
FIND ENDS

REARTIRE FOUND
LOOKFOR ENDS

The results were just as predicted. As before, subjects took longer in general to "see" smaller features; but they also took longer to see features that were not very strongly associated with the animal. In fact, the difference in the time needed to see more and less strongly associated features was exactly the same as the difference in the time other subjects needed to generate images of the same features. This result was exactly as expected if images of parts are generated at the time of query (and differences in association strength affect generation time) and then inspected (and differences in size affect inspection time). Thus we replicated our earlier finding that size affects the time needed to "see" images of parts, showed that it was not contradictory to the theory, and also verified a prediction of the theory.[4]

Transforming Images: Mechanisms versus Machinations

The findings on image transformation have been interpreted in two general ways. On the one hand, some researchers (including my co-workers and I) believe that they demonstrate something about the operation of the underlying mechanisms of imagery. On the other hand, some other investigators, such as Zenon Pylyshyn, have interpreted the findings on mental rotation, image scanning, and the like as showing that people have a good sense of how things operate in the visible world and can easily produce data that mimic what they believe they would have done had they seen the analogous real situation. In this case, propositional representations are used to compute the appropriate amount of time to wait before responding, and the data say nothing about how images actually operate. Mark Folk and I conducted several experiments that pit a prediction of our theory directly against one of our rivals'.

One such experiment was a study involving image rotation. First, the task. Subjects viewed a disk with a tick mark every sixty degrees, something like a clock with marks at every ten-minute interval (Fig. 8.2). They then were given two stimuli: a liter-sized soft drink bottle filled with lead buckshot and a thin dowel a yard long that weighed one ounce. When they handled both stimuli, almost all the subjects were shocked at how heavy the bottle was—sixteen pounds. They were then asked to image either the bottle or the dowel as if it had a pivot through the

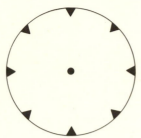

8.2. Disk with tick marks every sixty degrees. Subjects imaged objects mounted in the center and rotating around.

center and was mounted in the middle of the disk. Next, they were to image the stimulus turning, pointing at various tick marks as it revolved around the disk. The subjects were to press a button every time the bottle or stick pointed at a tick mark as they imaged it turning.

The crux of the experiment was that subjects were told to image the stimulus revolving in two different ways. They were to picture it turning as it would if they were actually rotating it physically or they were simply to "rotate the image." Now, according to Pylyshyn's theory, people interpret these two instructions in the same way: Their "imaged simulation" is really just a report of how they believe the stimulus would behave in reality. (This is supposedly why people tend to rotate images through the intermediate positions on a trajectory.) Therefore the results from both conditions should be the same: The bottle should take longer than the dowel to get going, because it is heavier, and it should take longer to slow down to a stop at the end of the spin. In contrast, if our theory is correct, we would expect the opposite results when subjects are told simply to rotate the image of the object. That is, in our view, rotation is a "region-bounded" transformation, in which one only processes the portion of the medium containing the image. Thus the larger the area processed, the more area must be processed at each step, and the more time the transformation will take. We therefore expected people to take longer to rotate the long dowel than the short bottle, even though the bottle was heavier. Furthermore, we did not expect any effects of "inertia" or the like, as Pylyshyn's theory did—after all, mental images do not really weigh anything!

We were pleased to find that our predictions worked out as hoped. As you can see in Fig. 8.3, when subjects were asked to

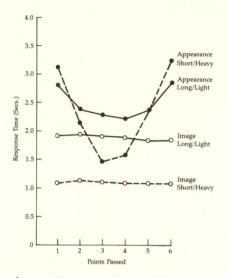

8.3. Results from the rotation experiment. "Appearance" instructions required subjects to image how the object would actually look while rotating, whereas "image" instructions required subjects to "rotate the image" itself.

imagine actually rotating the objects, the image of the dowel was rotated faster and the rotations of both stimuli displayed pronounced inertia effects (especially with the bottle). Subjects had trouble getting the objects in their images to start rotating and to stop rotating at the end. When asked simply to rotate their images—as opposed to imagining the objects actually rotating— there were no effects of inertia; the dowel took much more time to rotate; and rotation times generally were shorter than in the first condition.

This last point is an important one. It is not surprising that our knowledge of the laws of physics can influence the way we use imagery; after all, one of the values of imagery is as a simulation of possible real-world events. My colleagues and I would deny, however, that there is no more to image transformation than just applying such knowledge. If the mechanisms of imaging cause images to be "rotated" incrementally through the mental medium, then that operation is bound to take a certain amount of time. Any effects of knowledge should be added onto the effect of the imaging operation itself; so it is noteworthy that people took longer to mentally simulate a real rotation than to merely rotate an image.

There is, however, a counterexplanation for our findings. Perhaps people interpreted the different instructions differently, taking the directive "simply rotate the image" to mean they should pretend they were watching a smoothly rotating display. So we conducted a small control experiment. A second group of subjects was given the "rotate the image" instructions used in the previous experiment, but this time they were simply to estimate how much time the bottle and dowel would take to rotate past each tick mark in their images (Fig. 8.4). These estimates were almost perfectly correlated with the times of the subjects in the previous experiment who were asked to imagine the objects actually rotating: The second group of subjects guessed longer times for the bottle and their estimates showed effects of inertia. These subjects clearly did not interpret the "simply rotate the image" instructions to require "weightless" rotations or the like. Also, they clearly did not know how their imaging mechanisms actually worked; when asked to guess the results, they fell back

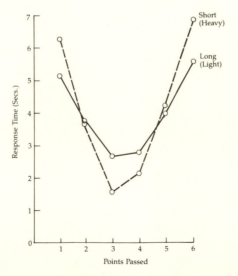

8.4. Results from control subjects guessing (incorrectly) the results from the "image" instructions in the rotation experiment.

on knowledge of the analogous physical situation and guessed wrong. These results are strong evidence against the view that imagery experiments just reveal what people think should happen and that their theories are rooted solely in a knowledge of how things work in the real world.

The results of this experiment, and others like it, are also important because they cast doubt on an evolutionary interpretation of the image transformation data. Recall that according to this theory we rotate objects along a trajectory because our imagery system evolved to mimic transformations as they occur in the real world. If so, why did instructions to do just this, to make the image mimic the analogous actual rotation, produce results so different from those obtained when people were asked just to "rotate the images"? The results lend real credibility to our theory, which predicted the results on the basis of hypothesized mental mechanisms, and they undermine the evolutionary theory—as well as Pylyshyn's nonimagery theory—which made the opposite predictions.

The Value of Predictions

The upshot of these experiments, then, is that our theory does fairly well in making some predictions that we might not otherwise expect and which would not follow from other theories. These findings therefore lend credibility to the theory, but they are not the end-all. For there is a major problem here, which you may have spotted: The theory was not concocted in the abstract, but on the basis of data that we had intentionally collected to determine how the theory should be constructed. At least some of our successful predictions were foregone conclusions, given the results we used to formulate the theory in the first place. This is not very impressive. To be worth its salt, a theory should also predict new data, unrelated to those used to formulate it initially.

The problem is that sometimes we cannot be sure whether the data being predicted are really *new* or just old findings in a new disguise. The results from the image generation study in which we varied size and complexity, for example, have a familiar ring in light of the experiments on image generation described in Chapter 6; there though, the results were from separate studies of the effects of size and of complexity on generation times. So are the results similar to the old ones or not? There does not seem to be any clear way of telling, one way or the other. Thus the theory's ability to predict data is important largely by contrast to what *might* have happened: Had the results contradicted any of our claims about structures and processes (e.g., had we found *no* difference in the times needed to form complex images at different sizes), the theory would have been in trouble.

EXTENDING THE THEORY

The most important use of the theory at this point, then, seems to be the same use we made earlier of the computer display metaphor: It provides a way of structuring the questions we ask so that, as answers accumulate, they begin to fill in our picture of the imagery system. Let us now consider how the computer model and the theory are fulfilling this role. In the rest of this chapter we will see how the model forces us to expand the theory itself, and in Chapter 9 we will see how it forces us to expand the general domain of our inquiry.

Adding the Third Dimension

Probably the most glaring shortcoming shared by the computer display metaphor that originally guided our theorizing and its computer model offspring is the treatment of images as two-dimensional displays. Our introspections suggest that images can be three-dimensional: We can scan around an imaged room or rotate an imaged object so that it may be seen from different angles. Research findings also indicate that people can manipulate images in three dimensions. The question is, How do images preserve three-dimensional information? Do they register a series of two-dimensional views, like snapshots, and simulate three-dimensionality with the help of perspective cues and other information that is inherently "flat"? Or can images actually depict spatial information in depth as well as in height and width? That is, is the medium like a fish tank in which the fish and plants actually move around or is it like a television picture of a tank, where motion and perspective effects make the display appear three-dimensional? Introspection cannot help us here.

Think about how we might construct the computer model so that it mimics whatever sort of three-dimensionality images have: We could shift around points in a two-dimensional matrix and program the FIND process to interpret depth cues in the way we do when viewing a photograph. Or we could posit a three-dimensional "spheroid" instead of a two-dimensional matrix and allow depth to be an intrinsic feature of an image. Instead of being flat, like a movie screen, the mental medium could have depth, like a box. Cells arrayed in three dimensions would be filled in to depict the spatial properties of surfaces on objects in direct, literal fashion. This does not imply a box of neurons in the brain any more than a two-dimensional medium implies an actual picture in the brain (see p. 20). The situation in the brain may be much like that in a computer when we set up a three-dimensional matrix. The cells are in three-dimensional relation to each other only because the computer retrieves information from them *as if* they were arranged in an actual box (see p. 22).

Steven Pinker, at the Massachusetts Institute of Technology, set out to study how images represent three-dimensional information. In his initial experiments, Pinker had subjects memorize the appearance of a three-dimensional scene that he had constructed by hanging toys at different places within a box (Fig. 8.5). The subjects then were to shut their eyes and image the box, focus on one toy, and scan to another. Pinker found that scan times increased in proportion to the actual three-dimensional distances between the objects, not the two-dimensional distances between objects that would have appeared in a photograph of the scene.

These results confirm that images can depict in three dimensions. But how? If you were trying to figure out how a watch works without opening it up, you would need to know more about it than just the fact that it keeps time. Hearing ticking sounds would help, especially if you listened for the subtle telltale signs of ratchets and escapements in action. So, let us examine some more data.

If the image medium functions like a sphere, a new question arises: Should the FIND procedures have access to any part of the medium—front, back, sides, top, and so on—or just what is visible from a given vantage point? If we think of the medium as something like a theater stage, it is conceivable that an image contains information about what is happening on the whole stage simultaneously; but it is also conceivable that the image holds only what can be seen from one particular vantage point—as if

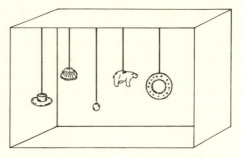

8.5. Toys hanging in a box used to test three-dimensional scanning.

the play were being broadcast on television, its three dimensionality reduced to the flat surface of the screen. In this case, viewing the scene from different angles would require a sequence of images, as when a television broadcast switches cameras.

To investigate this issue, Pinker asked a new group of subjects to memorize the scene of the toys hanging in the box. These subjects, however, were asked to image the scene as if they were looking through a rifle sight, focusing on one object, and then scanning to the next by shifting the sight. If images are processed from a particular point of view, as opposed to making information from all possible points of view available at once, the two-dimensional distances between the objects should dictate the time subjects need to scan between them. In contrast, if the medium really is three dimensional and we have direct access to information about an object's shape (as when one is feeling a statue), then the distance in three dimensions should still dictate the scanning time.

The results showed that scanning time was determined by the two-dimensional distances between the objects. What was really striking was that this remained true even when subjects first "mentally rotated" their image and "viewed" the scene from a novel point of view, one they had never actually seen. Even from an unfamiliar perspective, the time subjects took to sweep an imaginary rifle sight across the imaged box varied with the two-dimensional distances between the objects.

From these experiments we can draw two conclusions about images of three-dimensional scenes: First, images can depict information about the three-dimensional relations among objects in a scene, and second, images apparently are "viewed" from a particular vantage point. It seems, however, that we can rotate a scene in three dimensions to see how it would appear from other angles. Another set of studies carried out by Pinker and Finke showed that people can see emergent patterns as images rotate. Again subjects saw objects hanging in a tank, but this time the tank had transparent sides. The subjects were asked to image the tank rotated by a specified angle and then to draw the two-dimensional pattern formed by the four objects as seen at their new orientation. The subjects were remarkably good at recognizing the pattern as a parallelogram, even though this was not obvious when the tank was viewed from the original perspective.

Consider the two basic ways we could explain all these results. We could posit a three-dimensional medium, but with a FIND process that can only "see" its contents from one direction. If this is true, the next question is, How do people scan in three dimensions? One possibility is directly analogous to our computer model: by shifting the image of the focus object until it is centered in the medium. However, it does not feel this way. When you scan an image in three dimensions, it feels different from zooming in on the object—it is more like imaging a speck flying between the two objects. And, perhaps this is what happens, except that no actual speck is involved. That is, a second possibility is that we perform such a scan by imagining a nonexistent point through the scene and tracking its movement. This process probably would require more effort than two-dimensional scanning, in that it necessitates changing relationships between points in the image field rather than simply shifting an intact image across the medium, which would explain why scan times tend to be longer in three dimensions than in two dimensions.

The other alternative is to have not a spherical medium, but a two-dimensional medium that is processed in such a way that it mimics depth. Scanning in three dimensions would then take longer because the process takes into account the actual distance between points in the scene, rather than the distance between cells in the matrix. The distance would be stored as information somehow incorporated into the image itself. Perhaps depth information is implicit in the information in the cell; that is, just as we use different letters in our computer model to indicate how "bright" a point is, the mind could implicitly store the relative depth of each point along with the point itself. But this hypothesis has a serious difficulty: How would previously invisible parts of an object become visible as it is rotated in three dimensions? With a tanklike medium, this difficulty does not arise: The information is in the tank, just invisible. With a two-dimensional medium, information not shown on the visible surface would have to be stored in long-term memory, and new parts of the image generated as old parts are rotated out of sight. That is, more information must be encoded in memory than the image ever could depict at one time.

Steven Shwartz decided to test these two broad classes of models by examining the rates of rotation when imaged objects are turned in two and in three dimensions. If the tank model is correct and the mental medium has depth as well as height and width, Shwartz reasoned, then a given amount of rotation should take the same amount of time in either two or three dimensions. That is, whether an object is moved clockwise or counterclockwise (two dimensions) or back to front (three dimensions), all the information needed for the transformation is available in the image. But if the two-dimensional screen model is correct, then rotation should be slower in three dimensions than in two: Only in three-dimensional rotation would new information need to be filled in, which should require additional time. The results were clear-cut: There was a sizable difference in the rate of rotation, with three-dimensional transformations taking much longer than the equivalent two-dimensional rotations.

The evidence so far, then, is in favor of the model that to my mind seemed least obvious, a two-dimensional medium that can be processed so that three-dimensional images seem to occur. Once I heard about the evidence, however, my introspections started coming into line (this often happens!). One example is this simple exercise: Imagine a cube, seen so that one corner is directly in front of you; you cannot see the top or bottom, just the edge and two receding sides. Now rotate the cube so that you can see the front of the cube, the top, and one side. Look at Fig. 8.6. Is this what the cube in your image looks like? It is what mine looked like. But it is optically wrong. On the following page you will see what it should look like (Fig. 8.7). When a real cube is rotated this way, the front face and the side both are foreshortened. The cube in my image, in contrast—and those of most of the people I have asked—showed the front as a square and only

8.6. The cube as it appeared in the author's image.

the side foreshortened. This cannot be: If we can see the front and a side at the same time, the front (like the side) must be a trapezoid. But in our culture, we typically represent a cube with one face as a square; and so too in images. If one rotates an imaged cube by moving points around in a two-dimensional medium, it makes sense that cultural conventions on representing depth on a flat surface would be taken into account by the processes that shift the points. But if the cube were imaged in a three-dimensional medium, and merely rotated intact until a new part was visible, conventions would be unlikely to have any effect.

Our findings about the three-dimensional aspects of imaging show that the theory is fulfilling its role of leading us to ask new questions about how images are processed, questions that lead to productive research. The fact that our theory does fulfill its function of generating new questions is not, of course, sufficient grounds for concluding that it is correct, only that it is not useless. To the extent that we find coherent answers to the questions, the theory gains credibility: If it were wildly wrong, it could lead us to ask nonsensical questions that could not be answered because the guiding presuppositions are simply off base.

So far, we have delved into only one small section of the large territory still waiting to be explored, a mere peninsula on the continental mindscape. But even a continent can be explored systematically if one has a map, and our theory provides such a map of the terrain of mental imagery. In the following chapters we will use our theory to guide our explorations of other aspects of mental activity. In addition to uncovering further facts about the mind, we will derive some practical applications of these facts— for the mere ability to develop a technology from a theory is further support for the theory.

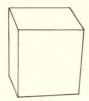

8.7. The cube as it should appear if the representation were optically correct.

9

Remembering Appearances

THE MIND APPARENTLY uses at least two kinds of representations, images and propositions. One additional question a theory of mental events must answer, then, is when various kinds of representations are used in mental activity. In this chapter we will consider a basic question: When are images and propositions used in remembering?

The value of experiments that study a single narrow, constrained task, such as rotating imaged objects, lies in what they tell us about larger issues. Because such experiments are highly specific, they enable us to reduce complex questions about how the mind works to a manageable level; that is, we can select a few variables we want to study, manipulate them, and evaluate the resulting data. The trouble, of course, is that there are so *many* narrow, constrained tasks we could study. How do you decide which are worth considering? In this book I have been arguing and demonstrating that thinking about how to program a computer to mimic a person is a good guide to asking questions. Thus in this chapter we will let the computer model structure the way we ask questions about remembering, and will collect data that will guide us in further developing our model.

DEPICTIONS AND PROPOSITIONS AGAIN

The experiments in which people decided whether features belong to objects showed that we can and often do remember things in more than one way. The same fact, such as the shape of a dog's ears, can be stored in a format that resembles either words or a picture. The fact is *about* visual information, but it need not be stored in a *format* that resembles the format of pictures. The depictive format carries information in the same way a picture does; for instance, it inherently specifies spatial relationships and is limited by the properties of the medium in which the information is presented. Although not literally pictorial, images in the mind—like pictures on the page—depict information (see Chapters 2 and 3).

The verbal counterpart is a descriptive propositional format that conveys information much as a sentence does. Propositional representations, you will recall, have a syntactic rather than a spatial structure; that is, symbols follow each other in a sequence that is in accord with certain rules of grammar. Verbal memories (e.g., of what someone said) that are stored propositionally do not appear to be filed away word for word; instead, they seem to carry the *gist* of the information in some condensed form that functions like a sentence. If someone were to ask you what Humphrey Bogart says to Ingrid Bergman at the end of the movie *Casablanca*, you probably can answer the question if you have seen the film, though you may not be able to repeat Bogart's exact lines.

Given that memories can be stored in images or propositions, two questions immediately arise: First, why does one form of information come to mind before the other? And second, what determines whether a particular fact will be stored as an image, a proposition, or both?

We can begin to look for answers to these questions by returning briefly to the much simpler question, What shape are a German shepherd's ears? When you first confronted this question, back in Chapter 1, you probably formed an image of the dog and inspected it for the answer. If you then formulated a verbal reply—"triangular," perhaps—you may still remember what you said. But suppose you are asked the questions several more times. Before long, you no longer have to generate an image to come up with your response. Although you may *have* an image when you answer the question, you do not *need* it, and you probably do not inspect the imaged object before you reply. After recalling the fact a few times, your mode of remembering the information has changed from depictive to descriptive.

Why does the image cease to play a role after you answer the question a few times? It seems that we learn the verbal answer as we say the words or think them over and over. It makes sense that the mind would find it easier to retrieve a few words from memory than to generate an image, inspect it, and translate the visual information into a verbal reply.

Then why use an image in the first place? A good guess would be because the information is not initially stored in a propositional format. Most of us have never had any reason (until now) to encode a verbal description of a German shepherd's ears. We store an image in memory when we look at the dog, but in the absence of a need to describe it in words, we simply leave it in its depictive form. If this explanation is correct, then perhaps the only way we can recall the information at all when first asked about the dog's ears is by using imagery. The alternative would be that we store a general verbal or propositional description of dogs' ears in general and deduce from that description the answer to any specific question about a particular dog: Dogs have long floppy ears; a German shepherd is a dog; therefore a German shepherd has long floppy ears. But in fact all dogs' ears are not shaped alike, so this method would not work. Besides, it would take a lot of effort to perform such a deduction every time we wanted a piece of information. It seems reasonable to suppose, then, that we use imagery when we have not thought about a visible feature of an object in the past—but have seen it—and when deduction is too laborious.

Although introspections and intuitions are valuable in hypothesizing about when imagery is used, one might question the validity of our conclusions. We did, in fact, ask a large number of subjects to decide whether certain objects had certain features and then to tell us whether they had used imagery in deciding. The items that subjects reported having to use images to evaluate turned out to be those that we had previously determined to be not often thought about, and not easily evaluated using deductive reasoning. However, these sort of introspective reports must be taken with a grain of salt, for reasons discussed earlier in this book. Thus we set out to explore the principles of image use more rigorously.

THE RACE BETWEEN WORDS AND PICTURES

Knowing that people apparently switch from using a depictive memory to using a propositional one when they think about an object's feature repeatedly still does not give us much insight into how either form of information is looked up. Do people always start out by generating an image? Or do they search for a verbal answer first and fall back on an image only if the information is not available in words? Still another possibility is that finding the answer to a question is like a horse race: Both kinds of information are looked up simultaneously and whichever one comes to mind first is the one that is used. Introspection and logic are not much help at distinguishing among these three mechanisms, so we devised an experiment. The task we gave our subjects was to decide which of two objects was bigger.

Say you were buying a pet for a friend's child, but had only a very small cage. The choice was between a mouse and a hamster, and you wanted to buy the smaller one. Which would it be? How would you decide? Many people report that they generate images of a mouse and a hamster and compare them. But what if the cage were huge, and you wondered, "Which is larger, a mouse or an elephant?" For this one, most people find images unnecessary; they "just know" that an elephant is larger. Similarly, say you went shopping for office furniture and came back to study the amount of room you had for the desk. You would probably find yourself imaging desks that are close in size to the available room, but you would "just know" that some are too big or too small.

If the comparison of "far" things (i.e., those disparate in size), like a mouse and elephant, is made propositionally, does this mean that somewhere in the mind is stored a statement that an elephant is bigger than a mouse? If so, our mental file of such observations must be enormous! A horse is bigger than a robin; an airplane is bigger than a breadbox—The list is almost infinite and therefore not a practical possibility.

A more plausible alternative is that we classify objects in general categories. We might have associated with "mouse" the label "very small," and with "elephant," the label "very large." These categories would be specified relative to a common standard— such as the human body—and there would probably be at least seven or so different ones (e.g., medium small, average, etc.). As was mentioned when we discussed our theory in Chapter 7, a common standard is needed because different categories are of different average sizes. Dogs, for example, are generally smaller than buildings; thus a large dog is still smaller than a small building. People do not err in deciding which is larger, a garage or a

Saint Bernard. Thus we must have the sizes indicated either directly relative to a common standard or directly relative to the category, but with the category then related to a common standard. In the latter case, we could store a Saint Bernard as a large dog but know that dogs are generally somewhat small things relative to us, whereas buildings are large things relative to us. In either case, when we look up "mouse" and "elephant," we can make a speedy comparison of their sizes by seeing which one is associated with a label that indicates a larger size relative to a common standard.

But do we search for "mouse" and "elephant" in our propositional files to begin with, and turn to images only if the data we seek are not encoded there? Or do we start with images and switch over? Or do we look up both formats at once and use whichever is more accessible? As was the case with the German shepherd question, the retrieval process happens so fast that we are not conscious of it—the answer seems automatic, as if it involved no effort at all. Clearly, experimentation is necessary to discover how the mind looks up information.

We began by describing three possible models for looking up information in terms of alternative ways of adding to our imagery computer program; that is, we assumed that information is stored as posited by the theory, and we thought about different ways of retrieving it. We identified each distinct step that would occur in a given type of retrieval process and arranged the steps in the sequence the program would have to follow to come up with the correct answer. Doing this clarified the differences in three processes; it also allowed us to generate precise predictions for each method of retrieving the information. As we consider each model below, we must see whether it can explain a central fact about comparing objects from memory: Objects that differ greatly in size (such as a mouse and an elephant) are compared much more quickly than objects of similar size (such as a mouse and a hamster), and objects with intermediate size discrepancies (such as between a mouse and a rabbit) are evaluated in an intermediate amount of time.

The first model hypothesizes that the mind begins by trying a propositional format when comparing the sizes of two objects from memory. (First, of course, the person must comprehend the task—that is, realize that he or she is to compare the sizes of two

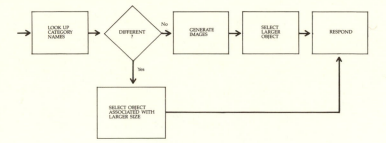

9.1. Flow chart for the propositions-then-imagery model.

named objects from memory.) Information about each object, stored in propositional form, is looked up and the size categories associated with the objects are found: For a mouse and an elephant, these would be something like "very small" and "very large." Next, these descriptions are compared. If they are different, as they are in this case, the object classified as larger is selected. If the two categories are the same, however—as they would be for objects very close in size, such as mouse and hamster—the categories cannot be used to make the decision. Thus images of the two objects side by side are generated and examined, and a decision about relative size is reached. This model explains the fact that subtle size distinctions take longer to make by positing that these judgments require more processing. That is, the closer in size two objects are, the more likely it is that the size categories are the same and imagery will have to be used— and this takes more time than when you can get away with only checking the categories themselves (Fig. 9.1).

The second model hypothesizes that the mind begins the comparison by looking up images. In this case, the appropriate images are generated and inspected very cursorily. If the size disparity between the two objects is substantial, the larger object can be distinguished almost immediately; if the difference in size is slight, there is a shift to using some sort of propositional representation that provides more detailed information (for instance, the size of each object in inches). This model, like the first one, explains the fact that small size distinctions take longer to evaluate by positing that these comparisons require more processing (Fig. 9.2).

The third model hypothesizes that the mind makes size com-

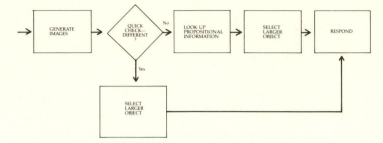

9.2. Flow chart for the imagery-then-propositions model.

parisons by looking up images and descriptions simultaneously. As soon as the task is comprehended, propositional information is retrieved at the same time images of the objects are generated. If both objects carry the same propositional size classification (such as "very small") or if imagery simply provides a faster answer, then the mind will end up using images. If, on the other hand, the propositional information is looked up faster and is sufficient to answer the question, this information will be used and the images ignored. Provided that the person has an image in storage, this model posits that imagery will be used in answering questions about features of an object in three circumstances: when a person has not thought about a property or been told about it, and thus has not stored a verbal description; when the distinction is relatively subtle and not captured in stored descriptions; and when it is more work to look up or deduce a description than

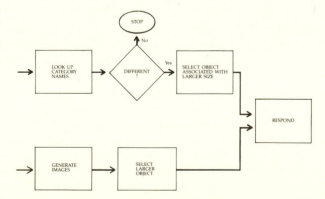

9.3. Flow chart for the imagery–propositions "race" model.

to rely on an image. In the last case, the description is in the process of being looked up when the sought information is found by using imagery (Fig. 9.3).

Testing the Models

We performed a number of experiments to try to identify the model that reflects the process people actually use to look up information. I will discuss only one of them here.[1] The technique was simple: We asked people to compare pairs of objects that we had previously selected to be very similar in size. We began by classifying objects according to size on the basis of ratings collected from 101 people; we then divided the objects into two groups, those above and those below the median size.[2] The subjects were given lists of the objects and told that those larger than the median size (lamp, watermelon, goose, beaver, and eagle) were to be considered "large," whereas those smaller than the median (football, blender, coffeepot, rooster, and arm) were to be considered "small." Thus we taught subjects the size descriptions they were to use in the comparison task to follow. They did not know there was going to be a comparison task, though, so they were not memorizing comparisons between objects on the spot.

The trick of the experiment was that we varied the amount of practice subjects had in learning the size associations. One group of subjects studied the items and categories until they could tell us the correct size category for each item twice in a row; the other group memorized the associations until they could categorize the objects correctly twelve times in a row. Our purpose in doing this was to increase the speed at which the second group could look up the objects' propositionally stored categories. We had previously established that the more practice subjects had, the faster they could later categorize the figures. The implications of this speeding-up process are quite different for the different models, as will become clear shortly.

After subjects had memorized the category descriptions, we asked them to compare the sizes of various pairs of objects. Half the pairs consisted of two objects in the same category (such as goose–beaver) and half were objects from different categories (such as watermelon–blender). Subjects were told to assume that the objects were of average size and to judge on the basis of visible surface area. Then we measured how long it took each group to make the size comparisons.

This experiment was designed so that each model would predict very different results. If propositional descriptions are looked up first, and then images, we reasoned, our subjects should not have to resort to imagery at all when the objects fall in different categories. The answer would be easily available in verbal form—"watermelon" is large, "blender" is small. The two groups of subjects should differ in overall speed, because those who had learned the descriptions more thoroughly would be able to look them up faster. Objects in the same category would take all subjects longer to compare than objects in different categories, because after the descriptions were looked up and found to be the same, processing would have to shift over to imagery. At that point, the more similar the objects were in size, the longer it would take subjects to compare them—the smaller the discrepancy, the harder it is to distinguish in an image (presumably because more precise—and hence time-consuming—FIND tests are required; cf. p. 136). In contrast, because size labels would be used by both groups when the objects are in different categories, we expect no effects of size discrepancy on these trials.

If images are looked up first and then descriptions, our expectations would be quite different. The subjects' amount of practice at learning the categories should have little or no effect on their response times, because according to this model, propositional size categories are not used to compare objects. If propositional information is used at all, it is detailed information about the size, and not about general categories. Presumably subjects would start by generating images of the objects and quickly comparing them. None of the pairs contained objects that were drastically different in size, so in many or all cases, processing would have to switch to propositional information. If the learned categories were made use of at all, it would only be to discriminate between objects in different categories. With objects in the same category, detailed information about each object's size (for instance, "a blender is about a foot and a half high and four inches in diameter") would have to be looked up and used to make the comparison. Perhaps most importantly, there should not be any effects of size disparity on response times. If the comparison is made by looking up detailed propositional information, it will not matter if an object one foot high is compared to one that is a foot three inches high or one two feet high; the numbers are not the same and one has only to find out which number indicates the larger size.

Finally, if the mind looks up images and descriptions at the same time, then the subjects' amount of practice at memorizing the objects' size categories should be critical. As was mentioned earlier, practice was shown to affect the speed with which the propositional descriptions could be looked up. A lot of practice thus should give propositional information an edge in the race between imagery and descriptions; with objects from different categories, the comparison should be able to be made very quickly on the basis of the learned labels. Subjects who did not receive a lot of practice, on the other hand, should not retrieve the propositional information very fast. Thus, even when objects are in different categories, there may be effects of size disparity, as would be expected if imagery were used. With objects from the same category, practice should not matter: Subjects might still retrieve the verbal descriptions quickly, but these categories would be useless; images would take over before propositional information could be used. The degree of size difference would affect the speed of the comparison, because the smaller the discrepancy, the harder it is to evaluate in an image.

If the third model is correct, then, response times should be fastest when subjects with a lot of practice at learning the size categories compare objects from different categories. And size disparity should not affect times in this case. This prediction is the same as for the first model. Unlike the first model, however, subjects who have learned the size labels less well should end up using images rather than propositional information to make the comparison. Therefore these subjects' response times should reflect the degree of size difference between the objects, because subjects are comparing the items themselves (in image form) rather than the artificial verbal labels we had them attach to the items. This should be true when objects are in the same category and when they are in different categories, because it is the visible size difference, not the category, that is being compared.

The results of the experiment were clear-cut: The mind retrieves and uses images and propositions at the same time. Size discrepancy had no effect for subjects who had thoroughly memorized

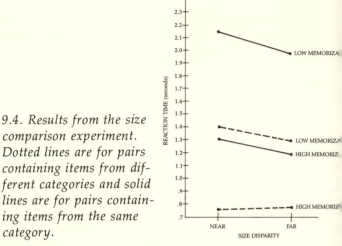

9.4. Results from the size comparison experiment. Dotted lines are for pairs containing items from different categories and solid lines are for pairs containing items from the same category.

the categories and compared objects in different categories, but in all other cases, the response times varied with the difference in size (Fig. 9.4).

But what evidence do we have that imagery per se was used in this task? I neglected to mention one other feature of the experiment. Subjects heard the names of the objects to be compared one at a time. Upon hearing the name of the first object they were asked to form an image of it, either at a very small size or at a normal size. They were to hold onto this image until the second object was named, at which point they were to decide which object was larger as quickly as possible. These people were told that they did not have to use the image, but would only have to hold onto it until the second word. As it turned out, when size descriptions were not well learned or when objects were in the same category, more time was taken when the initial image was small than when it was normal size. Subjects later reported that they had to "zoom in" on the object imaged at the small size prior to imaging the other object and comparing the two, whereas no such process was necessary with the normal-sized image. Evidentally, the objects must be at the same apparent "distance" before actual sizes can be compared.[3] Interestingly enough, there was no effect of the size of the initial image when subjects compared objects in different categories and the categories were strongly associated. This is just as one would expect if images were not used in making the comparison in this case, but were used in all the other cases. All things considered, then, the data strongly supported the view that images and descriptions are looked up at the same time and processed simultaneously.

ANSWERIF

We used the results of our experiments to program a new process in our general model, called the ANSWERIF process. To answer a question like, What shape is a rabbit's nose?, people commonly generate an image of the object and inspect the named part. If the question were simply, Does a rabbit have a nose?, most people probably would not bother with an image. The research findings indicate that we tend to search our propositional and depictive files simultaneously and use whichever format comes up first with the answer. When the computer model is given a command asking about a property of an object ("Answer if a rabbit has a nose"), the ANSWERIF process searches the object's propositional file for the appropriate entry (HASA.NOSE). Because highly associated features are near the top of the list, the program (like a person) can answer yes faster than for less associated features. If the ANSWERIF process searches the whole list and fails to find the feature, it tries another tactic. It looks up the object's superordinate category (such as "animal") and examines this propositional list. If it finds the feature there, it concludes that the object also has it.

At the same time—at least in theory—the ANSWERIF process also has called the IMAGE process to generate an image of the object, and the LOOKFOR process to search the image for the feature. Ideally, the two searches would be carried out simultaneously, but the computer (unlike the brain) can only carry out steps in sequence. The sequential nature of the model, then, is not "theory relevant" in this case. We have put the propositional path first because we know it is usually faster. The two do not depend on each other, though, so each one can be observed as if both were going on at the same time.

PUTTING IMAGERY TO WORK

Without question, imagery can be used to improve one's memory. A pioneer in using images for recall was the fifth century Greek poet Simonides. Simonides, the story goes, was performing his role as bard and orator at a banquet when he was called outside to receive a message. At just that moment the ceiling in the dining hall collapsed, mangling all the dinner guests beyond recognition. Nobody could tell, from an examination of the carnage, just who had been attending the dinner. This was a source of concern to potentially grieving wives and tax collectors. When asked who the hapless victims were, Simonides discovered that he could mentally picture the table and image walking around it, seeing all those seated with his mind's eye. Simonides reportedly found it quite easy to name everyone at the banquet by using this technique, and this observation led to the use of imagery as a general way of improving one's memory.

The product of Simonides' and his methodological descendants' efforts is usually called the *method of loci* (*loci* is Latin for *places*). The method of loci involves first selecting a series of familiar places—rooms in a house, say—among which one can imagine walking in sequence. To memorize a list, one mentally walks from place to place and leaves the image of one item on the list in each successive location (Fig. 9.5). To recall the list later, one again walks through the loci and "sees" what is in each spot. So, for example, if you wanted to remember a grocery list, you might image a loaf of bread next to the front door of your house, a carton of milk by the telephone, a head of lettuce in the bedroom, a dozen eggs in the bathroom, and so on. Once you get to the grocery store, you image strolling through the house and looking in each room for the item you imaged there. This technique is very effective, as you can discover if you take a few minutes to memorize some locations and try it out.

You may have found it odd that a technique invented by a Greek should have a Latin name. The reason for this is that the Roman orators developed Simonides' insight into an art. Cicero is usually credited with devising a way of teaching orators to remember long speeches, a technique that modern speakers also often find useful. The trick is to rehearse the speech by imaging the room in which it will be delivered. For each part of the speech, you pick out some part of the room, moving from location to location in an orderly way. At each successive location you mentally image an object or objects that will remind you of the next section of the speech. Then when you actually give the speech,

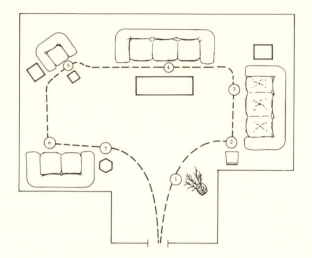

9.5. Selecting locations in a living room for the method of loci.

you can look from location to location and let the evoked images guide you in moving from topic to topic. For example, if your speech is about developments in marketing sugar in China, you might put an image of a Chinese consumer carrying a huge sack of sugar by the hall, an image of various consumers eating and drinking sugar products by the wall, and finally an image of negotiators signing an agreement near the window.

Since 1960 or so, Allan Paivio at the University of Western Ontario and other researchers have been investigating the relationship between images and memory that underlies Simonides' insights. For example, Paivio has demonstrated that concrete words (those that name picturable objects, such as *rock*) are easier to recall than abstract words (those that name nonpicturable things, such as *truth*). Paivio's theory is that concrete words can be memorized two ways, verbally and via imagery, whereas abstract ones can be memorized only one way, verbally. Thus we have two chances to remember a concrete word, by recalling either the image or the word itself, but only one chance to remember an abstract word.

More recently, it has been found that people learn concrete words more easily than abstract ones; if subjects are forced to memorize both types of words equally thoroughly, they show no later difference in recall. This finding fits with Paivio's theory, however. What the theory provides is an explanation of *why* we learn concrete words faster: That is, we can store more representations more quickly because two formats are available. Given enough time, people can presumably store as many representations of an abstract word as a concrete one, by storing the word itself over and over.[4]

Aspects of a stimulus also can affect how easy it is to remember. As was discussed in Chapter 4, objects in very small images are harder to recall than objects in normal-sized ones because the grain of the medium obscures their visible details. In addition, people remember pictures more easily than concrete words, and actual objects more easily than pictures. For instance, if someone asks you to recall some items he or she previously named, you are likely to have a harder time recalling them than if the person had shown you pictures of the objects or, better yet, had shown you the actual things. The difference could be due to the amount of information in the image: One can presumably glean more visual information from a three-dimensional object than from a two-dimensional representation of it.

Simonides took advantage of his discovery that images can aid recall to teach others how to use his techniques intentionally. Following up on this idea some 2,000 years later, Gordon Bower and his colleages at Stanford University used verbal instructions to study the way imagery actually helps memory. In a typical experiment, Bower asked people to memorize pairs of concrete words using one of three methods: simply repeating the association over and over (e.g., *dog–bike*), constructing separate images of the two named objects (e.g., a *dog* next to a *bike*), or constructing images of the two objects interacting in some way (e.g., a *dog* riding a *bike*). Interestingly, although subjects who used imagery in any way could remember the words better than those who used rote repetition, constructing an image of the objects interacting was by far the most effective memory strategy. One reason for this was discovered when another group of subjects was asked to make up sentences relating the objects in each pair. These people did almost, but not quite, as well as those asked to image the objects interacting. In other words, the sheer effort of thinking up an association between the two words seems to have fixed them more firmly in memory, presumably by adding them to the mental files in an additional form. This finding may have been affected by some subjects' using imagery to help construct their sentences; but from other data from similar experiments, it appears that redundancy alone—verbal as well as visual—has a strong effect on how well people remember things. The more ways an item is stored in memory, the easier it generally is to remember.

EXTENDING THE THEORY: WHEN ARE IMAGES USED IN REMEMBERING?

Research on mental imagery indicates that images are used to remember facts about objects or events in four situations: First, we use imagery if we have no appropriate description stored and cannot deduce the information from other stored descriptions. This situation often arises when we are recalling something we saw in passing, which did not seem important enough then to mentally describe in words. If I ask you how many windows there are in your kitchen, you have no choice but to use imagery (unless you have been asked the question before or have been told the answer and memorized it). Second, people use imagery if an appropriate description has been stored but is too difficult to remember. This is what happened in the size comparison experiment described earlier. Third, we use imagery if a description has been stored that would allow us to deduce the information, but the deduction is too cumbersome to make. This is often the case when one is recalling spatial relationships. For example, if I ask you which part of your car protrudes farthest to the front, you may well image it—even though you could have deduced that it would be the front bumper.

In all three of these situations, we use imagery because propositions are either absent or too difficult to dredge up. But we know that images are formed at the same time that propositions are recalled. So the fourth case where people use imagery to recall information is when images "win the race" because they are recalled faster than propositional information. This happens when one has had a lot of practice generating an image and has carefully memorized it, as can occur if one uses the method of loci.

These four points explain why we use imagery for tasks like remembering the overall spatial relations among pieces of furniture in a familiar room. You probably have never thought about each individual spatial relation between pairs of objects in your living room (the chair and the lamp, the chair and the sofa, the lamp and the sofa, and so on), and it would be difficult to deduce these relationships from your memories of where each object is. Imagery is more efficient. In addition, usually you want to remember something like the layout of a room because you want to think about these spatial relations (Where could I fit this new floor lamp?), which typically involves considering the overall effects of changing the configuration. Imagery is especially useful when we want to *reason* about spatial relations, simply because it portrays them all at once. In fact, this is a special type of visual thinking, which leads us to our next topic.

Visual Thinking

So FAR, our investigation of imaging has focused mainly on the properties of the representations and processes used in imagery. Probing properties in this way, though, is a bit like taking apart a car engine. As helpful as it is to understand the spark plugs, distributor, and so on, there comes a point where you want to know how the parts act together when the whole thing is running. Given that images occur in a spatial medium having a grain, size, and shape; are actively generated from their component sections; can be rotated and otherwise transformed; and so on, where does this get us? We are still faced with the fundamental issue debated by philosophers for more than 2,000 years: How and when are images actually used in human thinking and memory? We are in a much better position today to approach such questions than were the ancients, given what we now know about the way images are represented and processed. Although we cannot hope to answer this question completely at this tender stage in the history of cognitive science, we can demonstrate enough progress to justify optimism about the eventual outcome.

IMAGERY AND PROBLEM SOLVING

The spatial properties of imagery make it a natural way of approaching any spatial problem. If you want to get from one place to another, imagery is a useful way of thinking about possible routes. If you want to rearrange the furniture in a room, imagery allows you to try out a new decor before you go through the trouble of moving everything.

One of my favorite examples of this kind of practical use of visual images is a case where a friend called me in despair about his refrigerator. His freezer had turned into a solid block of ice and he had no idea how to defrost it. He had always simply moved when this happened before, but now the housing market was too tight for this kind of escape. He imaged what would happen if he simply unplugged the refrigerator: Melting ice would drip everywhere! So he imaged various pans placed at various locations in the refrigerator, and "looked" at them in his image to see if they would catch the water. He mentally moved the pans around, substituted new ones with different dimensions, and even mentally placed towels in a few spots just in case. But he still wanted advice before risking flooding his floor. He need not have worried; his imagery simulated very well what would have actually happened, and he could have gone ahead, placed his pans, and turned the refrigerator off.

In situations like this, imaging is valuable as a way of envisioning familiar things in new combinations so as to see how they would interact. If you wanted to drive a nail but you had no hammer, you might picture pounding the nail with another heavy object—a shoe or a book—to see whether what you have on hand has properties similar to those of a hammer. Besides being informative, using a mental simulation of the situation would save you the effort (and possible damage to your shoes and books) of a real trial run. In addition, visual thinking can be extended to situations that would be impossible to observe. This makes imagery a useful tool for scientists, as a story reported by the physicist Albert Einstein demonstrates. Trying to evaluate the properties of space and time, Einstein imaged himself traveling at the speed of light, pursuing a beam of light. He realized that if he did so, he would see light as an electromagnetic field at rest, with no velocity. But he also realized that "there seems to be no such thing, whether on the basis of experience or according to Maxwell's equations." Einstein's imagery, then, was one factor that inspired his own theory of relativity.[1]

Other engineers, inventors, and scientists also have reported using imaged simulations to test ideas. A particularly striking case is that of the inventor Nikola Tesla (who, among other things, invented fluorescent lights and the AC generator). Tesla claimed that when he was working on an invention, he could image a "picture complete in every detail, every part of the machine. The pictures were more vivid than any blueprint." Even more remarkably, Tesla claimed he could test his machines by using his imagery to conduct "dry runs," mentally setting them in motion for weeks—after which he would examine the parts of the machines for evidence of wear![2]

SIMULATION OR SYMBOLIZATION

In each of these examples, imaged objects or events are being used as substitutes for real objects or events. *Simulating* a situation mentally is a way of anticipating what would happen in the analogous physical situation. This is probably the most common form of visual thinking, but it is not the only one. Imaged patterns can also be used as *symbols*, standing for objects or concepts rather than depicting them literally. For example, consider the following simple problem: John is smarter than Dan. Phil is dumber than Dan. Who is smarter, John or Phil? Many people report that they find it easiest to answer this question by imaging a line with three dots on it. Each dot stands for one of the names in the problem; the order of the dots reflects the relative intelligences of John, Dan, and Phil.

Symbolic imagery is different from the simulation variety in several ways. First of all, the image does not depict an object as it might really appear, but is a symbolic representation. The dot that stands for Dan, for instance, bears no resemblance or relationship to a person. The dot stands for Dan because you defined it that way; it could just as easily have stood for Seymour.

Second, the purpose of using the image is not to "see what would happen"; that is, the goal is not to discover the properties of the imaged objects or the consequences of acting on them. Rather, the image is a notation, a visual aid to abstract thinking. Any manipulation of the material in the image is done to change its content, not to mimic a real situation. In the Phil, Dan, and John problem, we can add a dot or rearrange the order of the dots if we need to incorporate new information into the image.

A corollary of this point is that symbolic images must be interpreted twice. According to our theory, we first use the FIND process to evaluate what is being literally depicted—this dot is to the left of that other dot on the line. Then we have to use propositional associations to remember what the dots and lines stand for, translating this information into the terms of the problem: John is smarter than Phil.

Many problems can be imaged and solved in either simulation or symbolic form. The following problem is a frequently used example of how these two types of imaging can be applied to the same situation.[3]

A monk begins to climb a path up a mountain at 8:03 on Monday morning. The path is very tortuous, twisting and turning, becoming steep and rocky at times. The monk makes it to the top at 4:30, having stopped for a fifteen-minute lunch of dried bread and water at noon sharp. The monk then spends the entire night in meditation at the mountain top. At 8:03 the next morning he begins to descend the same path he used the previous day. Invigorated by his meditation, he makes very good time on his descent and arrives at the bottom at 1:05 in the afternoon.

The question: Was there any time of day (you need not say *when*) when the monk was at exactly the same point on the path on Monday and Tuesday?

This problem is an easy one if imagery is used to solve it, and either simulation or symbolic imagery is appropriate. In simulation mode, one need only image two monks leaving at the same time on the same day from the top and the bottom, and realize that their paths must cross (Fig. 10.1). Symbolically, one can image a graph, with the monk's height on the mountain plotted against time. An ascending line, representing the trip up, must cross the descending line of the trip down, and the point where they cross indicates the time at which the two heights were identical (Fig. 10.2).

It is also possible to solve this problem partly symbolically and partly by simulation by imaging one dot moving up the mountain path and another dot moving down. Simulation and symbolic imagery are not mutually exclusive; in fact, in imaging a problem or a situation, we typically blend elements of both. Most

10.1 Simulation as a means for solving the monk problem.

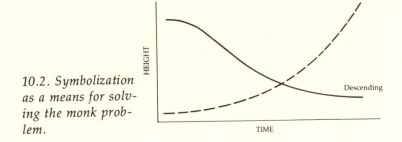

10.2. *Symbolization as a means for solving the monk problem.*

of our imaging falls somewhere on a continuum between the detailed simulation my friend used to defrost his refrigerator and the purely symbolic notation we might use for, "Who is smarter, John or Phil?"

Having stepped back and taken a look at varieties of visual thinking, how does this guide our research? What questions arise that must be further examined?

TESTING THE THEORY

So far we have been describing how imagery *could* work to help people solve problems, but we have not offered any real evidence that imagery *is* used in these ways. Thus it is worthwhile to test one prediction from our theory about when people use imagery to solve problems. Recall that in Chapter 9 we were led to fill in another component of our theory, specifying that people look for some types of information in images and in propositional memory at the same time. Whichever format provides the answer first is the one that is used. If this is true, then anything that speeds up a person's propositional fact retrieval should lessen the chances that he or she will have to rely on imagery. Suppose, for instance, that someone is given the sort of three-term series problem described above: George is smarter than Tom, and Jeff is dumber than Tom. Who is smarter, George or Jeff? Do people really have a tendency to solve this problem by imaging a line with three dots on it, each dot standing for one of the people?

Phil James and I reasoned that we could overcome people's tendency to use imagery on a problem like this if we had them learn the information so well in propositional form that they would not need an image. To test this prediction, we had subjects memorize the names of five people and associate a different intelligence category ("very smart," "very dumb," "average smart," and so on) with each one. We used categories in another dimension as well—beauty—so that subjects would have too much on their hands to try to memorize every possible comparison, given that someone's level of intelligence had nothing to do with his beauty. Two groups of subjects were tested, which differed only in how thoroughly the subjects had memorized the associations between the people and the categories. The subjects in one group had learned the associations to the point where, given a name, they could instantly snap back with that person's status in either dimension. The subjects in the other group had memorized the associations until they could repeat them back without error, but not so that they could respond to questions as quickly as the first group.

Next we confronted the subjects with a standard problem, such as, Is Herman more handsome than Stanley? Before the question, however, the subjects were asked to image a line with dots on it. On half the trials, the dots were to be centered in front of the subject's imaginary point of view, and hence presumably centered in the medium. On the other half, the dots were to be imaged way to the right, "in the corner of your mind's eye." We reasoned that if the subjects actually used the image in deciding who was smarter or more handsome, they should take longer when the images of the dots were in the less resolved periphery of the medium.

Sure enough, the group that learned the associations only moderately well needed more time to answer if the dots were imaged to one side. These people knew the correct associations—they did not make many errors—but they could not retrieve the propositional information fast enough to outrace the image. In contrast, the group that learned the associations thoroughly took the same length of time no matter which way the image was formed. They were able to recall the categories associated with the names so fast that they could compare them and make a decision before they finished inspecting the image.

The results, then, show that imagery is likely to be useful in solving problems like this, except in circumstances where the problem can be solved more quickly by using propositions.

Components of Visual Thinking

Whichever type of imagery we use, two steps in the imaging process are always used. First we must *generate* an image (using the PUT, PICTURE, and FIND processes) and at some point or points we must *"inspect"* it (using the LOOKFOR process and all the processes it depends on). Without both of these steps, either we have no image or we cannot use it, which amounts to the same thing. The type of image we generate and the way we interpret it depend on what we intend to use it for. If the problem is one that calls for symbolic imagery, the material in the image can be quite sketchy and schematic, but interpreting it may require considerable concentration. For example, suppose you are trying to tell someone how to get from one side of a city to the other. An image of a map consisting of only lines may be sufficient, but you have to remember what each of the lines means. The alternative, imaging what the city actually looks like, would save you effort in remembering the meaning of the imaged patterns, but would tax your ability to generate images to the extreme. Thus there sometimes is a "trade-off" between image generation and interpretation, with the effort saved in forming an image being repaid by increased effort in inspecting and interpreting it.

Another possible step in imaging is *manipulating* the image. This is a common part of the simulation form of imagery, as when we rearrange the furniture in a room. In Chapter 6 we considered some ways in which images can be manipulated and some of the means by which such transformations are accomplished.

Holding on to the Flickering Image

In addition to generating, inspecting, and transforming images, there is a fourth set of processes we have not yet considered that affects how well people can use imagery to solve problems. The problem of "reading" an imaged map, for example, involves *maintaining* the image. You cannot simply generate a mental image of a map and then inspect it at your leisure; you have to work at keeping each line from fading. The amount of information we can hold in an image at once is an important bottleneck on our ability to use images.

Say you wanted to design a new kind of ball for a game of outer-space soccer. Rather than kicking balls, the players would shoot at them to move them around. Thus the balls must be very tough, preferably made of steel plates. The plates are too thick to bend, so you want to cut out shapes and piece them together into a multifaceted sphere. If you cut the plates in the shape of hexagons, could you fit them together—with each side flush against the side of another hexagon—and then keep the hexagons rigid in a sphere? Try to image doing this. You need to generate a set of images of hexagons—using stored information in long-term memory to form patterns in the image medium—and then you need to shift these patterns together, perhaps using the PUT process to add new patterns from memory. And all the while you must use the REGENERATE process (discussed in Chapter 7) to maintain the image while you work with it.

Now compare the ease of fitting together imaged hexagons to that of constructing a ball from identical right triangles. Can you fit them together in a sphere? It is much harder to see that the hexagons cannot be folded into a sphere (if they are rigid, they fit into a plane, as is evident on many old tile floors) than to see this for the triangles. The REGENERATE process posited by our theory just cannot hold onto more than a few hexagons at once. With the triangles, however, you can first fit pairs of them together (one upside down, with their hypotenuses against each other) into rectangles. Then it is easy to see that rectangles fitted together are rigid and cannot be folded into a sphere. The reason the hexagon problem is so hard, then, is that we simply cannot simultaneously maintain accurate images of a sufficient number of hexagons to do the task. This limitation is a major constraint on the usefulness of imagery in visual thinking.

How sensitive is mental imagery to the sort of overloading evident in the hexagon problem? Unfortunately, most of us are very bad at holding much information in an image at once. This showed up dramatically in an experiment where subjects were asked to image a series of one-inch lines pointing in specified directions. For example, a subject might hear, "South, west, southwest, east, northeast, northeast." Each line was to be visualized, then connected with the previous one, so that subjects wound up imaging an erratic path two to ten line segments long. The directions were presented in random order and subjects heard the words *end point* at the end of the list. At that point they decided as quickly as possible whether the end of the path was above or below the starting point; this task forced them to image

FIVE SEGMENTS   EIGHT SEGMENTS

10.3. Connecting short segments to form a path in an image. The ease of holding the segments depends partly on how they can be organized.

the path and not simply rehearse the directions. Immediately after answering the question, the subjects drew the path (all had practice in drawing paths before the experiment). These people were a good cross section of society, not the usual college sophomores tested in psychology experiments. Although some of them were very good at the task, most of them were terrible, holding precise paths only when these consisted of at most a couple of segments.

One of the most interesting findings from this experiment was that people's scores did not always deteriorate when more segments were included in the image. Sometimes subjects remembered paths with more segments better than paths with fewer segments. For example, if a path happened to have two lines going in the same direction or forming a regular pattern, that path was remembered more easily than another one of the same length. (Fig. 10.3). Apparently, people were reorganizing the paths into fewer units, treating two lines in a row as one long line, organizing a regular pattern of several lines into one line that undulated, and so forth; and the fewer units in an image, the easier it was to hold.

The observations about image memory limitations also help explain some results from an experiment discussed in Chapter 6. In this experiment people were asked to image the same geometric figure as either a few overlapping shapes or a large number of adjacent ones. After showing that perceiving such a figure in terms of a few large units made it quicker to image (as was discussed before), we went on to show that the image also was easier to maintain once it was formed. The method used here was to ask subjects to image the figure and then push a button

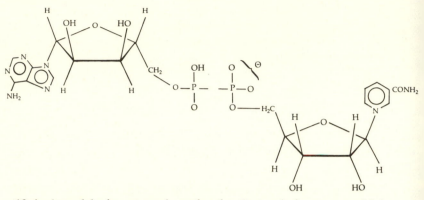

10.4. *A model of an organic molecule. O stands for oxygen, N for nitrogen, C for carbon, and H for hydrogen.*

as soon as they could "see" a certain subunit within it—say, a square. Even though you might expect a square to be easier to see in a figure described as containing four squares than in one containing just one square, the opposite was true. Subjects identified parts on the "simpler" figures faster than on the ones described as having more parts.

A practical implication of these findings is that the best way to hold as much information as possible in an image is to organize the whole image into a few units. Students learning organic chemistry often use this trick to learn the structures of large molecules (Fig. 10.4). A molecule is easier to remember if you memorize it in sections than if you try to recall the contents of the whole molecule at once. Furthermore, the evidence indicates that almost anyone can improve his or her ability to maintain images. With the path experiment, we found that subjects improved significantly the second time they tried it, even though they had had only ten minutes of practice. Most aspects of imaging seem to be innate capacities that only require use to develop; and unlike language, even adults are usually able to develop these capacities fairly readily.

Using the Components in Concert: Some Examples

Thus up to four kinds of imagery processes can be used to help solve a problem, and at least two of them—those involved in image generation and inspection—*must* be used. Not all visual problems involve transforming the image: The cross-city route question, for instance, requires no manipulation once a mental map is constructed. And not all problems involve holding onto an image: Envisioning how a couch would look against a wall generally does not require maintaining the image. Often, however, we use all four operations: generating the image, inspecting it, maintaining it, and manipulating it.

How successful an image is for a given task depends partly on how easy it is to perform these four steps. Some problems require considerably more complicated imagery than others. If you are simply interested in counting the number of pieces of furniture in a room, it is not necessary to take the time to image them in detail, nor is it necessary to hold onto complex images. If you are interested in which pieces can fit against a given wall, the rough sizes of the furniture are all you need. But if you are wondering whether a certain rug goes with a couch, you need to generate and maintain color and texture as well as shape and size.

The ease of using imagery to solve a given problem, then, is determined in large part by the ease of using the appropriate image generation, inspection, maintenance, and transformation processes. Because our theory specifies a number of the properties of these processes, it should tell us which problems will be difficult to solve by using imagery and why. As one example, consider the following problem. Suppose you are standing in the doorway of a house and gazing through the open door out onto the street. Rolling along the street from the left comes a wheel. The wheel has a black rim one inch across that looks like a black stripe. And one more thing: The wheel is very big—ten miles in diameter! The question is, What will the rim look like when the wheel first becomes visible as it rolls by the door, when it rolls halfway by, and when it is rolling away? In other words, how will the stripe along the rim appear through the doorway as the wheel rolls past? (See Fig. 10.5).

Because this problem requires judging subtle spatial relations (the stripe in the doorframe), the normal tendency is to use imagery in trying to solve it. But there is a problem: The wheel is so huge relative to the door frame that, if the wheel is not to overflow, the doorframe will be so small that you cannot see anything through it. Most people therefore image a smaller wheel, see what it looks like, and then try to guess what the larger one

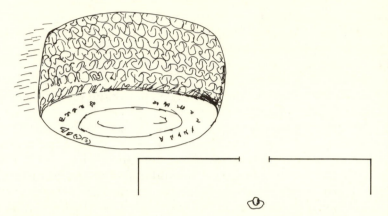

10.5. *The wheel and the door problem. What will the rim look like through the door frame? (Note: In the actual problem the wheel is ten miles in diameter.)*

would look like. Try this. If you image a smaller wheel, it will appear as an arc in the upper left of the doorframe, move down to the sill, and then rise back up to the upper right. This is accurate for a wheel of, say, twenty feet in diameter, but is incorrect for this gigantic wheel. This wheel is so large that any three- or four-foot segment of it will look like a straight line. Many people realize this, and correct the image: They see the wheel's rim as a slanted line coming down from the left corner until it is flat against the doorsill, and then a rising line becoming more slanted until it passes by the upper right corner. In fact, however, this too is incorrect: What you would see if a ten-mile wheel rolled past your door would be a flat line descending from the top of the doorframe, gradually going down to the sill, and then rising again. Such a large wheel would be touching ground very far to the left when its edge first became visible in the doorframe. The wheel would rise so gradually from its resting place that any four-foot segment seven feet off the ground (the height of the door) would appear flat.[4]

Why did imagery fail to help you to solve this problem correctly? For one thing, the constraints of the mental medium—its size and its grain—and the sensitivity of the FIND process that inspects it make it impossible to run an accurate simulation. You cannot make the wheel fit into the medium and still "see" anything through a correctly proportioned door. So we try to correct the image using propositionally stored knowledge (as was noted earlier, descriptive information can affect how we construct an image and transform it). For most of us, however, our propositional knowledge is inadequate to compensate for the errors in the image.

IMAGERY AND KNOWLEDGE

One of the most striking things about objects in images is how they mimic properties of real objects. They are not in fact objects; they are not even literally spatial. Yet they certainly act a lot like objects, passing through trajectories as they are rotated, and so on. In Chapter 8 we saw how knowledge of physical principles can affect mental rotation (although such knowledge is not *necessarily* used, as we also saw). Much of what happens when we form and manipulate an image in the course of thinking may be in part a reflection of our underlying knowledge and beliefs about what would happen if we were dealing with real objects. Consider the diagram in Fig. 10.6. If you move the piston on the left down to the line, how high will the water rise on the right side? To answer this question you have to know that water cannot be compressed and hence the volume filled will remain constant. Knowledge is clearly being used to guide imagery in this case, including rather detailed knowledge of physical relationships. But now consider the diagram in Fig. 10.7. Is the area of the inner square half the area of the outer one? In answering this question many people realize that they can mentally bend the corners of the outer square, which allows them to see that the corners will just cover the inner square. The corners in the image act as if they were corners of a sheet of paper. Even here knowledge is at

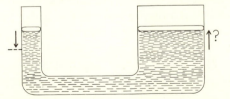

10.6. The piston problem. How high will the level on the right rise when the piston on the left is pressed down to the line?

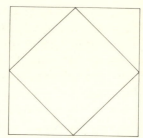

*10.7. What are the relative areas of the
two squares?*

work in constraining the image; we envision the figure behaving
as if it were drawn on or cut out of paper, not etched in stone.[5]

The interplay between properties of visual images and abstract
knowledge runs very deep in visual thinking. We are often
unaware that knowledge is influencing our images, and often are
not sure how best to use our knowledge to construct the best
image for a given purpose. We can frequently tell once we generate an imaged display what factors make it more or less effective, and we can change it or combine it with other images to
improve its usefulness, but we do not always know in advance
what display will do the trick in a given situation.

Our theory gives us some clues about what type of image is
likely to be useful in solving a given problem. To start with, consider problems that involve anticipating what would happen in
a physical situation, such as in the wheel and door problem. There
are two general rules here: The first is to picture the simplest
depiction of the situation possible (recall that we are not very
good at holding much detail in an image); therefore, do not image
a bicycle wheel (with spokes and rim) and a fancy door, but just
a circle and a rectangle. Second, picture the object or scene from
many vantage points: If you had imaged the wheel from different
distances and not just right alongside of the door, it would have
been easier to see that a tiny segment of an arc of the circle would
be a straight line. These two rules will not guarantee that you can
solve problems like this one, but they will help. One way they
will help is by reminding you of relevant pieces of knowledge,
such as what happens to arcs of circles when increasingly smaller
pieces of them are examined.[6]

With these guidelines in mind, try another problem: Suppose
a waterwheel is turning under a trickle of a waterfall and you

want to improve its efficiency. The wheel is attached to a mill and you need to use the weight of the water falling on the wheel to turn it with maximal force. All around the rim of the wheel are paddles. You can image the water splashing off the paddles; what sort of paddles will turn the wheel most forcefully? Cups are better than flat paddles: They hold the water, adding more weight on the way down. It might seem logical to have the cups pivot on axles, so that they are always upright. Doing this, however, would slow the wheel down, because the cups would remain full of water as they are hauled back up the wheel. You can see this by panning back and watching the whole waterwheel at work. The cups need to be rigidly mounted at the correct angle; this way, they will dump their contents at the bottom and not drag on the wheel as they ride back up (Fig. 10.8). Just forming the image of the wheel gives you a large part of the solution, but the leap to adding cups depends on your knowledge of physics. Seeing the water splash off the paddles provides the hint to add the cups, but the hint is only useful if you have the necessary knowledge.

It is well known that recognizing something is easier than recalling it. This is true for someone's name, for instructions on how to dig clams, and for solutions to problems. Thus much of the power of imagery comes from our ability to modify imaged objects and to see if the changes lead to anything. Folding the corners on a square can give us a clue on how to solve a geometry problem; seeing cups on the end of paddles can give us a clue on how to solve a physical problem. In many problems one must

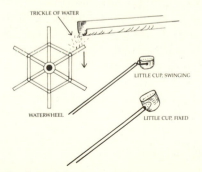

10.8. The waterwheel problem. How can you use the trickle of water more effectively?

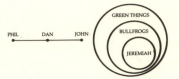

10.9. Rank-ordered concepts can be represented best by rank-ordered dots, whereas classes contained within each other can be represented best by circles within each other.

"play" with the material in an image, bending, folding, rotating, and moving parts around. As you do so, look for any relationships that provide hints on how to think about the problem. There is no substitute for the sharp eye (or mind's eye) in solving problems.

Giving advice on how to use imagery to solve simulation problems is a tenuous undertaking; but even less guidance is available for symbolic problems. As a general rule, try to make a physical model of the abstract relationship in the problem (such as a line with dots standing for people ordered in terms of intelligence). Critically, the image should be compatible with what it stands for: If you want to *rank-order* people's intelligence, a line with *rank-ordered* dots is a better tool than, say, concentric circles; but if you want to solve a syllogism, circles *within each other* are likely to work better than dots. Figure 10.9, for example, shows a symbolic image that could be used for the problem, Jeremiah is a bullfrog; all bullfrogs are green; what color is Jeremiah? In other words, the description of the display itself—as things ranked, contained, and so on—should match up with the description of the problem. It is often useful to try to image a chart or graph of the situation posed by the problem. In all cases, though, a major obstacle is often the amount of information that can be imaged at once. In general, we simply do not know much about how best to symbolize abstract knowledge, either on a page or in a mental image. The problem is to figure out "natural" rules connecting ideas with symbols, something nobody has yet done.

THINKING AHEAD

Thus, although our theory posits some properties of image representations and processes that affect problem solving (such as the grain and extent of the medium, the nature of the "race" between remembering images and propositions), it is a long way from telling us precisely how visual thinking proceeds. The theory is serving its role as a framework for asking questions, however, and as a means of framing answers. As we learn more about other aspects of mental activity, this will help us devise new ways to study thinking and eventually (we hope!) lead us to an understanding that is precise enough to guide us in further developing our computer model.

One way of studying mental activity that we have not yet explored involves taking advantage of what has up to now been a possible problem: the fact that people apparently differ widely in their thought processes. If we find that some people have trouble solving problems that require specific kinds of imagery, we can turn this knowledge into a tool for understanding the role of such image processes in thinking. Thus it behooves us now to consider individual differences in imagery ability.

11
People Are Different

As the long controversy over the role of images in thinking might suggest, people differ in their means of thought. You may have been puzzled from time to time when you have tried some mental imagery exercise—perhaps you found the instructions hard to translate into imagery or perhaps the very request seemed bizarre. In addition, you may have heard stories about some child you know who purportedly is exceptionally adept at playing spatial memory games (such as Concentration). Not only do people's imagery abilities differ from one individual to another, but age also seems to play a role.

Any general theory of mental activity should lend itself to explaining individual differences in thinking. It may have bothered you earlier when we talked about programming a computer to play gin rummy like a person. *Which* person? you may have wondered. The answer does not matter much if people are basically alike in their thought processes, differing only in terms of how and when they use the same underlying mental structures and processes.

Another challenge for our theory, then, is its ability to lend insight into that immutable fact of human nature, that people are different.

INDIVIDUAL DIFFERENCES

That people differ in their abilities to use mental images has been known almost since the birth of scientific psychology. In 1883 Sir Francis Galton, a researcher on intelligence, cousin to Charles Darwin and inventor of the dog whistle, wrote a book in which he devoted considerable effort to a discussion of mental imagery. Galton had invented a questionnaire asking people to describe various features of their breakfast table. This task seemed to elicit imagery, and it gave Galton an opportunity to probe its different aspects (such as how vivid and colorful objects appeared in people's images). Galton was very surprised when he first administered his questionnaire and discovered that many of his potential informants reported having no imagery at all! Upon reflection, he realized that he was the victim of a nonrandom sampling procedure: Most of his early subjects were his friends and associates, hardly the usual run-of-the-mill person. When a more varied sample was composed, Galton found that only about twelve percent of those he tested reported not being able to form mental images in response to the questions. The nonimagers, interestingly enough, tended to be lawyers and professional men of various sorts, leading Galton to suspect that imagery was a primitive thought mechanism unsuited to the higher kinds of thought.

A century later, one wonders how much Galton's early findings had to do with the effects of fashion on how people answer questions. A study published in 1965 gave the results of a poll of members of Mensa, a society composed of people whose scores on IQ tests are unusually high. The results were in sharp contrast to Sir Francis Galton's: Fully ninety-seven percent of these people reported experiencing vivid imagery. This finding is striking, because members of Mensa are much the same sort of people as those who denied having imagery when Galton asked his questions some eighty years earlier. What happened? Either people have changed in the interim or what they tend to say has changed. We cannot know the answer for sure, but I find it interesting that in the interim between the two studies a number of great thinkers, most notably Albert Einstein, professed to rely heavily on imagery in their work. Consider these words of Einstein's:

> The psychical entities which seem to serve as elements in thought are certain signs and more or less clear images which can be "voluntarily" reproduced and combined. . . . This combinatory play seems to be the essential feature in productive thought—before there is any connection with logical construction in words or other kinds of signs which can be communicated to others. The above-mentioned elements are, in my case, of visual and some muscular type. Con-

ventional words or other signs have to be sought for
laboriously only in a secondary stage, when the mentioned associative play is sufficiently established and
can be reproduced at will.

Imagery was definitely "in" by the time of the Mensa poll. It
is possible, of course, that the development of movies and television has induced people of our era to be more visual in their
thinking; at this point it is impossible to tell. A careful cross-
cultural study of an emerging country might give us some clues,
but such an investigation has yet to be carried out.

In any event, the idea that some people tend to use imagery
more than others has been widely accepted ever since Galton's
time. As often happens with popular ideas in psychology,
numerous tests were developed over the ensuing years to determine whether one is an imager or verbalizer, with occasional
success. For example, "visual imagers" show more regular
breathing patterns than "verbalizers" when they are working out
problems, presumably because implicit verbalizations disrupt
one's breathing pattern. But no earth-shattering distinctions have
been uncovered, which is a little surprising, given the large
amount of work that has gone into studying imagers versus verbalizers or other kinds of thinkers.[1]

Our theory led us to take a fresh approach to the question of
individual differences in imagery. One of the most salient features of the theory is that "imagery" is not a single ability, but a
collection of abilities. Although it is possible that people who are
good at one aspect of imaging are also good at the others, this
need not be so. For example, people who are especially skilled at
using the FIND process to classify patterns in their images may
never have had to develop an efficient REGENERATE process to
hold images in mind for a long time. If people's abilities at using
the various processes are relatively independent, then labeling
someone "good" or "bad" at using imagery in general may be a
serious misconception.

Not all previous tests have focused on sorting people into general categories based on overall imagery ability. In 1909 the
Englishman G. H. Betts devised a questionnaire on the vividness
of mental images. He asked his subjects to form various images
(e.g., of someone you frequently see) and to rate the vividness of

each image, using a scale ranging from 1 (for an image as vivid as an actual picture) to 7 (for no image at all). Similarly, in 1949 the American R. Gordon developed a questionnaire assessing how well subjects could control their images. This questionnaire presented a series of descriptions of a car in various situations, each of which required transforming the previous image in some way (having the car climb up a very steep hill, fall off a bridge into the stream below, and so on). Neither Betts' nor Gordon's questionnaire, however, succeeded in consistently predicting much that was noteworthy about people's imaging abilities.[2]

The notion that people differ in terms of the efficacy of specific structures and processes posited by our theory allows us to explain why Betts, Gordon, and others often failed. The items on every single one of these earlier tests invoke more than one process. Moreover, different items on the tests draw on different processes in different combinations. For example, asking a person to image a car in isolation may require only the IMAGE and PICTURE processes, but asking a person to image the car driving up a hill now also brings in the PUT and FIND processes (to image the car in its correct relationship to the road), as well as a transformation process. Thus when a person is asked to image a car, his or her rating of vividness, control, or whatever presumably will reflect mainly the effectiveness of the PICTURE process if the car is standing still. If the car is imaged in motion, on the other hand, the importance of the PICTURE process may be overshadowed by the contribution of other processes. Two people with different abilities could get the same score for entirely different reasons. If our theory is correct, then it is no surprise that people's scores on such tests do not necessarily predict differences in their performance in imagery tasks.

My colleagues and I set out to test the possibility that individual variations in the use of imagery spring not from an overall imaging ability, but rather from differences in people's handiness with the various structures and processes posited in our theory. We therefore tested people on a battery of tasks, each of which required using specific components of the imagery system. On any two tasks requiring a subject to use a similar combination of structures and processes, we reasoned, his or her performance should be similar. For one thing, the more processing two tasks have in common, the more likely it is they utilize

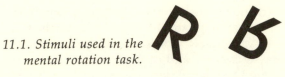

11.1. Stimuli used in the
mental rotation task.

a particularly good or poor process. For example, if someone is very bad at rotating images, then he or she should be bad at any task requiring rotation as one of its component processes.

We began by placing an ad in the *Boston Globe* asking for volunteer subjects. We recruited fifty people who varied widely in age (seventeen to forty-eight years), occupation (one subject reported being an unemployed clerk, another a television station owner), education (eleventh grade to Ph.D. candidate), and cultural background. These people were then tested for six hours each, spread over three days, on tasks like the following: One task required subjects to view a letter oriented at an angle and then form an image of this stimulus (Fig. 11.1). The subjects were asked to mentally rotate the letter clockwise until it was upright; at that point they were to decide whether it was normal or mirror reversed. From Lynn Cooper's earlier experiments we knew that people could follow these instructions, and our results gave us evidence that they actually did so. Like Cooper, we found that the length of time people took to perform the task increased incrementally for each degree the image should have been "rotated." We used speed of rotation as our measure in this task, because we knew it depended on the ROTATE and FIND processes. The theory also says that before examining a pattern to make a judgment, one always regenerates the image. So we also assumed that the REGENERATE process was used here, although it should not have affected rate of rotation.

We also used a task that was described in Chapter 10: Subjects heard a series of directions, four seconds apart, such as "North, west, southwest." The subjects were to begin by imaging a short line segment pointed in the direction first named, then attach a second line to its end pointed in the second direction, and so on. The number of line segments was varied from trial to trial and subjects were asked to draw the imaged pathway at the end of each set of directions. Our measure here was the accuracy of the drawings. According to our theory, subjects would have to use the PUT process to add each new segment correctly to the growing pathway, which involves the FIND and PICTURE processes (to find the end of the previous segment and then image a new one in the correct orientation). In addition, the REGENERATE process would be required to maintain the image over the course of its construction.

Each process posited in the theory was represented in at least a few of the tasks used in our experiment, and we varied the combinations of the processes. In addition to the tasks we made up to involve various components, we also had subjects take two of the standard imagery tests (which we had also analyzed in terms of the processes they should require).

After we had a score for each subject on each task, we evaluated the consistency of each subject's performance from one task to another. If people differ in overall imagery ability, we reasoned, then someone poor at one task should be poor at all the others; but if people are not just good or bad imagers in general, they should do well on some tasks, badly on some, and fair to middling on others. Furthermore, if people differ in how effectively they can use the various structures and processes involved in imaging, then their performance should cluster on tasks that make use of the same processes. And this is exactly what we found. The correlation between the similarity of processing components shared by two tasks and the similarity of a subject's scores on the two tasks was very high (the probability of this being due to chance was less than 1 in 1,000).

We also performed a number of statistical analyses on the correlations we observed among subjects' performances on the different tasks. These analyses revealed that people differed primarily with regard to three processes and one structural variable. First, the efficiency of a subject's FIND process was critical, even on tasks that were otherwise very different (e.g., assessing the ability to rotate an image versus the ability to "see" parts in an image). Some people simply were better than others at using the FIND process, which made them faster and more accurate at any task where they had to classify parts of an image. Second, people differed widely in the relative efficiency of the REGENERATE process. People who had trouble holding material in an image not only could not remember much information, but had a hard time using complex images in simple tasks. Third, people differed in the ease of generating images, which seemed to reflect differences in the efficiency of the PICTURE process. Fourth, people's images showed some interesting structural differences. Some subjects' images were "grainy," with details obscured; others had sharper images. Furthermore, there were wide variations in the maximal size of images. Although graininess and extent did not seem to be totally interrelated, sharper imagers did tend to be capable of "blowing up" their images to larger sizes.

In short, people do not differ simply in terms of "general imagery ability"; you are not just good or bad at imagery, but relatively good or bad at a host of separate imagery abilities; and these abilities can be explained in terms of differences in the structures and processes we posited in our theory. We tested some of these people a year later on other tasks requiring the FIND and REGENERATE processes and they showed similar differences. Apparently, then, a person's skill at various components of imagery often may be a stable part of his or her intellectual abilities. If this is true, we should be able to go back to the kinds of problems discussed in Chapter 10 and predict who will have trouble with which ones on the basis of the kinds of processing they do well or poorly. For example, if you do not have a very efficient REGENERATE process, you should have trouble seeing that a metal soccer ball cannot be constructed out of rigid triangles fitted together to fold into a sphere. But if you have exceptionally good grain in your spatial medium, you might be able to do the wheel and door problem easily (see Chapter 10). We have not yet examined this hypothesis, but it seems likely to be confirmed.

The kind of individual differences uncovered by these experiments may seem rather trivial in the general scheme of things. After all, how often do you confront the need to rotate an object in a mental image? The implications of our findings, however, go quite a ways beyond the types of tasks used in research. For example, when we were devising a test to assess the underlying processes in imagery, I took some of the test items to my local photographer to have slides made. This fellow was always interested in what he was photographing, so I decided to test him on the items. He did incredibly well! Perhaps this was due to the fact that he was a photographer and had had a lot of practice with mental imagery operations; or perhaps he *became* a photographer because he was good at imagery operations. It seems fairly clear that in at least some professions—photography, architecture, engineering, organic chemistry—imagery abilities may be critical. Most of us seem to be naturally good or bad at certain components, for whatever reason, and this may influence actual career decisions. Comfortingly, however, in most of our imagery experiments people definitely improved with practice. If practice underlies the lion's share of individual differences—an issue that has yet to be fully examined—then there may be hope for those people who see things poorly through the mind's eye. Although we may never be in a position to fit glasses to myopic mind's eyes, however metaphorically, we may be able to prescribe exercises to help people improve their inner vision.

COGNITIVE DEVELOPMENT

Young children are notorious visualizers. Many of the games children like to play involve visual thinking: Concentration and Old Maid, not to mention video games. Children also tend to have rich fantasy lives that are peopled with friends who exist only in their imaginations. Some children keep on depending heavily on imagery as they grow older, but most—at least in our culture—shift more and more to verbal abilities. To see why, let us return to one of my favorite questions:

What shape are a German shepherd's ears?

Most adults asked this question generate an image of the dog's head and inspect it for the answer. If the same question is posed over and over, however, soon the image is no longer needed; you can reply directly from verbal memory.

This simple example can be taken as a model of what happens as we get older. Adults depend on images mostly to call up facts about relatively unfamiliar properties; but to children, so many things are relatively unfamiliar that imagery may be their primary source of information. Over time, as they have occasion to draw on these depictive memories, they translate the facts they contain into propositional form. After this happens, they still have the option of using an image, but they no longer need it.

Our theory suggests other reasons why children should tend to use imagery more often than adults. Consider this question: Does a beagle have four legs? You probably have never asked yourself this before, yet you do not need an image to reply. Because a beagle is a dog, and dogs have four legs, you can quickly deduce the answer just from propositionally stored information. But children under age seven or so are notoriously poor at this sort of logical deduction. If a young child does not have the answer to a question like this one explicitly stored in direct association with the object—that is, in a list of propositions labeled by the object's name—then we expect that he or she will not go to the superordinate category, as an adult would, but will use an image.

The idea that children use imagery more than adults is hardly a recent one. The great Swiss psychologist Jean Piaget believed this. He and Bärbel Inhelder published a volume in 1971 called *Mental Imagery in the Child* studying the consequences of this claim. These studies, however, mostly relied on the child's either drawing an object or event in his or her image or describing it verbally. Unfortunately, young children are poor at making accurate drawings and are not generally very articulate. I decided it would be useful to obtain better evidence that young children really do use imagery more than adults.

Of all the experiments we did on this topic, my favorite was conducted in a book closet. It was the only space available at the school that was contributing my subjects, and I was glad of it: The books made for a cozy, relatively soundproof environment, and it was comfortable there for the six- and ten-year-olds who came in to be tested. Both age groups participated in two different tests. In the first test, they heard the name of an animal followed five seconds later by a possible feature of that animal. On half the trials the feature belonged to the animal and on half it did not. The children were told simply to "think about" features of the animal as soon as they heard its name and then to decide whether the feature was correct or incorrect as soon as possible once it was mentioned. In the second test, the children were specifically asked to image the animal on hearing its name (not even the six-year-olds had trouble understanding this instruction) and then to "look" on the animal in the image for the feature. I was struck by a couple of the younger children's remarks along the lines of, "Oh, you want me to do what I did last time again!" when I gave them these instructions.

In this experiment, as in the adult version described in Chapter 4, I chose the features so that the largest ones were the least strongly associated (I had first checked with a separate group of children to verify this). I expected that if my subjects used imagery, they would identify the larger features (e.g., "head" for cat) faster than the smaller ones ("claws"); and this was indeed the result for both the six- and ten-year-olds when they were told to form images of the animals. In contrast, when the ten-year-olds were not given any instructions about using imagery, they were faster for the small, highly associated features, just as the adults had been earlier. The six-year-olds, on the other hand, consistently answered faster with the large features, whether they were told to use imagery or not. However, when they had no instructions about forming an image, the difference in the time taken to evaluate large and small (but more strongly associated) features was much less than when they were told to use imagery. It was almost as if the effect of size versus association strength were being "watered down." This would make sense, I reasoned, if some of the six-year-olds were beginning to shift away from imagery to propositionally stored information.

Fortunately, I had anticipated this possibility from the start and had interviewed the children after the first session, when imagery instructions were not used. I asked each child to tell me how he or she had answered the question: By mentally picturing the animal and "looking" at it? By having a mental picture but not needing it? By not having a picture at all and "just knowing" the answer? By some combination of the strategies? Or were they not sure? For the most part, even the youngest children had no trouble identifying how they had reached their answers. The interesting thing was that when I broke down the data for the individual children according to their reported strategies, I found that most of the six-year-olds did in fact say they had used images, and these children did answer faster for the larger features. For the minority who said they did not use images, response times were faster for the smaller but more highly associated features, just as they had been for the older children and for adults. To my mind, this was convincing evidence that young children do in fact use imagery more than adults.

The question now becomes, So what? My hope is that we can use the theory to isolate the ways in which children are relatively precocious at using imagery. For example, if they are generally good with the PICTURE process but not with the PUT process, this would argue for developing teaching teaching techniques that use visual stimuli in a way that does not require the child to compose an image from parts when he or she later recalls the information. The idea would be to take advantage of the children's cognitive strengths in teaching. That is, we know that children are naturally inclined to use imagery; we can go one step further by figuring out the aspects of the imaging process in which they are particularly strong and using that knowledge to help them learn more successfully.

But this is just one direction in which practical applications could arise from research on mental imagery. Let us finish by looking more generally at a variety of potential applications of this research, and of research in cognitive science in general.

The Philosophical and the Practical

OUR INVESTIGATION OF MENTAL IMAGES, the quintessential "ghosts in the mind's machine," is a typical example of how cognitive scientists are currently studying the mind. Although cognitive science is often regarded as a subfield of psychology, the questions it asks and the tools it uses to answer them come from areas as diverse as linguistics, philosophy, and artificial intelligence, as well as experimental psychology. One of the beauties of this work is that it brings the most modern techniques of science and technology to bear on some of the oldest philosophical puzzles about human thinking. Let us recapitulate the problems we have dealt with over the course of this book and summarize our solutions, and let us move from the philosophical to the practical and see what will follow from research within the cognitive science framework.

THE PHILOSOPHICAL

Ghosts in the Mind's Machine

One problem we have addressed relates to Descartes' distinction between the intangible mind and the physical, mechanistic body. How can mental events, such as images, exist within and connected to a brain comprised of neurons, blood vessels, and the like? We began by splitting the problem into two problems, that of the nature of conscious experience and that of the nature of mental activities (such as remembering, perceiving, reasoning, and so on). We found a solution to the second problem, relating mental activities to the brain, by considering how processing occurs in a computer. Just as a computer can be described either at a physical level, in terms of its components and their operation, or at a functional level, in terms of its program and the tasks it performs, so can the brain. We can think of the computer's central processing unit (CPU) and memory locations as the means utilized by the program to get its job done. Similarly, the brain can be interpreted as the vehicle for performing the work of the mind.

The analogy between brain and computer also allows us to see how visual images can be picturelike without being actual pictures. The cathode ray tube (CRT) that displays information stored in the computer works by translating data encoded as bits into a physical, visible screen. The computer is able to interpret certain stored information as spatial images (whether or not it actually projects an image onto a CRT) because its CPU treats these data as if they were organized in a matrix; that is, these data function as if they were stored in a matrix, with some entries next to others, some diagonal from others, and so on. Thus, though the machine itself contains no actual screen, it can store and use material that is pictorial at the functional level. Our model suggests that the brain works this way too.

The Homunculus

A classic objection to the idea of the mind as anything more or other than the brain is that such a concept is tantamount to positing a homunculus, a little man inside the head. Must there not then be another little man inside *his* head? and so on. Thinking about mental imagery is an especially good way of dispatching this problem because the homunculus has so often been used as an objection to the very idea of mental images: What inner eye watches the screen inside the brain? We solved this problem with regard to imagery by positing that the "mind's eye" is a set of tests that categorize patterns as depicting examples of specific spatial classes. For example, if two lines meet at one end (in a functionally defined matrix) and diverge at the other, they form a pattern that is *pointed;* the tests that so classify the pattern correspond to the mind's eye. These kinds of tests are easily programmed into a computer and they pose no philosophical problems. The idea of processing in the computer effectively eliminates the need for a homunculus. The same idea can be applied to the brain, eliminating the need for homunculus to explain mental events.

Putting the World in the Mind

Another classic puzzle about the mind is the idea of mental representation. How can information about the world be "re-presented" in the nonphysical mind? How are we able to contemplate a thing in its absence? Many early philosophers believed that images were the answer: We can use an image to stand for an object because the image "looks like" the object and can be recognized in the same way we recognize the object when we actually see it. One major drawback to this idea is that images do not lend themselves to representing whole classes of things: Any given image must be an image of a particular object. One possible solution to this problem would be to have words (or propositional symbols corresponding to them) stand for classes. The trouble with this approach is that words are arbitrarily paired with the things they represent; how do we remember what a given word stands for? We cannot accomplish this by associating words with other words, because this would result in the same kind of infinite regression as the little man inside the head of the little man. . . . One way to sidestep this problem is to suppose that we associate a word with a set of images. The word stands for the category, and we know to pair it with the set of objects it represents because we have associated images of those different objects with the word in a memory. Once a sufficient number of words are grounded in this way, we can use them to define still more words.[1]

Another drawback to the idea that images are basic to putting the world in the mind is that images are inherently ambiguous. A picture (or image) of a sitting man could stand for "John," "bent knees," "sitting man," and so on. Although such ambiguity is theoretically a problem, it may be more apparent than real. The existence of perceptual principles such as the Gestalt laws of organization (see Chapter 5) effectively takes the teeth out of part of this problem: We are predisposed to organize visual patterns in certain ways and to see some parts as more important than others, and so on. These tendencies are evident even in very young infants and appear to be innate.[2] Once an image is organized, there probably are other principles that determine how it will be interpreted, as demonstrated by Eleanor Rosch's finding at Berkeley, that people name pictures in consistent ways. Thus you would not use the same picture to illustrate "bent knees" and "sitting man"; any given picture—and presumably image— will usually be given only one interpretation. Thus we have our cake and eat it too. Images can be used to establish nonarbitrary associations with objects in the world and can be linked with words (or propositions) to represent classes.

A Window on the Mind

Minds, by definition, are private. If we are to study mental events objectively, we need a way to make them publicly observable. How can we do this? The answer is not unlike the physicists' solution to the problem of how to discover new subatomic particles. In both cases, scientists make inferences from how the unobservable object of study—mind or particle—behaves in specific circumstances. The physicist might bombard an atom with a stream of electrons and observe its response. The cognitive scientist might give a person a problem and observe how quickly he or she responds. By measuring the *consequences* of mental activity—how long it takes, how many errors are made, and so on—we can make inferences about the activity itself. If mental images really do depict spatial extent, for example, then we would expect that progressively more time should be required for a person to scan greater distances across an object in an image, which turns out to be true.

Experience and Function

We divided mental phenomena into two general classes, those pertaining to experience and those pertaining to function. This book is concerned only with the latter, how the mind stores and uses information. One reason progress has been made in understanding such mental activity is that we know how to theorize about information processing. In contrast, we haven't the faintest idea of how to theorize about the nature of conscious experience per se. In fact, the experience itself may well be entirely epiphenomenal with regard to mental activity: The experience may play no part in how thinking actually gets done—just as the flashing lights on the outside of a computer play no part in the processing going on inside.

Strictly speaking, however, much of our data are findings about changes in the experience of imagery. We ask subjects to respond when they introspectively "see" something on an object in an image, or we ask them to "rotate" the objects in the image, and so on. One could look at much of the research on imagery as trying to explain changes in the experience of imagery by specifying the nature of the mental mechanisms that produce the experience. That is, the experience itself cannot be "processed"; it is in an altogether different category than things that can be processed (the philosopher Gilbert Ryle would call talk about "processing experiences" a *category error*). The assumption made here is that mental representations are processed when we have the experience of imagery, and the nature of such processing determines both the amount of time taken to do a task and the quality of the experience one has while processing is underway. Thus we assume that the way one "sees" something on an object in an image, "rotates" it, and so on, is by performing the requisite mental processing, which thereby results in the changes in the experience.

The cognitive scientist, then, can ask the following question: Why are particular experiences hooked up with particular mental activities? Recall that the properties of images apparent to introspection, such as the depiction of shape, did not necessarily have to reflect properties of the underlying mental representation (see Chapter 3). But we discovered that at least some of the properties of images evident to introspection really do reflect properties of the functional representation. This may not be an accident. If you stop to think about it, the "texture" of many experiences is related to the properties of the underlying cause of the experience in this way. A "sharp pain" is often caused by something jabbing into you; the burning feeling of an "acid stomach" is often caused by acid in the stomach. Instead of asking about the nature of experiences per se, the cognitive scientist will ask why particular experiences go along with particular mental activities.[3]

Toward a Theory of the Mind

Our next challenge was to consider what a theory of the mind would consist of and how to develop and evaluate one. The appropriate level of theorizing is determined in large part by the kinds of questions the theory is supposed to answer. The insurance agent seeking the cause of the fire is not interested in the physics of combustion, and the cognitive scientist seeking an understanding of mental events is not interested in the physical nature of nerve cells in the brain. A theory of mental activity should explain how people think, learn, use language, and the like. These questions center on issues about how information is stored and used, and the theory must provide answers that address these issues.[4]

A theory of information processing is one about how information is represented and operated upon. Our theory specifies a library or repertoire of the kinds of structures and processes that can be used to store and process visual information. The structures include types of *data structures*, which actually store the information, and types of *media* in which the data structures reside. By analogy, a television screen is a medium that functions as a space (when a person watches it) and the specific pictures are the data structures. The *processes* transform and compare data structures in various ways, allowing one to do things like scan across an image or generate it from a long-term memory encoding. For example, our theory of imagery posits a spatial medium— a "visual buffer"—in which images reside. The center of this medium is most resolved (in focus), and resolution decreases toward the periphery because the grain gets coarser. Our theory further states that an image is a pattern in this medium, and this pattern can be manipulated in various ways. For instance, gradual scanning is accomplished in part by a process (called SCAN in our theory) that shifts the pattern through the medium so that different parts are in the center and hence most sharply in focus; similarly, rotation is accomplished by a process (called ROTATE in our theory) that shifts the pattern around a pivot point. In both cases another process (called FIND in our theory) must be used to monitor the image as it is being shifted through the medium.

For every theory of structures and processes, there must be a theory of how these are used to perform any given task at a given time. Theories of the exact sequence of processing are descriptions of an *algorithm*. An algorithm is a set of steps that will result in a particular outcome, given a particular input. When a person scans an image, for example, the particular sequence of structures and processes he or she uses are described by the algorithm for the scan. In describing our computer model, the algorithm for scanning is represented by a flow chart. (Recall that scanning involves shifting the point of focus, not just seeing parts in an image.) In this case the algorithm specifies how the LOOKFOR process computes the direction of the scan and then uses this information to start the SCAN process shifting the image in the right way, which is then monitored by the FIND process, which guides the scan until a particular pattern is in focus. However, for every theory of structures and processes, there can be numerous theories of algorithms for a given task. For instance, when inspecting an image, the LOOKFOR process might let the image fade and then use the PICTURE process to generate the image in a new position in the image medium, so that a different pattern would be in the center and hence in focus. In doing so, the PUT and FIND processes would be used if multiple parts have to be arranged correctly. A complete theory must state why a particular algorithm is used at a particular time.

In this book we have concentrated our efforts at attempting to characterize the kinds of structures and processes that are available in the mind for using imagery to perform specific tasks. In doing so, we have also considered specific algorithms that describe when images are used to answer questions and how image generation, inspection, and transformation proceed.[5]

Models and Theories

A fundamental problem in the philosophy of science is, How does one get off the ground? How does one set out a theory where none existed before? We have found it useful to build models and to let them guide both our theorizing and empirical work. At the early stages we started with a rough model, the computer display metaphor, which helped to raise issues, such as the "matrix hypothesis." These issues then guided our experiments. Once we had enough data on key aspects of how people process images, we began to build a computer program that mimicked human mental processing. This model provided a more concrete and sophisticated way of testing the theory and raising new issues. That is, we could put specific input into the model and see what the computer does, which should correspond to what people do if the model (and the theory that guided its construction) is correct. And the experiments done to help flesh out the theory and model produced results (e.g., on the three-dimensional properties of images) that will need to be explained by all theories of imagery.

Evaluating the Theory

The final basic question we had to deal with was, How do we know whether our theory is correct? The classic answer to this question is to see whether the theory explains the data and is potentially disprovable (i.e., if any data could show that it is wrong). We showed that the imagery theory does in fact explain the data and provide testable predictions. However, in general, these criteria are better suited to fields with more highly developed theories which make very precise predictions. In cognitive science, theories are often embedded in models, and it is the models that are tested. One property of models is that they include components that are not "theory relevant"; for example, in our computer model, we were constrained to some degree by our programming language, the specific features of which were not germane to our theory of how the human mind represents and processes images. Thus the model itself cannot be taken at face value. Furthermore, models are often incomplete and will not even provide an explanation for all relevant phenomena.

Thus, in addition to our first two criteria for a theory—that it explain the data and be testable—we have proposed a third: that it have vitality. That is, a good theory should lead one to develop the theory further. Although working with models has drawbacks in some other respects, it enhances a theory's vitality. The very incompletenesses that make models difficult to disprove also make them vital: When we come up against a missing piece, we can collect new data to help us fill it in. This property of models in cognitive science was demonstrated at length in the last few chapters.

In summary, then, the new amalgam called cognitive science takes advantage of knowledge from a wide range of fields. From computer science it draws information about how computers and computer programs work; from philosophy it has adopted not only many of its basic questions and a general orientation toward the mind, but many of the fundamental ideas about information representation (e.g., "propositions"); from linguistics it draws a basic way of thinking about mental events and theories of language; and from cognitive psychology it draws methodologies and specific findings about human information-processing abilities. All this put together, a new and more vigorous approach to studying the mind has developed, which has resulted in new insights into some of the oldest puzzles about what we are.

THE PRACTICAL

We have just considered three criteria for evaluating the worth of theories of mental processing. However, there is yet another measure of a good scientific theory: its ability to provide a useful technology. We will conclude this chapter by considering some of the practical applications that can arise from our imagery theory and cognitive science theories of the mind in general.

Education

In Chapter 11 we used our computer model and theory of imagery as a way of discovering people's aptitudes for different parts of the imaging process. The idea has obvious implications for education. The usefulness of research for developing more effective educational processes is rooted in the notion that the most successful presentation of information is one that plays to the learner's strengths: If a new idea is conveyed in terms we can easily comprehend, it is likely to be easier to appreciate than if we have to shift our mental orientation in order to grasp it.

There are three realms in which our theory of imagery could be useful to designers of educational programs. The first is early education. Research so far suggests that children depend heavily on imagery in their early years, evidently up to the age of about seven. This finding argues for presenting information graphically to young children whenever practical. The rote memorization of statements of fact that was popular a century ago, for example, probably is not the most effective way to help children understand geography: You might describe "geography" as a description of the earth's surface; the "earth" as the planet or body on which we live; the shape of the earth as round, like a ball; and so on.

If children had to image the content of these statements, they could picture "surface" as a formica tabletop (that's the only type mother calls "surfaces"), a "body" as having two arms and two legs, a ball with stitches like a baseball, and so on. Keeping in mind that children may image the referents of words, one can take care to ensure that the right image is evoked, either by showing pictures and models or by using careful descriptions.

The great developmental psychologist Jean Piaget attributed much of the young child's problems in reasoning to a reliance on static mental images. For example, young children cannot anticipate how high the water will be when it is poured from one glass into another of a different shape. An understanding of the precise limitations of children's imagery would inform one on how not to use imagery in teaching. For example, if children's images are static, in that they cannot gradually transform their images (see them meld into a new shape), they may still be able to use "blink" transformations (erasing the first image and imaging the object anew in some altered way). If so, then it would make sense to shift from trying to teach the child rules of transformation to teaching him or her rules of formation. Learning how to "break up" an initial image and see it flow into a new shape is quite different from learning how to form a second image that is related to the first in some way. Similarly, if young children can form images easily, but have difficulty in maintaining them, then one should try to teach by inducing a series of rather simple images, and so on.

In addition, once one knew the specific limitations of children's imagery, one might be able to use the symbolic mode of imagery to teach even fairly "abstract" ideas. A line with dots along it, like the one used in Chapter 10 to solve three-term series problems, might help older children learn the elements of logic.

What about adults? Here is the second way in which theories of mental representation and processing can be useful in education. Consider a parable: Once upon a time the animals in the forest got together and lamented the sorry state of their offspring. The younger generation was hanging around waterholes, loitering on trail corners, and generally *not developing their potential.* So the adults decided to start a school to keep the young ones off the streets and do them some good at the same time. When the curriculum committee convened, each parent had a strong opinion to offer. The bears insisted that digging be taught; the birds chirped in that flying certainly should not be overlooked; "Nor can we forget climbing," said the squirrels. The young animals were gathered up and sent to the school. And soon the young birds were coming home with broken wing tips from trying to dig, the baby bears with broken backs from trying to fly, and so on.

The moral of this story is not simply that some of us are best fitted for some tasks and others for other tasks—this has the ring of a society of ants, each specialized for one particular function and good for nothing else. Rather, once you know what sort of creature you are, then there are two choices of how to approach a particular task. On the one hand, you can look for tactics that make use of your special talents: If you are a bird and want to dig, use your beak and claws; if you are a bear and want to fly, get into an airplane. On the other hand, you might practice the skills that are most obviously relevant. Unlike birds and bears, people can change themselves if they work at it (though how extensively imaging ability can be improved is still an open question).

By studying the ways in which people differ from one another—not just in general terms, such as a tendency to use imagery or words, but in terms of the underlying structures and processes operating in the mind—we can learn how best to present any information to a given person.

For example, suppose you're teaching a course in auto mechanics. By testing your students before the class starts, you discover that some of them have trouble with the REGENERATE process (a fairly common difficulty). Knowing that these students will have a hard time holding onto complex images, you might supply a diagram of a car engine for them to refer to as you describe each part. Another group has difficulty using the ROTATE process and cannot imagine the parts in motion; they will learn the operation of an engine most easily by observing a moving model, and so on. At the same time, you can encourage both groups to practice the skills they are weakest in.

Tactics like these will not obliterate the differences in how easily different people will learn different sorts of information; they are not intended to. They should, however, help people to learn to function reasonably well in our society.

Individual aptitudes are not the only important factor about imaging relevant to educational strategies. In general, people have more in common than not, at least with regard to how they use imagery. Some tasks are so much better approached one way than another that individual differences are all but irrelevant. Imagery

seems to be the best way of thinking about spatial, color, or tex-
tural relations that are relatively subtle, for instance. Gently
steering a sailboat to dock, anticipating how a sofa in a show-
room would look in a particular place in the living room, or
deciding whether a paint in the store has more yellow in it than
the paint on your living room walls all require imagery. Imagery
is also generally useful in situations where one needs to store a
lot of information about the appearance of an object or a scene.
If you want to be sure that nothing was stolen from your house
after a trip, you are better off memorizing an image of each room
than learning to recite to yourself, "Living room: stereo, television, oriental rug, . . ." These properties of images could well
be exploited more widely in the design of instructional programs
of all sorts. The most effective way of teaching anything—geography, the principles of the legal system, roller skating, or car
repair—depends on the student, the kind of information being
presented, and the uses the person will make of the knowledge
later. All three of these factors should be considered.

This leads us to the third aspect of education where understanding imagery can be valuable: helping people sharpen their
use of images for their own benefit. Quite a few of the ordinary
problems we encounter from day to day become easier to solve
with imagery. For instance, simple logic problems—"All apples
are X's; no X is a Y; can an apple be a Y?"—can be readily solved
with Venn diagrams. A Venn diagram is a convenient way of
expressing a syllogism or similar set of linked propositions in
visual form: A circle is used to represent each class described by
a proposition, and the way the circles overlap shows how the
classes relate. Drawing a Venn diagram is not always convenient
when we run into such a problem, but imaging one can be a
handy alternative. The only constraint is that the number of circles has to be small enough so as not to tax our limited capacity
to maintain images. It is such simple sets of propositions, in fact,
that form the underlying structure of much of the advertising we
are constantly exposed to. If people would get into the habit of
trying to discern this structure in television commercials and
newspaper and magazine ads, they would recognize that in many
cases the structure is badly flawed. For example, one fairly common oil company advertisement runs as follows: "Our country
requires huge amounts of energy. Oil is running out. Therefore

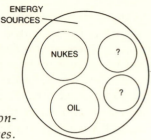

12.1. *A representation useful for reasoning about energy sources.*

we must turn to nuclear power." Whether the conclusion is correct or not is beside the point; the argument has no basis in logic (Fig. 12.1). If you image a Venn diagram, you can see that a big circle representing energy has lots of room for other circles when the one labeled *oil* is removed; the background is not a circle labeled nuclear energy, but a field for any sort of energy other than oil—solar energy, coal, wind, or whatever. Learning to recognize faulty arguments is almost a survival trait in a society such as ours, and any tactic that can foster this kind of thinking seems worth developing.

Human Engineering

Another potential contribution that theories of mental representation and processing could make is in the area we can loosely call product design. If you have ever thought about the structure of tools, appliances, and other human equipment, you have probably noticed that there are two sides to the principle "form follows function." A hammer is designed to bring down force on a nail, but it is equally tailored to the human hand and arm that supply the force. Given that all human beings are built fundamentally alike, some ways of constructing any given artifact are bound to work better than others. With simple tools, such as a hammer, the design principles derive mainly from physics and are fairly obvious. With more complex machinery, human psychology as well as physiology come into play. A well-planned heater control in a car, for instance, should raise the temperature as one turns a dial clockwise or slides a lever to the right (both directions are interpreted as "more" psychologically). A car with the reverse arrangement would be less easy to use. Manufacturers therefore try to anticipate problems like this, avoid them insofar as possible, and correct them when they do crop up.

The history of computers is rather interesting when viewed in this light. Over the decades since they were invented, they have become increasingly sophisticated not only in what they can do, but in how easily human operators can make them do it. Early computers were so arcane that it was a rare person who could get them to work. With continual advances in technology, the machines and programs have been redesigned over and over to make them easier to operate. For example, the programming languages have evolved from sets of 0's and 1's to English-like words. At this point, we are in a position to build computers that have not only switches and knobs designed for the human hand, but instruction sets and programs designed to be grasped by the human mind. Our theory of imaging may have some valuable insights to offer about how we might design computer systems that are more "user compatible" in this way:

Suppose we want to create a computer graphics system to help architects visualize what the finished building will look like if particular plans are used. The benefits of such a system are obvious; indeed, prototypes already exist. It is easy to think of features that would be useful: For one thing, we could have the computer alter parts of the building—add wings, delete windows, enlarge them, shrink them, move parts around. We could also vary the placement of the building, seeing how the sun hits it at different times of day, and so on. But how should we construct the program? One way would be to program the machine to mimic the way a person would think about the changes, that is, visualize it in his or her head. Thus the machine literally becomes an extension of the architect—a way of externalizing imagery. This would be a real boon, in that the computer could overcome some of the limitations of imagery, most notably in the vividness of the display and the number of items a person can hold in an image at once. Furthermore, if the machine operated the way we think, it should be easy to learn to use.

Understanding imagery is also potentially useful for designers of maps and diagrams that a person will later image. If you have ever tried to look up where you are on a detailed full-color map while driving, you can appreciate the possibilities. The ideal map or diagram for someone who wants to hold a route or location in mind should be organized so the person can see it as composed of relatively few units. Also, the details should be large enough to be "visible" in an image. It would be valuable, in addition, to know more about how people image color; for example, whether varying the number of colors affects how many shapes someone can image at once. If it does not—that is, if color and shape information are processed separately—then the use of color would greatly increase the amount of information someone can image at once, which would make it easier to use the map or diagram from memory. On the other hand, if color and shape both tax the same mental structures and processes, then it might be better not to make much use of color.

More generally, research designed to understand mental representation and processing should contribute to a specification of compatibilities between concepts and symbols. For instance, on a temperature map, certain colors clearly are best paired with certain temperatures: Blue is an easily understood symbol for cold, and red for heat. This sort of compatibility should be systematically studied, not just for colors but for a wide range of phenomena, such as patterns of movement and the like in dynamic computer displays. It is not obvious what the best way is to represent moving fluid, for example—moving dashes? dots? People appear to make some associations with given shapes, colors, and patterns of movement more readily than with others, and it would be beneficial to identify these tendencies and take advantage of them in designing visual displays.

Therapy

An understanding of the mind is a prerequisite for any science of psychotherapy. It is no accident that Freud was very interested in mental imagery, and it would be surprising if research on imagery did not have many different kinds of applications to psychotherapy. Let us consider a few possibilities.

For relatively mild problems, the most effective therapy may amount to a form of education. The therapist's goal in such cases generally is to diagnose the patient's unhappy view of self and the world and help him or her to change it. Most of what we mean by "personality" consists of representations in memory: After all, if a person were to forget absolutely every fact, skill, and habit, his or her previous personality would be virtually extinguished. All that would be left would be glandular tendencies and genetically determined predispositions. Thus changing many maladaptive aspects of personality can be viewed as changing certain information in memory that had been guiding the person's behavior. Much of the information on which we base our interactions in the world is rooted in our concepts of self and others, some of which probably is stored as mental images. This role of images may become apparent if you think about what is in your mind when you consider your co-workers' perceptions of you when you first arrive at work in the morning. It is not an accident that *perceive* means both "see" and "think of." Very often, therapists have said, patients remember themselves from a younger era, when they were less accomplished and more vulnerable. Bringing this image to the surface and updating it is a large part of the therapist's job. This process surely could be facilitated by a good understanding of how people retrieve images and replace one image with another.

Mental imagery already is being used in therapy to help people overcome phobias, irrational fears of some situation or thing, such as an incapacitating fear of snakes. It turns out that phobias often can be extinguished by a treatment program that makes use of images. A phobic person typically will become quite agitated and uncomfortable if asked to image the feared object or situation, almost as anxious as when faced with the real thing. The degree of fear varies according to the way in which the object is imaged: Someone with a snake phobia will be more upset imaging a snake crawling over his or her shoe than one off in the distance in a locked cage. The therapeutic strategy, therefore, is to have the phobic person form an image of the object that is relatively non-threatening and gradually learn to move to more aversive images while remaining relaxed. For example, the therapist might begin by asking the person to image a toy snake. When he or she can hold this image without becoming anxious, a slightly less innocuous object is tried; say, a very small real snake in a cage. Step by step, the person eventually comes to be able to image a live snake at close quarters. Once he or she is comfortable with an imaged snake, the person often can then face real snakes without fear. This is not too surprising, given the evidence that images are in many ways like percepts, but it is gratifying that this resemblance can be put to beneficial use.

Imagery research could help make this type of therapy—called *systematic desensitization*—more efficient by providing an initial diagnosis of a given person's strengths and weaknesses in imaging. Here again it helps to know that imagery is not an all-or-none ability, that people differ in how good they are at the various components of the imaging process, such as using the PICTURE process, the ROTATE process, and so on. Because many different sequences of images are possible in systematic desensitization, the images chosen should be of a type the patient in question can easily form. People who have trouble scanning images but who can generate new ones well probably will not gain much from trying to scan toward the feared object. They will be better off imaging the object at a distance and slowly zooming in on it, or forming a series of "still" images, each one a little larger. In addition, the complexity of the image is limited by the amount of information we are able to hold in mind at once. If the image is too complicated, so that some parts of it are always fading, the patient will not be able to maintain an object in an image that looks enough like the actual object for his or her relaxed response to be transferred to the real thing.

So far we have been talking about relatively mild mental disorders, many of which can reasonably be thought of in terms of concepts a person has that need "revamping." But some people's problems are more severe, putting them out of touch with reality. At least some of these maladies seem likely to be traceable to biochemical malfunctions in the brain, so that programs of reeducation may not hold much promise. Still, the kind of theory we have been developing here, and the accompanying methodologies for studying the mind, may be useful as a diagnostic tool. It is possible that certain of the more serious mental disorders affect specific structures and processes in the mind, in which case identifying the part of the system involved could help diagnose and perhaps even treat a patient. Some forms of schizophrenia, for example, are characterized by wild visual hallucinations. A faulty PICTURE process could cause involuntary images; so could a faulty FIND process. We can devise tasks that tap only one of these processes and thereby discover exactly where things are going wrong. Slightly different disorders may produce similar symptoms (such as hallucinations), but will respond best to different drugs. By pinpointing the problem, then, we not only understand it better, but can do a better job in diagnosis and treatment.

Artificial Intelligence

The field of artificial intelligence (AI) stands in a special relation to our approach to understanding the mind. Researchers in AI try to program computers to behave in intelligent ways, such as by solving problems, seeing, and understanding language. There are two general approaches to these challenges: performance mode and simulation mode. In performance mode, the computer is programmed to carry out some activity in the most convenient way possible, whatever that might be. No attempt is made to get the machine to do the job in the same way a person would. For example, some of the work on computer vision relies on lasers to establish the distance of an object from the camera. In simulation mode, in contrast, the computer is programmed to do things the way people do. We know that all the problems of AI are solvable in simulation mode: People are the proof. We talk, see, and so on. Thus if we program a computer to imitate a person in the right ways and give the computer a voice, eyes, and so on, it too should become "intelligent" (shades of HAL, the computer in *2001: A Space Odyssey*). As has been demonstrated with imaging, by getting the computer to go through the same steps people do, we can ensure that the machine will eventually carry out the required task.

The present work has obvious applications to this endeavor. If the mind really can use depictive images and if it does store images and use them as our theory describes, it makes sense to try to program the computer to do the job in the same way. For one thing, this often seems like the most efficient course. A case in point is one that involves creating a program to show a pile of toy blocks falling. The problem is to know where each block will be relative to the others at any given moment. If the blocks are imaged and the image is shifted through the spatial medium, this is easy to do. If the blocks are described propositionally, on the other hand, and various formulas are used to compute where they are at each millisecond, the computer's task is very difficult.[6] In general, the kind of image system we have been describing for people appears to be an efficient way for a machine to store and use visual information, for the same reasons it is a good way for people to do the same things. It took millions of years for the human mind to develop its capacities, and we can save a significant fraction of that time in our attempts to program machines if we take advantage of the solutions already worked out by and embodied in our own minds.

SCIENCE AND THE MENTAL IMAGE

Where, then, do these investigations leave us? We have unearthed much new information, but many clues remain to be followed up, and there are some large blank spaces. The glass is half empty; but it is also half full. Even if we never scientifically understand art, dreams, and literary images, we have accomplished more then J. B. Watson ever would have believed. And there does not seem to be a limit on what we can do with what we are learning. Imagery is only one small corner of the cognitive science enterprise, and similar progress is being made in numerous fields. These truly are exciting times in which to think about thinking.

Notes

CHAPTER ONE

1. Samuels and Samuels, 1975, p. xi.
2. E. B. Tichner, 1909, p. 22.
3. J. B. Watson, 1928, pp. 76–77.
4. Watson, 1928, pp. 75–76.

CHAPTER TWO

1. The original "Turing test" involved assessing an interrogator's ability to identify which of two people typing responses was a man, and which was a woman. A computer then replaced the man, and the accuracy of the interrogator's performance was now compared to the first case, allowing one to assess how well the computer could imitate a man (see Turing, 1950).
2. Recall that the goal is to understand how the mind works, not how we consciously *experience* it working; studying how computers work tells us nothing about the nature of conscious experience. We will return to the question of why the ghosts "feel" the way they do at the end of the book.
3. This is true even if the program is built into the circuitry of a special-purpose computer and is therefore part of the "hardware" (the machine itself) and not the "software" (the reprogrammable contents of memory). We are dealing with a way of talking about the machine's operation, not with hardware versus software.
4. See Putnam, 1973.
5. Although cognitive science is committed to the functional level of analysis, it is not committed to the particular way we now talk about this level. The vocabulary borrowed from the computer is the only one now available for characterizing information processing, but some other way of specifying information processing in the brain may ultimately prove more useful.
6. *Leviathan*, Part I, Chapter II, pp. 5–6.
7. The mind's eye does not *generate* the image; it does not put the points into the cells in the first place. Rather, it examines an image that is

already there. How mental images are formed is another question, which will be considered in Chapter 6.

8. These by-products are essential for studying the mind because they alert us that particular events are occurring. We do not need to use such hallmarks to help us to make inferences about the computer, however; we know how it works because we built and programmed it that way.

CHAPTER THREE

1. In the Bibliography are listed many of the papers published by researchers in the field. Although I often will mention only the head of a given laboratory, it should be understood that all of the people who collaborated on the papers deserve credit for the work.

2. Psychologists refer to propositional representations as "propositions," even though a proposition, strictly speaking, is the idea being conveyed, not the means of conveying the idea. Philosophers refer to the representation of the idea as a "sentence."

3. Thus it makes sense to talk of "large" and "small" images, where the size is relative to the spatial extent of the medium (i.e., the functional space in which images occur).

4. Although it is convenient to talk of the characteristics of different types of representations in the abstract, we should keep in mind that these characteristics emerge from the way in which information is processed. As we saw in Chapter 2, the same data can represent a number, an instruction, a letter, and so on, depending on how the data are processed. Thus when we use a symbolic description of a representation, we are assuming that the data are processed in such a way that the functional properties emerge.

5. It is always neatest when the data and introspections mesh, but we are not dependent on their doing so. If they do not, we simply reject the introspective reports: These reports include the subjects' interpretations of what occurred, and there is no reason why the subjects should necessarily be correct in their interpretations.

6. See Anderson (1978) for an example of such a propositional theory of image rotation.

7. Recall that when a person reports having the experience of imagery, we take this as an indication that an image representation is being processed. However, it is possible that image processing sometimes might not produce the experience—but without the experience as a hallmark, we have difficulty in knowing when to check to see whether image representations (i.e., mental images) are being processed.

8. See Pylyshyn, 1981.

CHAPTER FOUR

1. Plato, *Theaetetus*, Section 191.
2. These inferences rest on the assumption that the shape is symmetrical, which seems approximately correct; see Finke and Kosslyn, 1980.
3. For further details about the experiments on scanning, size, or the scope of the medium, see Kosslyn, 1980.

CHAPTER FIVE

1. This notion of object representation will work only if we make two assumptions: First, the process that compares an input to the stored images can "weight" some aspects of a given image as being more important than others (e.g., the width for sofas, which distinguishes them from chairs). Part of learning an object–concept is learning which aspects are most important, which can be represented by storing instructions for the comparison process along with the image (these instructions need have no "meaning" above and beyond how they affect this process). Second, the meanings of at least some words are innate, such as *or*, *and*, *of*, and so forth. Furthermore, relations like "is an instance of" and the idea of nouns, verbs, and so on probably are also innate, but representations of specific classes of objects seem likely to be learned (see Farah and Kosslyn, 1982).
2. *Leviathan*, Part I, Chapter II, p. 5.
3. See Finke, 1980, for a review of research on "levels of equivalence" between imagery and perception and a more detailed development of the basic approach.
4. Note that putting the two dots in a pair closer together would have resulted in a smaller angle in this task. Similarly, a looser definition of "overflow" would have resulted in a larger angle in the previous tasks: The field of attention fades gradually, and the absolute point of blur is not clear-cut.
5. See Bower, 1974.
6. Because imagery and perception share specialized "modality-specific" processing mechanisms, we can justify using perceptual terms—like *see*—without quotation marks when discussing imagery. However, I occasionally will use quotes in the remainder of this book to remind you that we are not speaking of actual seeing.

CHAPTER SIX

1. Some people claim to be haunted by imaged objects and events they cannot extinguish, usually of an emotionally charged incident. In this

case, presumably the unconscious mind does not *really* want to turn off the image, for whatever reason.

2. Strictly speaking, we should distinguish between the person's introspective experience of picturing an object in an image and the act of forming the image itself (i.e., the underlying representation). However, we assume that when people are asked to picture an object, they do so by forming the appropriate representation in the image medium. The instructions to "image" and to "picture" are thus synonymous, both requiring the unconscious mental acts that result in one's introspectively "seeing" an object appear in an image.

3. Because the word *rotate* is being used in a special sense, it should be in quotation marks; for the sake of readability, however, I have eliminated these in most cases.

4. See Sekuler and Nash, 1972.

5. For more details on the experiments on image generation and transformation, see Kosslyn, 1980.

CHAPTER SEVEN

1. Giving the musicians a score to follow is yet another step, equivalent to specifying an *algorithm,* as will be discussed later.

CHAPTER EIGHT

1. This generalization must be qualified in particular circumstances, however; see Chapter 7 of Kosslyn, 1980.

2. It has sometimes been said that psychologists have "physics envy"; and there is some truth to this. Physics is the quintessentially successful science (no one argues about whether there has been progress in physics) and we would do well to understand the secrets of its success.

3. For detailed explanations of most of the available data, see Kosslyn, 1980.

4. For additional details about the foregoing experiments, see Chapters 6 and 7 of Kosslyn, 1980.

CHAPTER NINE

1. For further details see Chapter 9 of Kosslyn, 1980.

2. These ratings were collected by Paivio, 1975.

3. For details of how this could be done, see Chapter 9 of Kosslyn, 1980.

4. For details about the work on learning, see Paivio, 1971.

CHAPTER TEN

1. See p. 53 of Einstein's autobiographical notes in Schilpp, 1949.
2. See O'Neil, 1944.
3. This problem is from McKim, 1980.
4. This problem was told to me by Shimon Ullman.
5. These problems were shown to me by Jill Larkin.
6. See McKim, 1980, for other guidelines.

CHAPTER ELEVEN

1. See Marks, 1977; White, Sheehan, and Ashton, 1977.
2. Versions of these tests are in Richardson, 1969. Marks, 1977, revised the Betts test, and seems to be having somewhat better luck with his improved version.

CHAPTER TWELVE

1. But also remember the additional requirements noted in footnote 1 of Chapter 5.
2. See Bower, 1974.
3. In fact, then, there are three problems: understanding mental activity, understanding conscious experience, and understanding the relationship between mental activity and conscious experience. An understanding of conscious experience may require an understanding of its relation to mental activity.
4. See Fodor, 1968, 1975; Putnam, 1973.
5. For detailed discussions of different levels of theorizing, see Marr, 1982, and Kosslyn, 1984.
6. See Funt, 1976.

Bibliography

Anderson J. R. 1976. *Language, memory and thought.* Hillsdale, N.J.: Erlbaum.

Anderson, J. R. 1978. Arguments concerning representations for mental imagery. *Psychological Review 85:249–277.*

Anderson, J. R., and Bower, G. H. 1973. *Human associative memory.* New York: Winston.

Angell, J. R. 1910. Methods for determination of mental imagery. *Psychological Monographs 13:61–107.*

Ashton, R., and White, K. 1975. The effects of instruction on subjects' imagery questionnaire scores. *Social Behavior and Personality 3:41–43.*

Banks, W. P. 1977. Encoding and processing of symbolic information in comparative judgments. In G. H. Bower (Ed.), *The psychology of learning and motivation: Advances in research and theory* (Vol. 2). New York: Academic.

Beech, J. R., and Allport, D. A. 1978. Visualization of compound scenes. *Perception 7:129–138.*

Betts, G. H. 1909. *The distribution and functions of mental imagery.* New York: Columbia University Press.

Bisiach, E., and Luzzatti, C. 1978. Unilateral neglect of representational space. *Cortex 14:129–133.*

Bisiach, E., Luzzatti, C., and Perani, D. 1979. Unilateral neglect, representational schema, and consciousness. *Brain 102:609–618.*

Block, N. 1980. *Readings in philosophy of psychology.* Cambridge, Mass.: Harvard University Press.

Block, N. (Ed.). 1981. *Imagery.* Cambridge, Mass.: MIT Press.

Boden, M. 1977. *Artificial intelligence and natural man.* New York: Basic Books.

Boring, E. G. 1950. *A history of experimental psychology* (2nd ed.). New York: Appleton-Century-Crofts.

Bower, G. H. 1970. Imagery as a relational organizer in associative learning. *Journal of Verbal Learning and Verbal Behavior 9:529–533.*

Bower, G. H. 1972. Mental imagery and associative learning. In L. Gregg (Ed.), *Cognition in learning and memory.* New York: Wiley.

Bower, T. G. R. 1974. *Development in infancy.* San Francisco: Freeman.

Brooks, L. 1967. The suppression of visualization by reading. *Quarterly Journal of Experimental Psychology 19:289–299.*

Brooks, L. 1968. Spatial and verbal components of the act of recall. *Canadian Journal of Psychology 22:349–368.*

Bruner, J. S., Olver, R. O., and Greenfield, P. M. 1966. *Studies in cognitive growth*. New York: Wiley.

Bundesen, C., and Larsen, A. 1975. Visual transformation of size. *Journal of Experimental Psychology: Human Perception and Performance* 1:214–220.

Chomsky, N. 1965. *Aspects of the theory of syntax*. Cambridge, Mass.: MIT Press.

Chomsky, N. 1967. *Current issues in linguistics*. The Hague: Mouton.

Clark, H. H. 1972. On evidence concerning J. Huttenlocher and E. T. Higgens' theory of reasoning: A second reply. *Psychological Review* 79:428–432.

Collins, A. M., and Quillian, M. R. 1972. Experiments on semantic memory and language comprehension. In L. Gregg (Ed.), *Cognition in learning and memory*. New York: Wiley.

Cooper, L. A. 1975. Mental rotation of random two-dimensional shapes. *Cognitive Psychology* 7:20–43.

Cooper, L. A. 1976. Demonstration of a mental analog of an external rotation. *Perception and Psychophysics* 19:296–302.

Dennett, D. C. 1978. *Brainstorms*. Montgomery, Vt: Bradford Books.

Descartes, R. 1911. *The philosophical works of Descartes* (Vol. 1, E. S. Haldane and G. R. T. Ross, trans.). Cambridge: Cambridge University Press.

Farah, M. J., and Kosslyn, S. M. 1981. Structure and strategy in image generation. *Cognitive Science* 4:371–383.

Farah, M. J., and Kosslyn, S. 1982. Concept development. In H. W. Reese and L. P. Lipsitt (Eds.), *Advances in child development and behavior* (Vol. 16). New York: Academic.

Fechner, G. T. 1966. *Elements of psychophysics*. New York: Holt, Rinehart, and Winston (originally published 1860).

Fernald, M. R. 1912. The diagnosis of mental imagery. *Psychological Monographs 58*.

Finke, R. A. 1980. Levels of equivalence in imagery and perception. *Psychological Review 86*:113–132.

Finke, R. A., and Kosslyn, S. M. 1980. Mental imagery acuity in the peripheral visual field. *Journal of Experimental Psychology: Human Perception and Performance 6*:126–139.

Finke, R. A., and Pinker, S. 1982. Spontaneous imagery scanning in mental extrapolation. *Journal of Experimental Psychology: Human Learning and Memory 8*:142–147.

Finke, R. A., and Pinker, S. 1983. Directional scanning of remembered visual patterns. *Journal of Experimental Psychology: Learning, Memory, and Cognition 9*:398–410.

Finke, R. A., and Schmidt, M. J. 1977. Orientation-specific color aftereffects following imagination. *Journal of Experimental Psychology: Human Perception and Performance 3*:599–606.

Finke, R. A., and Schmidt, M. J. 1978. The quantitative measure of pattern representation in images using orientation-specific color aftereffects. *Perception and Psychophysics 23*:515–520.

Fodor, J. A. 1968. *Psychological explanation: An introduction to the philosophy of psychology.* New York: Random House.

Fodor, J. A. 1975. *The language of thought.* New York: Crowell.

Funt, B. V. 1976. WHISPER: *A computer implementation using analogues in reasoning.* Ph.D. thesis, University of British Columbia.

Galton, F. 1883. *Inquiries into human faculty and its development.* London: MacMillan.

Glass, A. L., and Holyoak, K. J. 1975. Alternative conceptions of semantic memory. *Cognition* 3:313–339.

Goodman, N. *Languages of art.* New York: Bobbs-Merrill, 1968.

Gordon, R. 1949. An investigation into some of the factors that favour the formation of stereotyped images. *British Journal of Psychology* 39:156–167.

Hayes, J. R. 1973. On the function of visual imagery in elementary mathematics. In W. G. Chase (Ed.), *Visual information processing.* New York: Academic.

Hayes-Roth, F. 1979. Distinguishing theories of representation: A critique of Anderson's "Arguments concerning mental imagery." *Psychological Review* 86:376–392.

Hebb, D. O. 1968. Concerning imagery. *Psychological Review* 75:466–477.

Hesse, M. B. 1963. *Models and analogies in science.* London: Sheed and Ward.

Hinton, G. E. 1979. Some demonstrations of the effects of structural descriptions in mental imagery. *Cognitive Science* 3:231–250.

Hinton, G. E., and Parsons, L. M. 1981. Frames of reference and mental imagery. In J. Long and A. Baddeley (Eds.), *Attention and performance* (Vol. 9). Hillsdale, N.J.: Erlbaum.

Hock, H. S., and Tromley, C. L. 1978. Mental rotation and perceptual uprightness. *Perception and Psychophysics* 24:529–533.

Huttenlocher, J. 1968. Constructing spatial images: A strategy in reasoning. *Psychological Review* 75:550–560.

Huttenlocher, J., Higgins, E. T., and Clark, H. H. 1972. On reasoning, congruence, and other matters, *Psychological Review* 79:420–432.

Kaufman, L. 1974. *Sight and mind: An introduction to visual perception.* New York: Oxford University Press.

Keenan, J. M., and Moore, R. E. 1979. Memory for images of concealed objects: A reexamination of Neisser and Kerr. *Journal of Experimental Psychology: Human Learning and Memory* 5:374–385.

Kenny, A. 1968. *Descartes.* New York: Random House.

Kosslyn, S. M. 1975. Information representation in visual images. *Cognitive Psychology* 7:341–370.

Kosslyn, S. M. 1978. Measuring the visual angle of the mind's eye. *Cognitive Psychology* 10:356–389.

Kosslyn, S. M. 1980. *Image and mind.* Cambridge, Mass.: Harvard University Press.

Kosslyn, S. M. 1984. Mental representation. In J. R. Anderson and S. M.

Kosslyn (Eds), *Tutorials in learning and memory: Essays in honor of Gordon H. Bower.* San Francisco: Freeman.

Kosslyn, S. M., and Alper, S. N. 1977. On the pictorial properties of visual images: Effects of image size on memory for words. *Canadian Journal of Psychology 31:*32–40.

Kosslyn, S. M., Ball, T. M., and Reiser, B. J. 1978. Visual images preserve metric spatial information: Evidence from studies of image scanning. *Journal of Experimental Psychology: Human Perception and Performance 4:*47–60.

Kosslyn, S. M., and Shwartz, S. P. 1977. A simulation of visual imagery. *Cognitive Science 1:*265–295.

Kosslyn, S. M., Murphy, G. L., Bemesderfer, M. E., and Feinstein, K. J. 1977. Category and continuum in mental comparisons. *Journal of Experimental Psychology: General 106:*341–375.

Larsen, A., and Bundesen, C. 1978. Size scaling in visual pattern recognition. *Journal of Experimental Psychology: Human Perception and Performance 4:*1–20.

Lea, G. 1975. Chronometric analysis of the method of loci. *Journal of Experimental Psychology: Human Perception and Performance 2:*95–104.

Lindsay, P. H., and Norman, D. A. 1977. *Human information processing: An introduction to psychology* (2nd ed.). New York: Academic.

McKellar, P. 1965. The investigation of mental images. In S. A. Barnett and A. McLaren (Eds.), *Penguin science survey.* Harmondsworth, England: Penguin Books.

McKim, R. H. 1980. *Experiences in visual thinking.* Monterey, Calif.: Brooks / Cole.

Marks, D. F. 1973. Visual imagery differences and eye movements in the recall of pictures. *Perception and Psychophysics 14:*407–412.

Marks, D. F. 1977. Imagery and consciousness: A theoretical review from an individual differences perspective. *Journal of Mental Imagery 1:*275–290.

Marr, D. 1982. *Vision.* San Francisco, Calif.: Freeman.

Miller, G. A. 1956. The magical number seven, plus or minus two: Some limits on our capacity for processing information. *Psychological Review 63:*31–96.

Minsky, M., and Papert, S. 1972. *Artificial Intelligence Progress Report* (Memo 252). Cambridge, Mass.: MIT, Project MAC, Artificial Intelligence Laboratory.

Moore, T. V. 1915. The temporal relations of meaning and imagery. *Psychological Review 22:*177–215.

Moyer, R. S. 1973. Comparing objects in memory: Evidence suggesting an internal psychophysics. *Perception and Psychophysics 13:*180–184.

Moyer, R. S., and Bayer, R. H. 1976. Mental comparison and the symbolic distance effect. *Cognitive Psychology 8:*228–246.

Neisser, U. 1967. *Cognitive psychology.* New York: Appleton-Century-Crofts.

Newell, A., and Simon, H. A. 1972. *Human problem solving*. Englewood Cliffs, N.J.: Prentice-Hall.

O'Neil, J. 1944. *Prodigal genius: The life of Nikola Tesla*. New York: Washburn (reprinted 1981, Hollywood, Calif.: Angriff Press).

Paivio, A. 1971. *Imagery and verbal processes*. New York: Holt, Rinehart, and Winston.

Paivio, A. 1975. Perceptual comparisons through the mind's eye. *Memory and Cognition* 3:635–648.

Perky, C. W. 1910. An experimental study of imagination. *American Journal of Psychology* 21:422–452.

Piaget, J., and Inhelder, B. 1971. *Mental imagery in the child*. New York: Basic Books.

Pinker, S. 1980. Mental imagery and the third dimension. *Journal of Experimental Psychology: General* 109:354–371.

Pinker, S., and Finke, R. 1980. Emergent two-dimensional patterns in images rotated in depth. *Journal of Experimental Psychology: Human Perception and Performance* 6:244–264.

Pinker, S., and Kosslyn, S. M. 1978. The representation and manipulation of three-dimensional space in mental images. *Journal of Mental Imagery* 2:69–84.

Podgorny, P., and Shepard, R. N. 1978. Functional representations common to visual perception and imagination. *Journal of Experimental Psychology: Human Perception and Performance* 4:21–35.

Postman, L. 1974. Does imagery enhance long-term retention? *Bulletin of the Psychonomic Society* 3:385–387.

Putnam, H. 1960. Minds and machines. In S. Hook (Ed.), *Dimensions of mind: A symposium*. New York: New York University Press.

Putnam, H. 1973. Reductionism and the nature of psychology. *Cognition* 2:131–146.

Putnam, H. 1978. *Meaning and the moral sciences*. London: Routledge and Kegan Paul.

Pylyshyn, Z. W. 1973. What the mind's eye tells the mind's brain: A critique of mental imagery. *Psychological Bulletin* 80:1–24.

Pylyshyn, Z. W. 1979a. Validating computational models: A critique of Anderson's indeterminacy of representation claim. *Psychological Review* 86:383–394.

Pylyshyn, Z. W. 1979b. Imagery theory: Not mysterious—Just wrong. *Behavioral and Brain Sciences* 2:561–563.

Pylyshyn, Z. W. 1981. The imagery debate: Analogue media versus tacit knowledge. *Psychological Review* 87:16–45.

Reed, S. K. 1974. Structural descriptions and the limitations of visual images. *Memory and Cognition* 2:329–336.

Reed, S. K., and Johnsen, J. A. 1975. Detection of parts in patterns and images. *Memory and Cognition* 3:569–575.

Richardson, A. 1969. *Mental imagery*. New York: Springer.

Richman, C. L., Mitchell, D. B., and Reznick, J. S. 1979. Mental travel: Some reservations. *Journal of Experimental Psychology: Human Perception and Performance* 5:13–18.

Ryle, G. 1949. *The concept of mind*. London: Hutchinson.

Samuels, M., and Samuels, N. 1975. *Seeing with the mind's eye*. New York: Random House.

Schacter, S., and Singer, J. 1962. Cognitive, social and physiological determinants of emotional state. *Psychological review* 69:379–399.

Schilpp, P. A. (Ed.). *Albert Einstein: Philosopher–scientist*. La Salle, Ill.: Open Court, 1949.

Schwartz, R. 1981. Imagery—There's more to it than meets the eye. In N. Block (Ed.), *Imagery*. Cambridge, Mass.: MIT Press.

Segal, S. J. 1971. Processing of the stimulus in imagery and perception. In S. J. Segal (Ed.), *Imagery: Current cognitive approaches*. New York: Academic.

Segal, S. J., and Fusella, V. 1970. Influence of imaged pictures and sounds on detection of visual and auditory signals. *Journal of Experimental Psychology* 83:458–464.

Sekuler, R., and Nash, D. 1972. Speed of size scaling in human vision. *Psychonomic Science* 27:93–94.

Shepard, R. N. 1978. The mental image. *American Psychologist* 33:125–137.

Shepard, R. N., and Cooper, L. A. 1982. *Mental images and their transformations*. Cambridge, Mass.: MIT Press.

Shepard, R. N., and Metzler, J. 1971. Mental rotation of three-dimensional objects. *Science* 171:701–703.

Shwartz, S. P. 1979. *Studies of mental image rotation: Implications for a computer simulation of visual imagery*. Ph.D. thesis, Johns Hopkins University.

Simon, H. A. 1972. What is visual imagery? An information processing interpretation. In L. W. Gregg (Ed.), *Cognition in learning and memory*. New York: Wiley.

Smith, E. E. 1978. Theories of semantic memory. In W. K. Estes (Ed.), *Handbook of learning and cognitive processes* (Vol. 5). Hillsdale, N.J.: Erlbaum.

Sternberg, S. 1966. High-speed scanning in human memory. *Science* 153:652–654.

Stevens, S. S. 1975. *Psychophysics: Introduction to its perceptual, neural, and social prospects*. New York: Wiley.

Tichner, E. B. 1909. *Lectures on the experimental psychology of the thought processes*. New York: MacMillan.

Turing, A. M. 1964. Computing machinery and intelligence. A. R. Anderson (Ed.), *Minds and machines*. Englewood Cliffs, N.J.: Prentice-Hall (originally published 1950).

Watson, J. B. 1913. Psychology as the behaviorist views it. *Psychological Review* 20:158–177.

Watson, J. B. 1928. *The ways of behaviorism*. New York: Harper.

Watson, J. B. 1930. *Behaviorism*. New York: Norton.

Weber, R. J., and Bach, M. 1969. Visual and speech imagery. *British Journal of Psychology* 60:199–202.

Weber, R. J., and Castleman, J. 1970. The time it takes to imagine. *Perception and Psychophysics 8:*165–168.

Weber, R. J., and Harish, R. 1974. Visual imagery for words: The Hebb test. *Journal of Experimental Psychology 102:*409–414.

Weber, R. J., Kelley, J., and Little, S. 1972. Is visual imagery sequencing under verbal control? *Journal of Experimental Psychology 96:*354–362.

Weizenbaum, J. 1976. *Computer power and human reason.* San Francisco: Freeman.

White, K., Sheehan, P. W., and Ashton, R. 1977. Imagery assessment: A survey of self-report measures. *Journal of Mental Imagery 1:*145–170.

Winston, P. H. (Ed.). 1975. *The psychology of computer vision.* New York: McGraw-Hill.

Wittgenstein, L. 1953. *Philosophical investigations.* New York: MacMillan.

Wundt, W. 1894. *Lectures on human and animal psychology* (S. E. Creighton and E. B. Tichner, trans.). New York: MacMillan.

Wundt, W. 1912. *An introduction to psychology* (R. Pintner, trans.). London: Allen.

Yates, F. A. 1966. *The art of memory.* Chicago: University of Chicago Press.

Index

abstract ideas:
  as essentially imaginal, 7–8
  see also concepts
abstract words, remembering of, 173–74
adaptation phenomenon, 67–69
afterimages, 80–81
algorithms, 210–11
alphabet, computer representations of, 16–17
ambiguity, 6, 207–8
  Gestalt laws and, 89–90
ANSWERIF process, 171
architecture, computer graphics systems in, 218
Aristotle, 5
artificial intelligence (AI), 14–15, 222–23
association strength:
  in computer model data, 120
  generation time and, 144, 148
  inspection time and, 58–59, 144–48
atom, Bohr's model of, 115

behaviorism, 7–11
  demise of, 9–11, 13
  experimental methodology of, 74–75
  language as viewed in, 11
  mental events discredited by, 7–9, 12–13
  stimuli and responses in, 8–10, 11
Berkeley, Bishop, 6
Betts, G. H., 196–97
Bisiach, Edoardo, 70, 78
bits, 16
blindness, imagining abilities and, 78
"blink" transformations, 214

Bobrow, Danny, 43
Bohr, Niels, 115
Bower, Gordon, 174
brain:
  biochemical malfunctions in, 221
  -computer analogy, limitations of, 26–27
  damage to, 69–71, 78, 83
  mind relationship with, 3–4, 18–19, 205–6
  noise errors in, 139–40
  physical vs. functional descriptions of, 18, 205–6
  physiology of, 24–25
  symbols manipulated by, 19, 20
breathing patterns, of "visual imagers" vs. "verbalizers," 196
Brooks, Lee, 76
bytes, 16–17

cathode ray tubes (CRTs), 17, 206
central processing, 79–80
  imagery at level of, 80–83
central processing units (CPUs), 15–17, 26, 27, 206
cerebral cortex, 79
children:
  imagery abilities of, 201–4, 213–14
  static images held by, 214
  teaching techniques geared to, 203–4, 213–14
Chomsky, Noam, 10–11, 13
Cicero, 172
classes:
  of objects, representations of, 5, 6, 72–73, 207, 227
  symbolic imagery for, 192

cognitive development, 201–4
    shift in propositionally stored
        information in, 202, 203
    teaching techniques and, 203–4,
        213–14
cognitive psychology, 212
cognitive science:
    approach of, 18–19, 29–30, 212–
        13
    practical applications of, 203–4,
        213–23
    vocabulary of, 225
color imagery, 81
colors, in maps and diagrams, 219
complexity:
    generation time and, 142–43
    see also detail
computer display metaphor, 20–
        28, 30, 153, 206, 211
    for generating of images, 21–22,
        91–92, 93–96
    limitations of, 26–28
    matrixlike phenomena in, 22–
        25, 27, 83, 93–96, 116, 206
    for "mind's eye," 25, 54–55
    for rotation of images, 106–9
    for scanning of images, 114
computer display screens, 17
computer graphics systems, in
        architectural design, 218
computer model of imaging, 110,
        116–59, 210–12
    active memory structures in,
        117–19
    data structures in, 113–14, 117,
        119
    evaluation of, 212
    existing data explained by, 131–
        41
    fading of images in, 125, 130,
        137–38
    generating of images in, 122–
        25, 131–36, 141, 142–43
    goals of, 116, 131
    grain in, 118, 125–26
    as guideline for future research,
        153–59, 160, 164
    inspecting of images in, 122,

125–27, 136–38, 141, 143–48,
        211
    long-term memory structures
        in, 117, 119–22
    maintaining of images in, 122,
        125, 130, 137–38
    mental medium in, 117–19, 210
    novel scenes, 124–25
    predictions generated by, 141–
        53
    propositionally stored informa-
        tion in, 120–21, 122, 123, 132
    remembering in, 171
    scanning in, 128–29, 210–11
    size of images in, 121, 125–26
    skeletal images in, 121–22, 123,
        132
    spontaneous use of imagery in,
        141
    superordinate information in,
        121, 171
    transforming of images in, 122,
        127–30, 139–40, 141, 148–52
computer programs, 16
    decriptive vs. depictive repre-
        sentations in, 36
    images utilized in, 222–23
    mental processes imitated by,
        19–20
computers, 13–28
    artificial intelligence concept
        and, 14–15
    electronic advances in, 14
    memory-CPU interactions in,
        15–17
    mental processes related to, 11,
        13, 17–28
    performance vs. stimulation
        mode of, 222
    physical vs. functional descrip-
        tions of, 17–18, 205–6
    symbols manipulated by, 13, 19
    "user compatibility" of, 218
computer science, 212
concepts:
    of classes of objects, 5, 6, 72–73
    compatibility of symbols and,
        217–19

as essentially imaginal, 7–8
Cooper, Lynn, 105–6, 108, 198

data, existing:
    computer model of imaging
        and, 131–41
    explained by good theories,
        111–12
data structures, in computer
    model, 113–14, 117, 119
deductive reasoning, 162, 175, 202
depictive representations, 33–36,
    160–61
    properties exclusive to, 33, 36
    propositional (descriptive) rep-
        resentations vs., 34–36, 41–
        47, 57–60
    see also images, mental
Descartes, René, 205
descriptive representations, see
    propositional representations
detail:
    generation time and, 95–96,
        131–32, 135
    grain related to, 54, 56–62, 174
    inspection time and, 60–62, 136,
        137–38
detector cells, 25
diagrams, imagery principles
    and, 218–19

education:
    imagery abilities and, 203–4,
        213–17
    in psychotherapy, 219–20
    of young children, 203–4, 213–
        14
Einstein, Albert, 141, 178, 195–96
emotion:
    behaviorists' interpretations
        of, 8
    experience of, thought factor in,
        31
evolution, image transformations
    and, 139, 152
experimental methodology:
    of behaviorism, 74–75

in imagery studies, 37–41,
    208–9
see also introspection
eyes:
    "mind's eye" vs., 73, 128–29
    visual information transmitted
        from, 78, 79, 128
    see also "mind eye"

fading of images, 139
    in computer model, 125, 130,
        137–38
    inspection time and, 137–38,
        143–44
    sectional nature of, 119, 130
Farah, Martha, 142–43
field-general transformations, 129
FIND process:
    ability differences in, 196, 197,
        198, 199, 200
    faulty, in hallucinations, 221
    in generating of images, 122,
        123, 124, 125, 132, 136, 142,
        183
    Gestalt laws and, 138
    in inspecting of images, 125,
        126, 137, 138, 168, 188, 211
    in symbolic imagery, 179
    three-dimensionality and, 154,
        156
    in transforming of images, 129,
        139, 140, 210, 211
Finke, Ronald, 51, 78, 80–81, 84,
    85–86, 156
Folk, Mark, 148–52
forgetting, 53–54
formats:
    defined, 36–37
    multiplicity of, 51–52, 160–61
Freud, Sigmund, 38, 112–13, 219
Fusella, Vincent, 75

Galton, Sir Francis, 194–95, 196
generating of images, 92–104, 228
    ability differences in, 199–200
    assembling of image sections
        in, 98–104, 132–36

generating of images (*continued*)
  association strength and, 144,
    148
  cell-by-cell activation in, 96–98
  complexity-size relationship in,
    142–43
  computer display metaphor for,
    21–22, 91–92, 93–96
  in computer model, 122–25,
    131–36, 141, 142–43
  detail-time relationship in, 95–
    96, 131–32, 135
  different types of parts related
    to time in, 102, 135–36
  inspection process in, 102, 142–
    43
  number of parts related to time
    in, 96–99, 132, 135
  simple activation model of, 93–
    96, 98
  simple retrieval vs., 21–22
  size-time relationship in, 94,
    95, 108, 132, 136, 142–43
  spatial reference points in, 100–
    102
  storage mechanisms and, 92–99,
    103–4
  verbal or propositional infor-
    mation in, 100, 101, 102, 132,
    136
  in visual thinking, 183, 186–87
  see also regenerating of images
Gestalt laws of organization, 88–
  90, 207
  four general principles in, 88
  as inborn or strongly habitual,
    89–90
  inspection time and, 88–89, 137,
    138
  storing of images and, 96, 99
Gordon, R., 197
grain and resolution:
  at center vs. edge, 65
  in computer model, 118, 125–26
  individual differences in, 200
  size of image and, 54, 55, 56–62,
    118, 137, 142–43, 174
grammar, 33, 34

hallucinations, 221, 227–28
HASA entries, 120, 126, 144, 171
Hesse, Mary, 115–16
Hobbes, Thomas, 21, 73
homunculus concept, 12, 22, 25,
  206
Hume, David, 73

imageless thought, 37–38
IMAGE process, 132, 135, 136,
  171, 197
  functions of, 122–23, 124–25
imagery abilities:
  blindness and, 78
  brain damage and, 70–71, 78, 83
  career decisions and, 200–201
  changing fashions and, 195–96
  of children, 201–4, 213–14
  hindered by visual perception,
    75–77
  individual differencess in, 194–
    201
  practice as factor in, 201
  standard tests of, 196–97, 199
  teaching methods and, 203–4,
    213–17
  various structures and pro-
    cesses in, 196–200
images, mental:
  of abstract concepts, 7–8
  after-, 80–81
  as basic elements of thought, 5–
    6, 7–8
  for classes of objects, 5, 6, 72–
    73, 207, 227
  cognitive science approach to,
    29–30
  color, 81
  in computer programing, 222–
    23
  concept-symbol compatibility
    and, 217–19
  conscious experience of, 30–32,
    208–9, 226, 229; *see also* intro-
    spection
  defined, 30
  as epiphenomenal, 32

as frequently experienced phenomena, 1

memory improved by, 171–75

multiple interpretations of, 6

nonpictorial interpretations of, 30–32

observation methodology for, 37–41, 208–9; *see also* introspection

percepts vs., 72–75, 90, 91–92

philosophical speculations on, 4–6

pictorial properties of, 32–37, 41–47

psychological speculations on, 6–13

in psychotherapy, 219–21

representation function of, 3, 72, 207–8

slide projector metaphor for, 2–3, 4, 21

stabilized, 67–69

static, of children, 214

as unscientific topic, 7–9, 12

see also skeletal images; symbolic imagery

imaging:

at central processing level, 80–83

computer-brain analogy of, *see* computer display metaphor

knowledge factor in, 148–52, 189–91

as primitive thought mechanism, 195

processes of, *see specific processes*

structures of, *see* matrix, mental; medium, mental

as subvocal thinking, 8

theory of, 113–16, 209–12; *see also* computer model of imaging

visual perception vs., 72–90, 128–29, 141, 227

Inhelder, Bärbel, 202

inspecting of images, 29

association strength and, 58–59, 144–48

by children, 202–3

in computer model, 122, 125–27, 136–38, 141, 143–48, 211

detail-time relationship in, 60–62, 136, 137–38

in generation process, 103, 142–43

Gestalt laws of organization and, 88–89, 137, 138

sectional fading and, 137–38, 143–44

size-time relationship in, 56–62, 136, 137, 144–48

in visual thinking, 183, 186–87

intelligence, artificial (AI), 14–15, 222–23

introspection, 12, 162, 209, 226, 228

defined, 4

externalizing of, 38–40

limitations of, 4, 7–8, 32, 37–38, 100

knowledge, imagery guided by, 148–52, 189–91

Kulpe, Oswaldo, 37–38

language:

conscious experience of, 31–32

depictive representations vs., 33–36

experience of imagery vs., 31–32

grammar in, 33, 34

learning of, 5, 11, 33

see also propositional representations; words

Leviathan (Hobbes), 73

linguistics, 10–11, 212

logic problems, Venn diagrams and, 216–17

LOOKFOR process:

in inspecting of images, 125–26, 137, 183, 211

LOOKFOR process (*continued*)
  in remembering, 171
  in transforming of images, 129
Luzzatti, Claudio, 70

Macbeth (Shakespeare), 74
McCollough effect, 80–81, 141
maintaining of images, *see* regen-
    erating of images
manipulating of images, *see*
    transforming of images
maps, imagery principles and,
    218–19
matrix, mental:
  computer display metaphor for,
    22–25, 27, 83, 93–96, 116, 206
  in image generation, 93–98
  interpreting of, 25
  spatial characteristics repre-
    sented in, 22–25, 154
  in visual perception, 83, 86–87
medium, mental, 53–71
  in computer model, 117–19, 210
  defined, 54
  forgetting and, 53–54
  grain or resolution of, 54, 55,
    56–62, 65, 118, 125–26, 137,
    142–43, 174, 200
  identifying properties of, 54–55
  shape of, 62, 66, 85, 118
  simultaneous awareness vs.
    maximum scope of, 84–85
  spatial extent of, 55, 62–66, 71,
    83–86, 118, 129
  standard image size and loca-
    tion in, 123
  three-dimensionality and, 154,
    156–58
  in visual perception, 55, 71, 83–
    86
memory, 92–93
  active, structures in, 117–19
  of computers, 15–17, 26, 206
  of images, limitations on, 184–
    86
  image size and, 60–62, 174
  improved by imagery, 171–75

long-term, structures in, 117,
    119–22
  personality rooted in, 219–20
  philosophical speculations on,
    4–6
  three levels of, 57–58
  see also remembering; storing of
    images
Mensa society, imagery poll of,
    195, 196
Mental Imagery in the Child (Piaget
    and Inhelder), 202
method of loci, 172–73, 175
methodology, *see* experimental
    methodology
Metzler, Jackie, 38–39, 105
mind:
  brain relationship with, 3–4,
    18–19, 205–6
  demise of research on, 7–9
  philosophical speculations on,
    4–6
  psychological investigations of,
    6–13
  revivification of interest in, 12–
    13
  theory of, 209–10
"mind's eye," 3, 225
  computer display metaphor for,
    25, 54–55
  interpretive tests of, 25, 86–90,
    206
  maximum scope of, 85–86
  real eyes vs., 73, 128–29
models:
  in building of theories, 114–16,
    212
  see also computer model of
    imaging
motivation, as factor in imaging,
    143

neurons, 24–25
Nobel Prize, 19
noise errors, 139–40
novel scenes, 21, 103

computer display metaphor
and, 91–92
in computer model, 124–25

objects:
classes of, 5, 6, 72–73, 207, 227
in images, real objects mimicked by, 189–90
oblique effect, 82–83
optic chiasma, 78
optic nerve, 78

Paivio, Allan, 173–74
PAN process, 126, 127, 128, 137
patterns:
emergent, in three-dimensional
rotations, 156
organizing of, 89–90; see also
Gestalt laws of organization
sub-, recognition of, 88–89
Pennington, Nancy, 81–82
Perani, Daniela, 70
perception, visual, 5, 71
adaptation phenomenon in, 67
Gestalt laws of organization
and, 89
imaging vs., 72–90, 128–29, 141,
227
imaging hindered by, 75–77
matrixlike processes in, 83, 86–
87
mental medium in, 55, 71, 83–
86
neural mechanisms of, 78–79
processing levels of, 79–83
percepts:
images different than, 90, 91–92
images resembled by, 72–75,
220
performance mode, 222
peripheral processing, 79–80
Perky, C. W., 74
personality, as representations in
memory, 219–20
philosophical speculations, 4–6,
212

phobias, overcome by mental
images, 220–21
physics, 228
laws of, obeyed in image transformations, 104–6, 139–40,
148–52, 189
Piaget, Jean, 202, 214
PICTURE process:
ability differences in, 197, 199,
200, 203–4
faulty, in hallucinations, 221
in generating of images, 122,
123, 125, 132, 135, 183
in inspecting of images, 125,
211
in regenerating of images, 138
in transforming of images, 139
Pinker, Steven, 51, 154, 155–56
Plato, 53–54
Podgorny, Peter, 86–87
Popper, Karl, 112
predictions:
of computer model of imaging,
141–53
generated by good theories,
111, 141
testability of, 112–13
problem-solving, see visual thinking
processes:
in computer model, 122–30, 210
defined, 113–14
see also specific processes
product design, mental representation and processing in, 217–
19
programs, see computer programs
propositional (descriptive) representations, 33–36, 161, 226
characteristics of, 34
children's use of, 202, 203
in computer model, 120–21,
122, 123, 132
depictive representations vs.,
34–36, 41
in generating of images, 100,
101, 102, 132, 136

propositional (*continued*)
  images vs., in problem-solving,
    181–82
  images corrected with, 189
  in remembering, 160–71, 175
  scanning of, 43–45, 47
Proust, Marcel, 92–93
psychology, 6–13
  scientific methods in, 6–7, 9
  see also behaviorism
"Psychology as the Behaviorist
    Sees It" (Watson), 7–8
psychotherapy, 219–21
  maladaptive aspects of person-
    ality in, 219–20
  for phobias, 220–21
PUT process:
  ability differences in, 197, 198–
    99, 203–4
  in generating of images, 122,
    123–25, 132, 135, 183, 184
  in inspecting of images, 125,
    126, 211
  in regeneration of images, 138
  in transforming of images, 139
Pylyshyn, Zenon, 31, 148, 149

rank-order, symbolic imagery for,
    192
Reed, Stephen, 87–89
REGENERATE process:
  ability differences in, 196, 198,
    199, 200, 215
  function of, 130
  in inspecting of images, 125,
    137–38
  in visual thinking, 184
regenerating (maintaining) of
    images:
  in computer model, 122, 125,
    130, 137–38
  sectional fading and, 119, 130
  in transformation process,
    107–9
  in visual thinking, 183–86, 187
region-bounded transformations,
    129, 149
relativity theory, 141, 178

remembering, 160–76
  of abstract vs. concrete words,
    173–74
  in computer model, 171
  deductions in, 162, 175
  imagery-propositions "race"
    model of, 165–67, 169–71, 175
  imagery-then-propositions
    model of, 165, 166, 168–69
  images vs. propositions in,
    160–71, 175–76
  propositions-then-imagery
    model of, 164–65, 168, 169
  of words vs. pictures or objects,
    174
  see also memory
resolution, *see* grain and resolu-
    tion
RESOLUTION process, 125–26,
    129
responses, in behaviorism, 8–9,
    10, 11
Rosch, Eleanor, 207
ROTATE process, 129, 198, 210,
    215
rotation of images, 29
  ability differences in, 198
  angle-time relationship in, 38–
    41, 108
  computer display model for,
    106–9
  in computer model, 210
  oblique effect and, 82–83
  physical laws obeyed in, 104–6,
    139–40, 148–52, 189
  as region-bounded transforma-
    tion, 149
  size-time relationship in, 107–9
  size transformations simultane-
    ous with, 109–10
  in three dimensions, 155–56,
    157–58
Ryle, Gilbert, 12, 209

SASA entries, 144
scanning:
  of propositional representa-
    tions, 43–45, 47

in visual perception, 128–29
scanning of images:
  adaptation phenomenon and, 69
  affected by subjects' cooperation, 49–51
  computer display metaphor for, 114
  in computer model, 128–29, 210–11
  distance-time relationship in, 41–51, 60, 114
  size or scale and, 47–49, 60
  of three-dimensional images, 154–55, 156
SCAN process, 126, 127, 137, 210, 211
Schachter, Stanley, 31
schizophrenia, 221
Schmidt, Martin, 80–81
Schwartz, Steven, 106–9, 116, 157
Seeing with the Mind's Eye (Samuels and Samuels), 2
Segal, Sydney, 75
Shakespeare, William, 74
Shepard, Roger, 38–39, 86–87, 104–5
Simon, Herbert, 19
Simonides, 172, 173, 174
simulation, 192
  imaging processes in, 183
  in solving spatial problems, 177–78
  symbolization vs., 179–81
simulation mode, 222
Singer, Jerome, 31
size:
  comparison of, images vs. propositions in, 163–71
  in computer model, 121, 125–26
  generation time and, 94, 95, 108, 132, 136, 142–43
  grain or resolution and, 54, 55, 56–62, 118, 137, 142–43, 174
  inspection time and, 56–62, 136, 137, 144–48
  memory and, 60–62, 174
  rotation time and, 107–9

scanning time and, 47–49, 60
spatial extent of medium and, 55, 62–66
standards and categories for, 163–64
transforming of, 109–10, 127–28
visual angle as measurement of, 63–64
skeletal images:
  as always present, 144
  in computer model, 121–22, 123, 132
  encoding of, 122
slide projector metaphor, 2–3, 4, 21
spatial relations:
  imagistic reasoning and, 176, 177–78
  see also three-dimensionality
speeches, memory techniques for, 172–73
stabilized images, 67–69
stimuli, in behaviorism, 8–9, 11
storing of images, 89, 92–99, 103–4
  in chunks, 98–99
  computer model for, 117, 119–22
  Gestalt laws of organization and, 96, 99
  in organized units, 96–98
  "simple activation" model of, 93–96, 98
  see also memory
strokes, brain damage caused by, 69–71
structures:
  in active memory, 117–19
  defined, 113, 210
  in long-term memory, 117, 119–22
  see also matrix, mental; medium, mental
subpatterns, recognition of, 88–89
subvocal thinking, 8
superordinate categories, 121, 171
symbolic imagery, 192, 214
  imaging processes in, 183

symbolic imagery (*continued*)
  propositional problem-solving
    vs., 181–82
  simulation vs., 179–81
symbols:
  compatibility of concepts and,
    217–19
  manipulated by brain, 19, 20
  manipulated by computers, 13,
    19
systematic desensitization, 220–21

Tesla, Nikola, 178
theories:
  existing data explained by, 111–
    12
  future research structured by,
    113
  of imagery, 113–16, 209–12; *see
    also* computer model of imag-
    ing
  of mind, 209–10
  models in relation to, 114–16,
    212
  predictions generated by, 111,
    141
  testability of, 112–13
therapy, *see* psychotherapy
thinking:
  imageless, 37–38
  philosophical speculations on,
    4–5
  as reponse to stimulus, 9
  subvocal, 8
  see also visual thinking
three-dimensionality, 2–3, 153–58
  point of view and, 154–55
  rotation and, 155–56, 157–58
  scanning time and, 154–55, 156
  of visual perception, 78
  see also spatial relations
Tichner, E.. B., 7, 37
transformations, "blink," 214
transforming of images, 104–10
  in computer model, 122, 127–
    30, 139–40, 141, 148–52

deformations in, 139–40
evolutionary theory of, 139, 152
field-general vs. region-
  bounded operations in, 129
nonimagery theory of, 148–52
novel scenes created by, 21–22,
  91–92, 103
physical laws obeyed in, 104–6,
  139–40, 148–52, 189
as regeneration process, 107–9
in size, 109–10, 127–28
in visual thinking, 183, 187
see also rotation of images;
  scanning of images
Turing, Alan, 14
Turing test, 14, 225
2001: A Space Odyssey, 222

unconscious, 38
unilateral visual neglect, 69–71,
  78, 83

Venn diagrams, 216–17
verbalizations:
  in assembling of images, 102
  breathing patterns and, 196
visual angle, 63–64
visual perception, *see* perception,
  visual
visual thinking, 177–93
  abstract knowlege in, 189–91
  in children's games, 201
  guidelines for, 190, 192
  imaging processes in, 183–87
  limitations of, 184–86, 187–89
  propositional problem-solving
    vs., 181–82
  simulation vs. symbolization
    in, 179–81
  spatial problems solved by, 176,
    177–78
  Venn diagrams in, 216–17
Von Neumann, John, 15–16

Watson, John B., 7–9, 10, 37

Weber, Robert, 102
words:
    abstract vs. concrete, remem-
        bering of, 173–74
    computer programs for, 17
    in mental representations, 5

multiple images associated
    with, 72–73, 207
    see also language
Wundt, Wilhelm, 6–7, 37

ZOOM process, 126, 127–28, 137